2026
중등영어 교사임용

임용고사 합격에 반드시 필요한
일반영어 및 문학에서 만점을 추구한다.

Reading Writing & Booster

합격을 넘어
평생 가는 영어 실력!

Preface

중등교원 영어 임용 시험에서 합격하려면, 반드시 일반영어 및 문학 부분에서 높은 점수를 받아야 합니다. 이 책은 일반영어와 문학에서 만점을 받기를 원하는 수험생이 스스로 공부할 수 있는 방법을 체득할 수 있도록 도와주기 위해 쓴 책입니다. 일반영어와 문학에서 만점을 받기 위해서는 정확하고 빠르게 지문들을 읽으면서, 문제에서 요구하는 내용을 파악하고 요약하여, 지시사항에 따라 답안을 정확하고 빠르게 쓸 수 있어야 합니다.

물론 서술형과 요약형 문제의 답안을 잘 쓰는 것도 중요한 일이지만, 수험생의 입장에서 가장 고민스러운 유형은 기입형 문제입니다. 대개, 총 6개에 달하는 기입형 문제는, 일반영어와 문학 선체 24짐(2025년도 기출문제 기준) 중 절반에 해당하는 12점의 배점이 주어져 있어서, 매우 비중이 큰 문제 유형입니다. 기입형 문제의 정답을 찾기 위해서는 먼저 글의 요지를 빨리 파악하고 앞뒤 문맥의 논리와 연어(collocation)를 고려하여 영어적 관점에서 가장 적합한 단어를 본문에서 찾아내야 합니다. 기입형 문제의 정답을 고를 때에도 글의 요지를 빨리 파악하는 것이 중요한데, 그러기 위해서는 평소 독해력을 최대한 높이고 속독 능력을 갖추는 것이 필수적입니다.

정확하고 빠른 독해력은 글을 읽고 이해하는 능력으로서만 중요한 것이 아니라, 말하고 듣고 쓰는 능력을 향상시키기 위해서도 반드시 필요합니다. 특히 임용고사 2차 시험의 심층면접, 지도안 작성을 비롯한 수업 실연에서 높은 점수를 받기 위해서는 영어 자체를 잘 할 수 있도록 노력해야 합니다. 1차 시험 결과가 발표되고 나서 한 달이 채 안되는 기간 내에 시행되는 2차 시험에서 좋은 결과를 얻으려면, 1차 시험 준비를 하면서 2차 시험까지 생각하며 공부해야 합니다. 즉, 평소 좋은 글을 많이 읽으면서, 자신이 2차 시험에서 활용할 수 있다고 생각하는 유용하고 좋은 문장들을 많이 암송하거나 필사하며 외워두고, 또 직접 입으로 발음을 하는 연습을 해야 합니다. 그래야만 1차 시험에 합격했다는 결과를 받고 나서도 당황하지 않고 2차 시험까지 마무리를 잘 하여 최종 합격할 수 있습니다.

Reading & Writing

이 책에서는 이와 같이 1차 시험뿐만 아니라 2차 시험에서도 고득점을 받을 수 있는 바람직한 영어 공부 방법을 제시합니다. 단순히 글을 잘 이해하고 답안을 정확하게 서술할 수 있는 능력을 뛰어 넘어, 말과 글을 통해 영어로 자신의 뜻을 명료하고 정확하게 표현할 수 있도록 도와드립니다. 그렇게 탁월한 영어 실력을 갖출 수 있어야, 단순히 임용시험의 합격에 만족하는 것이 아니라, 나중에 학교 현장에서 학생들에게 영어가 얼마나 재미있는지 알려줄 수 있고, 또 실력있는 교사로서 존경을 받을 수 있습니다.

이 책이 임용고사를 준비하면서 일반영어와 문학에서 항상 고민을 하고 있던 많은 수험생에게 자신감과 희망을 줄 수 있기를 바랍니다.

2024년 12월 22일

김병두

Contents

❏ 머리말 ··· ii

PART 01 일반영어와 문학 만점을 위하여 _ 7

1. 일반영어와 문학에서 어려움을 겪는 이유 ··· 8
2. 올바른 영어 독해 공부 방법 ··· 18

PART 02 속독을 위한 영어 구문 분석 _ 25

1. 모르는 부분의 추론은 다음과 같은 네 가지 원칙을 따르자 ···················· 26
   1. 지시어(구)의 대상을 찾는다. ··27
   2. 문맥 속에서 상호 관련된 어구에 주목한다. ··31
   3. 설명 또는 비교의 대상을 찾는다. ··34
   4. 논리적으로 접근한다. ··38

2. 어려운 부분을 쉽게 파악하는 방법 ··· 41
   1. 같은 말을 반복하지 않고 다른 표현으로 바꿔 서술하는 영어의 특성 ········42
   2. 재술 구조 ···45

3. 속독의 원칙 (The Rudiments of Speed Reading in English) ················· 48
   1. 속독의 원칙 1: 주제를 빨리 파악한다. ··48
   2. 속독의 원칙 2: 문맥의 길잡이가 되는 안내어에 주목한다. ··················51
   3. 속독의 원칙 3: 앞의 내용에 기반하여 뒤에 올 내용을 예측하며 읽으면 읽기 속도를 높일 수 있다.
      ··56

PART 03 장문 독해 지문 _ 59

1. 일반영어 ··· 60
   01. What Suffering Does ···60
   02. The bluster imbalance ···64
   03. Three Myths About the Brain ···68
   04. The distorting reality of 'false balance' in the media ···················72
   05. Dangerous Divisiveness ···76
   06. Teaching Is Not a Business ···80

07. Inequality Is a Drag ········· 84
08. Relax, your kids will be fine ········· 88
09. Harvard Alums Still Say They Went to College in Boston ········· 92
10. The Structures of Growth ········· 96
11. Diet Lures and Diet Lies ········· 100
12. The Mental Virtues ········· 105
13. Is American democracy headed to extinction? ········· 109
14. Hello, Stranger ········· 113
15. Introspective or Narcissistic? ········· 118
16. The one fight to have before your wedding ········· 123

2. 문학 지문 ········· 127

1 소설 ········· 127

01. An American Tragedy by Theodore Dreiser ········· 127
02. The Age of Innocence by Edith Wharton ········· 136
03. Call of the Wild by Jack London ········· 139
04. Anne of Green Gables by Lucy Maud Montgomery ········· 146

2 시 ········· 156

01. Love is Not All (Sonnet XXX) by Edna St. Vincent Millay ········· 156
02. To Science by Edgar Allan Poe ········· 157
03. "Under the greenwood tree" by William Shakespeare ········· 158
04. I Should Not Dare To Leave My Friend by Emily Dickinson ········· 159

3 희곡 ········· 160

01. The Crucible by Arthur Miller ········· 160
02. Man and Superman by George Bernard Shaw ········· 163
03. A Streetcar Named Desire by Tennessee Williams ········· 165
04. The Glass Menagerie by Tennessee Williams ········· 168

❏ 장문 독해 지문 번역 _ 171

1. 일반영어 지문 번역 ········· 172
2. 문학 지문 번역 ········· 204

Reading & Writing
Booster

PART 01

일반영어와
문학 만점을 위하여

일반영어와 문학에서 어려움을 겪는 이유

　임용고사를 준비하는 수험생들이 가장 고민하는 것이 일반영어와 문학이다. 다른 과목들은 공부하면 그래도 지식이 쌓이고 점수가 어느 정도는 나오는데, 일반영어와 문학은 아무리 해도 실력이 늘지 않고 공부하는 방법도 잘 모르겠다는 이야기들을 많이 한다. 앞으로 영어 교사가 되어 학교에서 학생들에게 영어를 잘 가르쳐야 할 예비 교사들이 일반영어와 문학에 자신이 없다면, 과연 교사로서 자격이 있을까? 영어학과 영어교육학이 훌륭한 교사가 되기 위한 자질을 높이기 위한 과목이라면, 일반영어와 문학은 수업 시간에 학생들에게 가르치는 내용과 직결되는 부분이다. 그러므로, 영어 교사가 되고 싶은 사람은 단순히 시험에서 합격하는 차원을 넘어 영어 자체를 잘 할 수 있도록 노력해야 한다. 그래야 교사가 되너라도 학생들의 고충을 잘 이해하고 그 문제를 해결하도록 잘 도와줄 수 있다.

　사실, 영어독해만 잘해도, 일반영어와 문학 부분에서 하는 고민을 크게 덜 수 있다. 그런데 왜 독해가 안 되는가? 그 이유를 먼저 알아야 한다. 간단하게 몇 가지만 정리해 보자.

　첫째, 영어 문장을 이해할 때 영어의 품사대로 한국어 단어를 집어 넣고 "직역"하여 생각하는 습관을 바꾸어야 한다. 직역하여 해석하는 방식이란 영어 문장에 특정 영어 단어의 한국어 일대일 대응어를 그대로 끼워 넣어 해석하고 난 다음, 그 말이 무슨 뜻인지 생각해 보는 것을 말한다. 이러한 직역 방식을 사용할 경우, 글의 내용이 추상적이라서 어렵거나 문장 구조가 복잡하면 우리 말 구조도 덩달아 복잡해지게 된다. 더군다나 읽는 속도도 떨어진다. 그래서 글 전체의 요지를 이해하지 못하게 된다. 그럴 때 흔히들 이런 이야기를 한다. "해석은 되는데 무슨 말인지 모르겠다."

　무슨 뜻일까? 결국은 글의 요지를 이해하지 못했다는 것이고, 그렇기 때문에 기입형 문제나 서술형 문제에 빠르고 정확하게 답안을 쓰지 못하게 된다. "해석은 된다"는 말은 기계적으로 단어들을 넣어서 일차적인 직역은 할 수 있다는 것이다. 하지만 결국은 숨은 뜻이나 메시지를 이해하지 못했다는 것이니, 그 문장을 읽으면서 고개를 끄덕이는 것이 아니라 갸우뚱하게 된다. 항상 내가 글을 정확하게 읽었는지 확인하고 싶다면, 읽으면서 고개를 끄덕이고 있는지 갸우뚱하고 있는지 생각해 보면 된다.

좀 더 자세히 살펴 보자. 먼저 아래에 있는 아주 간단한 예문을 보자.

Ignorance of the law is no excuse.

이 문장은, "법의 무지가 변명이 될 수는 없다."로 한국어로 단순직역하는 것이 아니라 "법을 모른다고 해서 핑계거리가 될 수는 없다"로 옮기는 것이 우리 말도 더 자연스럽고 이해하기도 더 쉽다. 흔히 우리는 영어 문장에서 단어가 주어 자리에만 있으면 무조건 "은/는/이/가"라는 주어를 나타내는 조사 중 한 개를 미리 넣고 생각하는 습관이 있다. 이 습관이 영어 문장에 대한 이해를 가로막는 가장 큰 문제이다. 이 문장의 경우에도 단순히 주어로 잡는 것이 아니라 "그 법에 대해 모른다고 해서"라고 부사적으로 처리할 경우, 훨씬 자연스럽게 이해할 수 있다. 위 문장에서 "of"는 언뜻 보기에는 소유격의 "of"와 같아서 기계적으로 "~의"라고 옮기면 될 것 같지만 사실 의미상으로는 "모른다"는 동사적 성격을 가진 명사 ignorance의 대상이 되는 the law와 연결해 주는 목적격으로서의 "of"의 성격을 가지고 있다.

위 문장을 서술적인 문장으로 바꾸어 보면, 다음과 같다.

Even though you are ignorant of the law, there is no excuse for that.
Even though you do not know about the law, it cannot be used as an excuse.

마찬가지로, There is a lot of public ignorance about how the disease is spread. 라는 문장도 "그 질병이 어떻게 퍼져 나가는지에 대한 많은 대중의 무지가 있다"라는 식으로 기계적으로 해석해 놓고 생각하는 것보다는 "그 병의 전염경로에 대해 흔히 잘 모른다"라고 이해하면 훨씬 더 생생하게 이해할 수 있다. 위 문장들의 공통점은 사물이 주어가 된다는 점이다. 소위 "물주구문"이라는 용어로도 많이 이야기하는 유형이다. 이러한 구문의 경우, 영어의 주어를 우리말에서 주어로 잡지 말고 부사적으로 해석하는 것이 좋다.

이제 주어가 조금 더 긴 문장을 살펴보자.

Failure to submit assignments by the due date will result in an automatic failing grade.
His failure to return her phone call made her realize that something was wrong.

위의 두 개 문장에서 첫 번째 문장의 주어는 "Failure to submit assignments by the due date"이고 두 번째 문장의 주어는 "His failure to return her phone call"이다. 주어가 조금 더 길어졌지만, 이제는 충분히 어떤 방식으로 이해해야 하는지 쉽게 이해할 수 있을 것이다.

이 두 개의 문장도 부사적으로 처리해 보자.

> **Failure to submit assignments by the due date will result in an automatic failing grade.**
> 제 날짜에 숙제를 제출하지 못하면, 자동적으로 낙제점수를 받게 된다.
>
> **His failure to return her phone call made her realize that something was wrong.**
> 전화했는데도 그의 전화가 없는 걸 보고, 그녀는 무엇인가 잘못되었다는 것을 직감했다.

이런 문장을 처리할 때에는 항상 주어와 동사의 관계를 잘 보고 처리하면 된다.
이제 조금 더 복잡한 문장을 보자.

> **Concern about the effects of global warming has fostered renewed interest in the Earth's recurrent ice ages.**

이 문장의 경우에도, 주어는 Concern about the effects of global warming 이다. 이 부분을 먼저 처리해야 한다. 이 부분은 단순히 명사구로 된 주어이지만 의미상으로는 "지구온난화의 여파에 대하여 우려하고 있다"는 서술적 의미가 담겨 있다. 하나의 문장으로 만들면, Many people are concerned about the effects of global warming. 라고 볼 수 있다. 그 다음 동사 부분을 보니 has fostered 이다. 결국 *A* has fostered *B*. 라는 단순 구조, 소위 3형식 문장이다.

그럼 이 문장을 한 눈에 쉽게 이해하면 어떻게 될까? "지구온난화의 여파에 대한 우려로 인해, 지구에 빙하기가 다시 발생할 수도 있다는 점에 대해 새로운 관심이 나타나고 있다."로 생각하면 된다. 이런 식으로 생각하면 속독이 가능해진다.

이번에는 난이도를 많이 높여서, 아주 복잡해 보이는 문장을 보자.

> **The attempt to conceive imaginatively a better ordering of human society than the destructive and cruel chaos in which mankind has hitherto existed is by no means modern: it is at least as old as Plato, whose "Republic"' set the model for the Utopias of subsequent philosophers.**

한 문장에 불과하지만 독해 공부를 하는데 있어서 시사하는 바가 큰 문장이다. 언뜻 보면 아주 복잡해 보이고 명료하게 이해하기 힘든 문장처럼 보인다. 이런 문장의 경우에는 단순히 직역식으로 한국어의 일대일 대응어를 끼워 넣는 방식으로는 이해할 수 없다. 하지만, 글의 구조를 잘 보고 논리적으로 차근차근 풀어 나가면 충분히 잘 이해할 수 있다. 위 문장의 경우에는 "The attempt to conceive imaginatively a better ordering of human society than the destructive and cruel chaos in which mankind has hitherto existed"가 주어이다. 이 때, 이 주어 부분의 의미를 빨리 이해해야 하는데, 무조건 한국어 단어를 영어의 어순에 끼워 넣지 말고, 논리적으로 잘 풀어 나가야 한다. 우선 "The attempt to conceive ~"하는 부분은 "~한 것을 생각해보려는 시도"로 생각한 다음, "a better ordering of human society than the destructive and cruel chaos in which mankind has hitherto existed"라는 구절이 무엇을 가리키는지 보아야 한다.

먼저 "인류가 지금까지 살아왔던 파괴적이고 가혹한 혼란상태 (the destructive and cruel chaos in which mankind has hitherto existed)"라는 것이 무엇을 의미할까? 역사적으로 볼 때, 극소수의 특권층이 부와 권력을 장악하고 있던 "불평등한 사회"를 말한다는 것을 빨리 간파해야 한다. 항상 표면적으로 나타난 단어의 뜻보다 숨은 뜻을 찾아내는 습관을 들여야 한다. 그 다음에는 "그보다 더 나은 사회환경 (a better ordering of human society than)"이라고 했으니, 논리의 흐름상 뒷부분에 나오는 유토피아 (Utopia)를 가리킨다는 것을 알 수 있다. 이렇게 앞 뒤 맥락에서 무엇을 의미하는지 알아 내는 것이 중요하다. 그리고 is by no means modern 도 "절대 현대적이 아니다"라고 하면 어색하다. 뒷부분에 "거슬러 올라가면 최소한 플라톤의 경우에도 찾아볼 수 있다 (it is at least as old as Plato)"고 했으니, "단지 오늘날 나타난 것은 아니다"라고 해 주어야 한다.

그래서 "The attempt to conceive imaginatively a better ordering of human society than the destructive and cruel chaos in which mankind has hitherto existed is by no means modern: it is at least as old as Plato, whose "Republic"' set the model for the Utopias of subsequent philosophers" 라는 문장을 전체적으로 우리 말로 자연스럽게 번역하면,

"인류가 지금까지 살아왔던 파괴적이고 가혹한 혼란 상태보다 더 나은 사회 환경, 즉 유토피아를 구상해보려는 시도는 단지 오늘날에만 나타난 현상이 아니다. 그러한 구상은 거슬러 올라가면 최소한 플라톤의 경우에도 찾아볼 수 있는데, 플라톤이 저술한 "국가"는 그 이후의 철학자들에게 유토피아에 대한 일종의 모범적 기준을 제시해 주었다." 라고 옮기면 된다. 사실 이 글은 철학자 버트란트 러셀이 공산주의에 대한 자신의 생각을 피력한 내용이다.

이와 같이 사물이 주어인 경우, 그리고 주어가 길게 되어 있는 경우는 기계적으로 한국어 단어를 끼워 넣고 직역식으로 해석한 다음 생각하는 것이 아니라, 논리적 구조를 빨리 파악하고 직관적으로 읽어 나갈 수 있도록 연습해야 한다.

그럼 왜 이렇게 논리적으로 한 번에 이해하지 못하고, 먼저 기계적으로 "직역"하고 나서 다시 "의역"이라는 과정을 거치는 잘못된 습관을 가지게 되었을까? 여러분들이 다녔던 학교나 학원 수업에서 선생님들이 설명할 때도 그렇고, 각종 참고서들의 해석본도 거의 모두 그렇게 해석해 놓았기 때문이다. 이런 문제는 지금도 고쳐지지 않고 있다. 초등학생이든 중학생이든 처음에 영어를 접하면 영어와 한국어의 어순이 달라 설명하기 힘드니 품사별로 고정시켜 놓고 한국어 단어를 끼워 넣어 설명하는 것이 편하기 때문이다. 그 습관을 어느 시점에는 바꿔 주어야 하는데, 그대로 가지고 있으니 제대로 이해하지 못하고 직역하는 습관이 굳어진다.

또 영어 참고서들도 직역 위주로 번역을 해 놓아 내용을 제대로 이해할 수 없게 해 놓았다. 솔직히 참고서의 해석을 보면 번역의 관점에서 문제가 많다. 참고서의 번역이 잘 되어 있어야, 청소년기부터 영어를 제대로 배울 수 있다.

영어는 사물 주어가 발달한 언어이다. 특히나 사물 주어가 추상적이고 길어질 경우에는 어렵

게 느껴지는 경우가 많다. 그런 경우에는 앞에서 설명한 것처럼 의미를 생각하면서 풀어서 이해하면 훨씬 쉽게 이해할 수 있다. 이와 같은 간단한 원리만 알아도, 사물주어가 나오는 복잡한 문장들이 전처럼 어렵게 느껴지지 않을 것이다. 지금까지 여러분들이 공부해 온 글 중에서 잘 이해가 안되었던 부분이 있으면, 이와 같이 사물 주어를 처리하는 방법을 적용해 보기 바란다. 아마, 그 전에는 이해하지 못했던 글들이 좀 더 쉽게 느껴질 것이다.

두 번째, 잘못된 습관은 영한사전에 의존하는 습관이다.

앞에서 제일 먼저 고쳐야 할 습관으로 지적한 기계적 직역 습관은 바로 이 습관과 연결되어 있다. 또 다음에 언급할 세 번째 나쁜 습관, 즉 어휘를 익힐 때 영어 단어와 일대일 대응어인 한국어만 함께 외우는 습관과도 관련이 있다. 이 세 가지 습관을 고치지 않으면 제대로 된 영어 실력을 키울 수 없다.

영어를 처음 배울 때는 어쩔 수 없었을지 몰라도 일정 시점이 지나면 영영사전을 많이 보는 습관을 들여야 한다. 영영사전을 많이 본 사람들은 느끼겠지만, 단어의 의미를 정확하게 익히고 활용 능력을 높이기 위해서는 반드시 영영사전을 보아야 한다. 물론, 처음에는 영영사전의 설명을 정확하게 이해하는데 부담을 느끼고, 또 영어로 된 설명을 한국말로 어떻게 표현해야 할지 잘 모른다는 생각 때문에 기피하는 경우가 있다. 그러다 보면 점점 영영사전을 못 보게 된다.

하지만 영영사전을 찾아보는 과정을 통해서 영어에 대한 직관력을 키울 수 있다. 그리고 실제로 영영사전을 많이 보는 과정 자체가 독해력을 키우는 과정이기도 하다. 다양한 영영사전의 정의들을 빨리 판단해야 하고, 또 패러프레이징한 예문들을 보면서 이해력도 키우고 표현력도 키울 수 있기 때문이다.

예를 들어 다음과 같은 예문들을 보자.

> He was *defined* by his passions.

이런 문장이 나오면 흔히 "직역"식으로 해석하여 "그는 그의 열정에 의해 정의된다"라고 "끼워 넣고 거기에서부터 무슨 뜻인지 이해하려고 한다. define 이라는 단어를 보면 "정의하다"라는 영한사전의 1차적인 한국어 대응어가 가장 먼저 떠오르기 때문이다. define과 같이 쉬어 보이는 단어는 아는 단어라고 생각하기 때문에 영영사전을 찾아 보지 않는다. 그런데 우리 말로 "그는 그의 열정에 의해 정의된다"하면 무슨 뜻인지 금방 와 닿지 않는다. 그러니 "해석"은 되는데 "이해"가 안된다는 느낌이 남는 것이다.

하지만 위 문장을 이해하기 쉽게 제대로 번역하면,

> "그 사람의 열정은 그 사람의 진면목을 보여준다"
> "그 사람은 열정이라면 누구에게도 지지 않는다"

"그 사람은 열정의 화신이다."

"그 사람은 진짜 열정적이다."

"그 사람은 열정 빼면 시체다."

등등 우리 말로는 다양하게 번역할 수 있다.

실제로 learnersdictionary.com에서는 이 문장에 대해 "his passions showed what kind of person he was"라고 패러프레이징하고 있다. "그 사람의 열정을 통해 진정한 그의 모습을 볼 수 있다"는 식의 의미라는 것이다.

영영 사전에서는 define 의 여러 의미 중에 "to show or describe (someone or something) clearly and completely"라는 의미가 있다는 것을 설명하고 있다.

마찬가지로 "It is his work that really defines him." 라는 예문도 "그 사람의 작품을 보면 그의 진면목을 볼 수 있다." 라고 번역하는 것이 가장 한국어적인 번역이다.

영영사전의 중요성을 언급한 김에, 우리가 알고 있는 쉬운 단어인데도 오해할 여지가 있는 단어들을 영영사전을 통해 좀 더 살펴보자. 다음 예문은 be about something 이라는 표현을 보여주는 예문이다. 단순히 "~에 관한 것이다"라고 직역해서는 의미가 잘 통하지 않는다.

예를 들어 다음과 같은 예문을 생각해 보자.

Good management is all about motivating your staff.
A good marriage is all about trust.

위 두 문장은 한국어로 어떻게 이해하는 것이 가장 정확할까?

첫 번째 문장은 "경영에서 가장 중요한 것은 직원들이 의욕적으로 일할 수 있는 환경을 만들어 주는 것이다." 두 번째 문장은 "결혼에서 가장 중요한 것은 서로에 대한 신뢰이다"라고 각각 번역할 수 있다. 두 번째 문장의 경우, 영어로 다시 표현하면, "Trust is the most important part of a good marriage."라고 할 수 있다.

또 영업의 본질에 관하여 설명한 다음과 같은 문장이 있다. "Sales is not about selling anymore, but about building trust and educating." 이런 문장을 직역하여 번역하면 어떻게 될까?

"영업은 더 이상 파는 것에 관한 것이 아니라 신뢰를 구축하고 교육하는 것에 관한 것이다." 라고 번역하면 무슨 말인지 어느 정도 유추는 할 수 있겠지만 제대로 된 한국어 문장이라고 할 수 없다. 이와 같은 직역단계를 거치는 단계에만 머물면, 역시 "해석은 되는데 이해가 안된다"고 고개를 갸우뚱하게 된다. 하지만 이 문장을 보자마자, "영업이 과거와는 달리 그냥 물건만 판다고 끝나는 것이 아니라, 고객과의 신뢰를 쌓고 또 고객이 좀 더 제품이나 서비스에 대해 유익한 정보를 알 수 있도록 도와주는 것"이라는 의미까지도 이해할 수 있어야 고개를 끄덕이며 읽을 수 있는 것이다.

　영영사전에서는 이렇게 쉽게 이해할 수 있도록 친절하게 잘 설명하고 있다.
macmillandictionary.com에서는 be about something 이라는 표현에 대해 이렇게 설명하고 있다.

> **be about something**: used for saying what the most basic or important aspect of a particular job, activity, or relationship is

다음 문장도 살펴 보자.

> She helped him put his life in proper perspective.
> Seeing how difficult their lives are has really put my problems into perspective.

　위 두 문장은 한국어로 어떻게 이해하는 것이 가장 정확할까? 첫 번째 문장은 "그녀 덕분에 그는 자신의 삶에 대해 제대로 조망해 볼 수 있게 되었다." 또 두 번째 문장은 "그들이 얼마나 힘든 삶을 살고 있는지 보고 나니, 나의 문제점들도 넓은 시야를 가지고 바라볼 수 있게 되었다."고 번역할 수 있다.
　macmillandictionary.com에서는 perspective 에 대해 이렇게 설명하고 있다.

> **perspective**: a sensible way of judging how good, bad, important etc. something is in comparison with other things.

　영영사전의 설명이 처음에는 어려워 보이지만, 예문들을 더 많이 보면, 훨씬 쉽게 이해할 수 있다. 그래서 영영사전을 볼 때에는 반드시 예문들을 함께 봐야 한다. 그래도 정확하게 이해하기 힘들다면 그 단어를 구글 등의 검색 사이트에 넣어, 검색 결과 나오는 문장들을 5개만 보면 어감을 이해할 수 있다. ChatGPT와 같은 인공지능 소프트웨어를 활용하면 원하는 만큼 예문을 볼 수 있으니, 잘 활용하면 단어의 뜻뿐만 아니라 용례도 정확하게 기억할 수 있다. 그런 방식으로 단어를 익힐 경우, 오래 기억에 남는다.

　society도 살펴 보자. Henry David Thoreau의 Walden 중 Solitude에 관한 글을 보면, I experienced sometimes that the most sweet and tender, the most innocent and encouraging society may be found in any natural object. 라는 문장이 나온다. 이 문장에서는 society를 사회라고 하는 한국어로 옮기면 안된다. 이 문장에서는 함께 있는 상태를 의미한다. 즉 자연과의 조화를 의미하는 것이다.
　그래서 자연스러운 한국어로 번역하면,
"나는 가끔 자연 속에 있을 때, 가장 다정다감하고 가장 순수하고 기분 좋은 벗과 함께 있는 듯한 느낌을 가진다"고 번역해 볼 수 있다. 여기에서 society는 the company or friendship of other people 의 의미이다. company라는 표현도 이와 같은 의미이다.

예를 들어, 다음과 같은 문장이 있을 수 있다.

I turned the radio on for company.

위 문장의 의미는 "심심해서 라디오를 틀었다"는 뜻이다. 즉, "so that I wouldn't be lonely."로 패러프레이징할 수 있다.

하나 더 예를 들어 보자.

If you're confused about the new system, you're in good company.

위 문장의 의미는 "새로운 시스템이 헷갈리는 건 다들 마찬가지야."라는 뜻이다. 그래서 이번에도 패러프레이징하면 other people are also confused와 같은 의미로 볼 수 있다.

또 social 이라는 표현도 단순히 "사회적인"이라는 직역하는 것이 아니라, 영영사전에서 설명하고 있는 것처럼 "liking to be with and talk to people"이나 "happy to be with people"의 의미를 가진다는 점을 생각하면 He is a social drinker. 나 He only drinks socially.라는 문장을 보았을 때 "그 친구는 술을 좋아하지는 않지만 분위기상 한 두 잔은 할 줄 안다."라는 의미라는 것을 알 수 있다. 영영사전의 설명을 보면 "he only drinks alcohol at parties and other social events."라고 할 수 있다. 또, "This is not a social call. I'm afraid I have some bad news."라는 예문 역시 "그냥 놀러 온 것이 아니고, 사실은 좋지 않은 소식이 있어."라는 의미이다.

그 밖에도 다음과 같은 예문도 영영사전의 중요성을 잘 보여 준다.

"You want to be careful, I think you've drunk too much."라는 문장은 "조심하는 것이 좋겠어. 너무 많이 마셨어"라는 의미이고, "You don't want to go there alone."라는 문장은 "혼자서는 가지마"라는 뜻이다.

위 예문에서 볼 수 있는 것처럼, 영영사전을 보면 you want to 는 "하라"고 조언하는 말이고 you don't want to는 "하지 말라"고 경고하는 표현이라는 설명을 볼 수 있다. 영영사전에서는 아래와 같이 자세히 설명하고 있다.

you want to/you don't want to do something: used for advising or warning someone that they should/should not do something

또 dynamic을 명사로 사용하면 변화나 결과를 초래하는 요인을 의미한다.

> dynamic: something that causes change or growth in something else

그러므로, Disease was a central dynamic in the decrease in population.라는 문장은 "질병은 인구 감소에서 핵심적인 요인이다"라고 번역할 수 있다.

dynamic은 문맥에 따라, 아래의 사전적 정의처럼 특정집단 내의 분위기나 관계를 의미하기도 한다.

> dynamic: the way that two or more people behave with each other because of a particular situation

이러한 관점에서 보면, the dynamic between a doctor and a patient는 "의사와 환자 사이의 관계"를 말하고, the teacher-student dynamic는 "선생님과 학생 사이의 관계"를 말한다. 반면에, "The dynamics of this class are different from those of other classes."라고 하면, "이 반의 분위기는 다른 반의 분위기와 차이가 있다"로 이해할 수 있다.

지금까지 이 글을 읽다 보면, 한 가지 의문이 들 것이다. 영한사전에는 한국말 대응어가 있지만, 영영사전에는 한국말 대응어가 없는데 어떻게 적절한 한국어를 찾아낼 수 있느냐는 것이다. 바로 앞에서 설명한 dynamic만 해도 때로는 "요인"이라는 말로 옮기기도 하고 때로는 "관계" 또 때로는 "분위기"라고 하는데 그걸 어떻게 찾아내느냐는 의문이 들 수 있다.

적절한 한국어를 찾아내는 방법은 먼저 영영사전의 정의를 통해 단어의 의미를 이미지로 익히고 예문을 읽으면서 스스로 빈칸을 채우는 퀴즈를 푼다고 상상하면서 읽어보는 것이다.

예를 들어 "The dynamics of this class are different from those of other classes."라는 문장을 읽으면서 "이 반의 _____는 다른 반의 _____와 다르다"라고 생각하면서 _____, 즉 빈칸에 들어가기에 가장 적합한 표현을 찾으면 된다. 그런 연습을 계속하면 직역과 의역을 거치는 독해, 즉 두 단계를 거치다 보니 읽는 속도도 떨어지고 내용이 조금만 추상적이거나 자신이 모르는 주제일 때는 "해석은 되는데 이해가 안된다"는 느낌을 가지는 것이 아니라 처음부터 한 단계만으로도 의미를 파악하고 숨은 뜻과 논리도 이해할 수 있는 실력을 갖출 수 있다.

세 번째 지적하고 싶은 나쁜 습관은 영어 단어와 한국어 일대일 대응어만 따로 외우는 습관이다.

첫 번째 언급한 기계적 직역 습관, 두 번째 지적한 영한사전에 지나치게 의존하는 습관과 더불어 또 한가지 고쳐야 할 습관은 단어를 대하는 태도와 단어를 외우는 습관이다.

영어를 공부하다 보면 단어 때문에 고민하는 경우가 많다. 물론, 단어는 매우 중요하다. 글을 읽고 이해할 때, 구문이 익숙하지 않고 내용을 잘 몰라도 단어의 의미만 정확하게 알고 있어도 내용을 유추하기가 쉽기 때문이다. 그래서 잘못 생각하면 "단어만 알면 독해는 다 할 수 있는데, 단어를 몰라서 그래. 그러니 단어만 죽도록 외우면 된다"고 생각할 수 있다.

하지만, 영한사전에서 영어 단어와 한국어 일대일 대응어만 따로 외우거나 아주 까다로운 어휘들만 모아 놓은 어휘 책에서 같은 방식으로 단어만 많이 외우는 것은 별 효과가 없다. 지하철을 타거나 버스를 타고 다니다 보면 중고생뿐만 아니라 다양한 영어 시험을 준비하는 성인들도 단어만 따로 외우는 모습을 자주 볼 수 있다. 대개의 경우, 종이 한 장을 반으로 접어 왼쪽에는 영어 단어, 오른쪽에는 한국어 대응어를 적어 기계적으로 외우는 식이다. 그렇게 단어만 외우는 것은 당장에는 무엇인가 하고 있는 것 같아 마음의 위안이 될지는 모르지만, 효과가 없을 뿐만 아니라 오히려 장기적으로는 독이 될 가능성이 있다. 장기적으로 "독"이 될 수도 있다고까지 말하는 이유는 독해가 안 되는 것이 사실은 앞에서도 지적한 것처럼 문장을 보는 시각이 잘못되어 있고, 단어의 어감을 정확하게 이해하지 못하여 나타나는 현상인데, 단순히 단어 때문인 것으로 착각하게 만들기 때문이다. 그 결과, 단어만 많이 외우면 된다는 생각 때문에 오히려 잘못된 습관을 고쳐야 한다는 필요성을 절감하지 못하게 되니, 장기적으로는 오히려 독이 될 수 있다.

만약 난이도가 높은 각종 영어 독해 시험에서 원하는 점수를 얻고, 더 나아가 좀 더 차원 높은 글, 즉 The Economist, New York Times, New Yorker 등의 권위 있는 신문이나 시사 잡지, 또 그 밖에도 다양한 문학작품이나 고전을 원서로 읽으려면, 다양한 글을 많이 읽으면서 주제 지식을 많이 늘려야 한다. 그런데 단어만 따로 외우다 보면 읽는 양 자체가 절대적으로 부족하게 되고 단어의 의미를 너무 좁게 이해하게 되어 결국은 독해력 향상의 발목을 잡는 결과가 나타나는 것이다.

일반영어와 문학 때문에 고민하는 임용시험 수험생들은 지금까지 설명한 세 가지의 나쁜 습관만 버려도 분명히 달라지는 것을 느끼게 될 것이다.

올바른 영어 독해 공부 방법

　이제부터는 독해력을 향상시키기 위하여 어떻게 해야 할지 생각해 보자. 가장 먼저, 앞에서 설명한 그릇된 습관을 버리고 나서, 영어로 글을 읽는 재미를 느끼고 다양한 수준과 내용의 글을 기회가 있을 때마다 읽어보는 습관을 들여야 한다.

　독해력을 늘리기 위해 가장 먼저 지적하고 싶은 것은 우선 많이 읽는 것이다. 영어 독해 때문에 고민하는 사람들 중에는 "정독"이 더 중요한지 "다독"이 더 중요한지 질문하는 경우가 많다. 물론 두 가지 모두 중요하지만 구태여 꼽으라고 한다면 "다독", 즉 우선 많이 읽는 것이 중요하다. 많이 읽다 보면 자꾸 의문이 생기게 되고 그 의문을 해결하는 과정에서 나름대로 해결방안을 찾게 되기 때문이다. 우선 읽는 양이 많아야 질적인 변화도 일어난다.

　물론 그 과정에서 영영사전을 많이 찾아보고 또 모르는 부분이 나오면 최대한 유추를 한 다음에 구글 등의 온라인 검색을 통해서 수시로 찾아보는 습관을 들여야 한다. 검색을 할 때에는 단순히 문서 내용만 보는 것이 아니라 이미지나 동영상들도 보는 것이 좋다. 훨씬 더 입체적으로 공부할 수 있기 때문이다.

　어떤 시험이든 시험을 준비하는 사람들은 특히 자신이 혼자서 공부하고 고민하는 시간을 늘려야 한다. 특히, 강의에 대한 의존도가 높은 사람들, 특히 온라인 강의를 많이 듣는 사람들은 혼자서 공부하는 시간을 늘려야 한다. 어떤 시험이든, 수험생은 혼자 공부하는 시간이 절반 이상이 되어야 한다. 강의는 30% 면 충분하고 호흡이 잘 맞는 사람들과 스터디하는 것이 20% 정도 되는 것이 적절하다. 혼자서 공부하다 보면 잘 풀리지 않아서 답답할 때도 있지만 결국은 그런 과정을 거쳐야 기억도 오래 남는다. 당장에 시간을 아낀다고 강의에만 의존하거나 누군가가 정리해 놓은 어휘들만 외우는 방식으로는 실력을 향상하지 못하고 항상 제자리 걸음을 걷는 듯한 느낌을 가질 수 밖에 없다. 자신이 스스로 해결할 수 있는 능력을 키우지 못하기 때문이다.

　공부에 많은 시간을 투자하는데도 원하는 성과가 나오지 않는다면 혹시 강의에 지나치게 의존하고 있지 않는지, 혼자 고민하고 문제를 해결하는 것이 두려워서 그런 것은 아닌지 생각해 보아야 한다. 모르는 단어나 구문이 나오거나 논리가 이해가 되지 않을 때에도 그렇고, 우리

말로 어떻게 옮겨야 할 지 막막할 때에는 앞에서 이미 설명한 것처럼 스스로에게 빈칸 문제나 퀴즈를 낸다고 생각하고 해결해 보라.

그래도 잘 안되면 구글에 이해가 안 되는 문장을 통째로 넣어 검색해 보거나 영영사전에서 표현을 찾아보면 웬만한 것들은 해결할 수 있는 단서들이 있다. 그러면 스스로 해결할 수 있다. 그런데, 혼자서 읽고 공부하는 것이 막막한 사람들이 보통 하는 이야기는 "내가 해석한 것이 맞는지 알 수가 없어서 읽어봤자 의미가 없는 것 아니냐. 어차피 확인도 안 되는데 그래도 읽어야 하느냐"는 것이다.

결론부터 이야기 하자면, 그래도 많이 읽어야 한다. 많이 읽다 보면, 어느 시점이 지나서 자신도 모르게 이해력이 높아지고 영어에 대한 직관력이 생긴다. 그리고 모르는 단어도 자꾸 보면 눈에 익고, 그러다가 사전을 한 번 찾아보면 잊어버리지 않게 된다. 그러니 스스로를 믿고 우선 읽는 양을 늘리기 바란다.

둘째, 앞에서도 이미 설명한 것처럼 영영 사전을 반드시 봐야 한다. 그렇다고 영한 사전은 보지 말라는 이야기는 아니다. 때로는 영한 사전에 있는 한국어 단어가 더 명료할 때도 있다. 두 사전을 같이 비교하면서 보는 것이 좋다. 하지만 점차 공부하다 보면, 영영 사전이 훨씬 도움이 된다는 것을 실감하게 될 것이다. 사전 찾는 것을 시간낭비라고 생각하면 안된다. 사전을 찾고 그 단어의 정의와 예문들을 보는 자체가 독해 공부이다. 반드시 예문들을 읽고 소리내어 몇 차례 발음을 해 보라. 가능하면 예문들은 외우는 것이 좋다. 그렇게 하는 것이 서술형 답안을 쓸 때에도 도움이 되고, 2차 수업 실연에서도 유용하게 사용할 수 있기 때문이다.

셋째, 영어와 한국어의 차이점을 명확하게 알고 영어의 관점에서 글을 읽고 이해해야 한다. 한가지 분명한 차이는 영어는 다양성을 추구하는 반면 한국어는 통일성을 추구한다는 점이다.

예를 들어, 과거 언론 매체의 기사들을 보면 영어에서는 북한을 지칭할 때, North Korea나 Pyongyang 뿐만 아니라 the rogue nation, the Stalinist nation, the hermit nation, the isolated nation 등으로 다양하게 사용한다. 이와 같이 영어에서는 다양하게 사용하는 반면, 한국어에서는 "북한"이라고 하나로 통일성 있게 사용하는 것이 좋다.

또, 뉴욕타임즈의 한 기사에서 미국의 연준(the Fed)에서 기준 금리를 0.25% 인상하기로 했다는 기사가 실린 적이 있었다. 그 중 다음과 같은 문장이 있었다.

The Federal Reserve raised its benchmark interest rate on Wednesday and signaled that it expects additional rate increases next year in a display of measured confidence in the economy that came despite financial market worries and political pressure to suspend rate increases.

번역을 한다면 "연방준비제도는 수요일 기준 금리 인상을 단행하며, 내년에 추가 금리 인상이 예상된다고 시사했다. 이는 금융 시장에 대한 우려와 금리 인상을 보류해야 한다는 정치적 압박에도 불구하고 경제 상황에 대해 조심스럽게 자신감을 나타낸 것으로 보인다."라고 할 수 있다. 이 문장에서, raise its benchmark interest rate라는 표현은 기준 금리를 인상한다는 의미이다. 그런데, 그 문장 이후 뒷부분에, "Mr. Powell insisted on the wisdom of the

Fed's plans to raise borrowing costs while investors dumped their holdings."라는 문장이 나온다. "파월 의장은 (주식시장의) 투자자들이 주식을 대거 매도하는 와중에도 연준의 금리 인상 계획이 현명한 판단이라고 주장했다."는 뜻이다

이 문맥에서 "raise borrowing costs" 역시 기준 금리 인상을 의미한다. 빌리는 비용이란 금리이니 말이다. 하지만 영어에서는 이와 같이 같은 표현을 반복하여 사용하지 않고 반드시 다른 말로 바꾸어 표현한다. 이 경우에도 한국어는 "금리 인상"이라는 하나의 표현만 사용한다.

넷째, 논리적으로 사고하고 추론할 수 있어야 한다. 영어 독해력을 높이기 위해서는 독해의 두 가지 요소에 집중해야 한다. 글을 읽으면서 전체적인 요지와 흐름을 빨리 잡는 한편, 구체적인 인과 관계와 내용도 정확하게 이해해야 한다. 이미 앞에서도 설명한 것처럼 단순 직역식으로 문장을 보는 것이 아니라, 보편적이고 상식적인 논리를 바탕으로 논리적으로 추론하면 읽어야 한다.

예문을 통해 살펴 보자. DNA를 방대한 양의 정보를 저장하는 매체로 활용할 수 있는 가능성을 다룬 Economist 기사에 다음과 같은 문장이 있었다.

> But, as is often the case, natural selection knocks humanity's best efforts into a cocked hat. DNA, the information-storage technology preferred by biology, can cram up to 215 petabytes of data into a single gram. That is 10m times what the best modern hard drives can manage.

물론 특히 영국 영어에서는 A throw B into a cocked hat 이라는 숙어가 아래 예문의 경우처럼, "A 가 B보다 훨씬 낫다"라는 의미라는 사실을 모르면 이해하기 힘든 문장인 것은 사실이다.

> The old design was good, but this new one knocks/beats it into a cocked hat.
> "과거의 디자인이 좋은 것은 사실이다. 하지만 새로운 디자인이 과거의 그 디자인보다 훨씬 낫다."

하지만 그 숙어의 뜻을 알았다고 해서 예로 든 문장을 제대로 이해할 수 있는 것은 아니다. 전체 문맥의 논리를 이해해야 하기 때문이다. 예를 들어 위 문장 중 natural selection knocks humanity's best efforts into a cocked hat 부분을 번역할 때 직역을 한다고 생각해 보자. "자연 선택은 인간의 최고의 노력보다 훨씬 낫다."라고 하면 무슨 말인지 알 수 없다. "natural selection"은 다윈의 진화론 중 핵심적인 개념인 "자연선택설"을 의미한다. 하지만 이 경우에는 생물의 유전의 기본적인 단위인 DNA를 상징적으로 나타내는 표현으로 볼 수 있다.

따라서 위의 문장을 번역하면, "대개의 경우처럼, 저장 매체의 경우도 인간이 아무리 최첨단 기술을 동원하여 노력해도 자연을 따라갈 수는 없다. DNA 저장 정보 장치는 단 1그램의 DNA에 215 페타바이트의 정보를 저장할 수 있다. 이와 같이 방대한 용량은 현재 존재하는 가장 큰 용량을 가진 하드 드라이버의 저장 용량의 1천 만 배이다."라고 할 수 있다.

다섯째, 상상력을 발휘하여 전체적인 이미지와 스토리를 떠올릴 수 있어야 한다. 이러한

상상력은 물론, 어떤 글이든 읽을 때 필요하지만, 특히 문학 작품을 읽을 때 중요하다.
예를 들어, Stephen Crane의 소설 The Red Badge of Courage 중 Chapter 2에는 다음과 같은 문장이 있다.

> He was afraid to make an open declaration of his concern, because he dreaded to place some unscrupulous confidant upon the high plane of the unconfessed from which elevation he could be derided.

복잡하고 추상적으로 느껴져서 쉽게 이해하기 힘든 문장이다. 이런 글은 스토리를 상상할 수 있어야 이해할 수 있다. 주인공 Henry Fleming은 십대의 어린 나이에 남북 전쟁 당시 북군의 일원으로 참전한다. 이 부분은 헨리가 전투를 앞두고 두려움을 가지고 있는데, 그 부분에 대해 다른 사람에게 털어놓을까 고민하는 부분이다.

이 문장은 우선 표현들 때문에 특히 짐작하기 힘들 수 있다. 하지만 글을 읽다가 문장의 구조나 단어들을 통해 명쾌하게 이해되지 않을 때, 즉 나무만 보아서는 잘 모를 때 또는 미시적으로 접근해서 큰 그림이 잡히지 않을 때에는 전체적인 맥락 속에서 유추하는 것이 필요하다. 다시 말하여, 숲을 본다고 말할 수도 있고 거시적 관점에서 추론한다고도 할 수 있다. 어쨌든 직관적으로 추론을 해 보고 거꾸로 검증하는 의미에서 문장 구조를 보는 것이 좋은 방법인 경우도 있다. 이 경우, 그렇게 접근하면 오히려 이해하는 것이 쉬워진다. 앞 부분에서는 자신이 걱정하고 있는 걸 공개적으로 말하기(to make an open declaration of his concern)는 두려웠다고 했다. 그 다음에 because ~라고 했고 더군다나 deride 라는 동사가 나왔으니, "왜냐하면 ~ 비웃음 거리가 되지 않을까 걱정이 되었기 때문이다"라는 의미가 나와야 한다는 것을 알 수 있다.

그럼 이 문장을 이해하는 방법을 구체적으로 살펴 보자. 이 문장을 이해하려면 우선 개별적인 표현들의 이미지를 떠 올려야 한다. 우선 "unscrupulous confidant"는 쉽게 말하면 믿을 만하다고 생각하고 털어놓지만 나중에 뒤통수를 칠만한 사람을 의미한다는 것을 알 수 있다. 물론 사전적인 의미를 보면 "unscrupulous"는 "not honest or fair"의 의미이고 "confidant"는 "a trusted friend you can talk to about personal and private things" 즉, 믿을만한 사람을 의미한다. 그 다음에 좀 더 까다로운 표현을 살펴보자." high plane of the unconfessed"는 속내를 드러내지 않는 사람들 (the unconfessed) 에게서 느낄 수 있는 초연한 경지(high plane)를 말한다.

이 부분을 이해하려면, 역시 영영사전에서 각각의 단어를 어떻게 설명하고 있는지 예문과 함께 보는 것이 도움이 된다.

1. plane: a level of thought, existence, or development

    예문 He uses meditation to reach a higher spiritual plane.

    예문 I don't consider the two writers' stories as being on the same plane.

2. the unconfessed: people who have not confessed;

  예문) The unconfessed cannot be forgiven.

"placed some unscrupulous confidant upon the high plane of the unconfessed"라는 부분을 좀 더 자세히 분석해 보면 "placed someone upon the high plane of ...."부분은 "...한 지점에 누군가를 놓는다는 식으로" 물리적 이미지를 만들어 설명하고 있다. 그리고 from which elevation he could be derided에서 elevation은 high plane과 직결되는 내용이다. 당연하지만, 높은 곳에 있으면 고도(elevation)가 높아진다. 그리고 which는 the high plane of the unconfessed 가 선행사인 관계형용사이다. 이와 같이 복잡한 문장 구조이지만, 문장을 나누어서 보면 좀 더 명료하게 이해할 수 있다. 뒷부분을 단문으로 만들어 보면, "He could be derided from the high elevation of the unconfessed."라고 보면 된다.

그래서 "그는 두려워하고 있다는 사실을 드러내지 않았는데, 그 이유는 믿을만하다고 생각해서 상대방에게 자신의 속내를 드러낼 경우, 상대방은 두렵다는 내색을 하지 않았기 때문에 그와 같이 유리한 상황에서 자신을 비웃지나 않을까 겁이 났기 때문이다"라고 번역할 수 있다.

이런 문장들은 이해하기도 쉽지 않다. 그래서 영영사전을 통해 각각의 단어에 대한 어감을 정확하게 이해하고 논리적 상상력을 통해 그 의미를 파악하는 연습을 많이 해야 한다. 그러면 점차 복잡한 문장 구조를 어렵다고 기피하지 않고 오히려 즐길 수 있게 된다.

여섯째, 문장을 이해할 때에는 단순히 단어별로 보는 것이 아니라 흐름으로 읽으면서 의미 단락을 넓혀 가야 한다. 때로는 앞에서 이미 언급한 논리적 상상력을 바탕으로 이미지를 만들어 이해하는 것이 도움이 된다.

다시 예문을 하나 살펴 보자.

Gary Younge 라는 흑인 작가가 사회의 관용과 포용의 정신을 강조한 글에 다음과 같은 문장이 있다.

The problem is not with people taking sides, or even the sides they've taken, but the apparent inability of many to venture beyond their own trenches to see what kind of truce is possible.

이 문장의 경우에도 그냥 영한사전의 한국어 일대일 대응어를 끼워 넣어서는 정확하게 이해할 수 없다. 그럴 경우, 이미 앞에서도 이야기한 것처럼, "해석은 되는데 이해가 안된다"는 말이 나오기 쉽다.

이런 문장을 보면 단어를 하나씩 보는 것이 아니라 여러 개의 단어들로 구성된 메시지를 찾아야 한다. 이 문장을 우리 말에 가장 자연스럽게 재구성해 보면 "문제는 사람들이 진영논리에 따라 편가르기를 하는 것(people taking sides)이나 심지어 그들의 진영 논리(the sides they've taken)가 아니다. 오히려 문제점은 많은 사람들이 자신의 아집(their own trenches)에서 과감히 벗어나(venture beyond) 서로 어떠한 공감대를 형성할 수 있을지(what kind of truce is possible)를 알아보지 못하는 것 같다는(the apparent inability)는 점이다."라고 배열할 수 있다.

이와 같이 문장을 보려면 개별적인 단어의 정확한 의미도 알아야 하지만, 메시지를 논리적으로 읽어야 한다. 그렇게 이해하면 구체적이고 명료하게 이해할 수 있다.

일곱째, 가능하면 앞에서부터 문장들을 처리하면서 이해하는 문장구역 (sight translation) 또는 문장시역이라고도 하는 방식으로 연습하면 문장의 구조를 파악하고 의미를 빨리 이해하는 데 도움이 된다. 방법은 간단하다. 영어로 된 문장들을 읽으면서 바로 한국어로 번역하는 연습을 하는데, 입으로 통역처럼 한국어로 옮기는 것이다. 이러한 방법으로 연습할 경우, 문장의 의미단락별로 이해할 수 있고 한국어를 자연스럽게 다듬을 수 있다는 장점이 있다. 통역대학원에서도 통.번역 연습을 할 때 중요하게 생각하는 훈련 방식이고 연사의 문장이 끝나지 않은 상황에서 동시통역이 가능할 수 있는 것도 문장구역 연습이 잘 되어 있기 때문이다. 이러한 방식은 속독이 특히 중요한 임용시험을 준비하는 수험생들에게는 매우 유용한 독해 방식이다.

간단하게 예를 들면, 과거 Economist에 실린 기사 중에 "Agriculture is war by other means."라는 문장이 있었다. 이 간단한 문장도 직역을 하면 명료하지 않다. 만약 직역을 한다면 "농업은 다른 수단에 의한 전쟁이다."라고 번역할 수 있을 것이다. 하지만 그 보다는 앞에서부터 문장구역 방법으로 처리하고 때로는 문장을 나눌 필요가 있으면 나누어 이해하는 것이 더 좋은 방법이다. 만약 문장구역식으로, "농업도 일종의 전쟁이다. 다만 수단이 다를 뿐이다."라고 하면 더 분명하고 명료하게 의미를 전달할 수 있다.

여덟째, 영어로 된 글을 빨리 정확하게 읽고 이해하려면, 영어뿐만 아니라 한국어로도 독서량을 크게 늘려야 한다. 모든 분야에 대한 지적인 호기심과 노력이 반드시 필요하다. 특히, 과학적인 내용을 다루는 지문의 경우에는 구체적인 사실들 사이의 상관관계를 이해할 수 있을 정도의 지식이 반드시 필요하다. 소위 문과에 해당하는 전공을 선택한 사람들은 특별히 과학에 평소 관심이 있는 경우가 아니면, 과학기사들을 읽을 때, 어려움을 겪는 경우가 많다. 그리고 소위 이과에 해당하는 사람들은 철학, 종교 및 인문학 등 추상적이고 관념적인 내용을 다루는 지문에서 어려움을 겪는 경우가 많다. 그러므로 지적인 성장뿐만 아니라, 영어 독해력을 향상시키기 위해서도 다양한 분야의 좋은 책들을 많이 읽어야 한다.

이와 같이 영어를 영어답게 공부하고 글의 문맥을 이해하는 방법을 익히면, 비약적으로 영어 독해력을 높일 수 있고, 결국에는 임용고사에서 일반영어와 문학에서 고득점을 올릴 수 있다.

Reading & Writing
Booster

PART 02

속독을 위한 영어 구문 분석

1

모르는 부분의 추론은
다음과 같은 네 가지 원칙을 따르자

1. **지시어의 대상을 찾는다.** (Identify the referential expressions.)
   정관사, 각종 대명사 및 지시 대명사, 그리고 another, other, such 등의 표현이 지칭하는 대상을 빨리 판단하면 속독이 가능하다.

2. **문맥 속에서 상호 관련된 어구에 주목한다.**
   (Pay attention to contextually related expressions.)

3. **설명 또는 비교의 대상을 찾는다.**
   (Look for the subject of explanation or comparison.)

4. **논리적으로 접근한다.**
   (Approach logically.)

각각의 원칙을 예문과 함께 좀 더 구체적으로 살펴보자.

1 지시어(구)의 대상을 찾는다.
(Identify the referential expressions.)

① 단문으로 구성된 아래 예문을 통해 지시어(구)의 대상을 찾는 연습을 해 보라. 색으로 표시한 부분은 의미상 서로 관련이 있는 부분이므로, 쉽게 추론할 수 있다.

1. Life is full of unpredictable changes, but wisdom allows us to navigate this uncertainty with grace.

2. Communication can often lead to misunderstandings, but clarifying our intentions can dissolve this confusion.

3. Human ambition frequently leads to conflict, but empathy has the power to heal this division.

4. Technological advances sometimes cause societal disruptions, but thoughtful policies can mitigate this upheaval.

5. Prolonged exposure to stress weakens mental resilience, but self-care practices can counteract this deterioration.

6. The allure of an ancient artifact surpasses all other fascinations.

7. A mentor's guidance to his pupil stands apart from all other influences.

8. The bond between twins transcends all other connections, uniquely characterized by shared experiences and innate closeness.

9. "I still find it perplexing that you've allowed such a trivial issue to perturb you," Richard observed, waving away her agitation as though it were an insignificant breeze.

10. "I cannot comprehend why this has stirred such a tempest within you," Clara said, her words cutting through the tension with a veneer of detachment.

11. "It baffles me that you would let something so inconsequential unsettle you," Sebastian noted, his dismissal of her unease thinly veiled beneath a polite smile.

12. The resonance of a poet's words, woven from the fibers of their innermost thoughts, transcends all other expressions of language and art, shaping meanings that cannot be imitated.

13. The historian's meticulous reconstruction of an era through fragmentary records surpasses all other forms of intellectual inquiry, for it intertwines evidence with imagination to resurrect the past.

14. The bond shared between siblings who have endured life's hardships together resists comparison to any other human connection, for it is tempered by shared suffering and unspoken understanding.

15. A philosopher's pursuit of truth, untethered from worldly distractions, stands apart from all other endeavors of the human mind, as it ventures into realms both abstract and eternal.

16. The allure of a masterpiece crafted with an artist's vision, labor, and soul transcends all other creations, for it carries within its form an ineffable depth that defies replication.

② 비교적 짧은 문단으로 더 연습해 보자.

1. Ecosystems are delicate networks sustained by the intricate interplay of flora, fauna, and environmental factors. Yet, human activity disrupts the balance through deforestation, pollution, and overexploitation of resources, leading to biodiversity loss, climate instability, and the collapse of natural systems.

2. Languages evolve over time, shaped by cultural shifts, technological advancements, and the movement of people. With each passing generation, words fall out of use, grammatical structures morph, and entirely new expressions emerge. This transformation reflects not only linguistic creativity but also the ever-changing nature of human communication.

3. Public trust in institutions has declined steadily due to corruption, inefficiency, and perceived lack of accountability. Citizens feel increasingly alienated as those in power fail to address pressing concerns such as inequality and climate change. This disillusionment breeds apathy and skepticism, eroding the foundational confidence necessary for governance and societal cohesion.

4. Identity is a multifaceted construct, encompassing race, gender, nationality, and countless other dimensions. However, societal pressures often force individuals

into reductive categories, ignoring the fluidity and intersectionality of their lived experiences. This oversimplification perpetuates stereotypes and stifles authentic self-expression.

5. International cooperation is critical for addressing global challenges like climate change and pandemics. Yet, differing national priorities, economic disparities, and political ideologies often hinder progress. This fragmentation weakens the collective response, leaving humanity vulnerable to crises that require unified action.

③ 조금 더 긴 문단으로 더 연습해 보자.

1. The symphony created by a composer, borne of countless hours of thought and inspiration, stands apart from all other manifestations of human creativity. Unlike the transient melodies of a folk song or the structured repetition of a pop anthem, the symphony is an epic narrative, each movement revealing a chapter in a story that transcends time. Its uniqueness lies in the way it intertwines harmony and dissonance, order and chaos, forging a language that speaks directly to the soul. No other form of artistic expression combines such mathematical precision with emotional depth, allowing each listener to interpret its meaning in their own way. The symphony's power to evoke universal truths, while remaining deeply personal to each audience member, distinguishes it from all other art forms.

2. An architect's design for a monumental structure rises above all other interpretations of space and form. Unlike the utilitarian construction of a simple dwelling or the ornate detailing of a historical edifice, a monumental design seeks to embody the aspirations of a culture, a people, or even an epoch. It challenges the natural boundaries of gravity and material, redefining what is possible within the framework of human ingenuity. All other structures fade in comparison to the monument's ability to merge functionality with symbolism, crafting a space that invites reflection, awe, and unity. Through its enduring presence, the monument reminds us of the transcendent ideals that inspire its creation.

3. The scholar's devotion to uncovering the truths of history surpasses all other intellectual pursuits, for it entails an unyielding commitment to piecing together fragments of the past with meticulous care. While a scientist explores the laws governing the physical universe and a philosopher delves into the nature of

existence, the historian walks a delicate line between evidence and interpretation. No other discipline demands such a profound empathy for those long gone, combined with the rigorous objectivity required to reconstruct their lives. A single artifact or obscure document may hold the key to unlocking an entire narrative, transforming our understanding of what once was. In this way, the historian's work bridges the temporal chasm between the present and the distant past.

4. The ocean's call to those who venture across its vast expanse differs from all other experiences offered by nature. Unlike the serenity of a forest or the majesty of a mountain peak, the ocean offers a paradoxical allure, embodying both tranquility and tempestuous power. Its depths hold mysteries no other landscape can rival, containing life forms, currents, and phenomena still largely unknown. The sailor, the explorer, or even the casual wanderer drawn to its shores feels an undeniable pull—a connection to something primordial and infinite. No other element of the natural world mirrors the ocean's capacity to inspire both fear and fascination, leaving those who encounter it forever changed by its relentless motion.

5. A mentor's influence on a young mind transcends all other relationships in the realm of education and personal growth. While a teacher imparts knowledge and a parent provides support, a mentor occupies a singular role, guiding through example, wisdom, and understanding. This bond defies simple categorization, as it intertwines instruction with inspiration, correction with encouragement. Unlike any other form of guidance, the mentor's influence extends beyond the immediate goal, shaping not just skills but the very character of the mentee. Through their unique insight into potential and challenges, a mentor empowers an individual to achieve what they themselves might never have imagined, leaving a legacy that no other relationship can replicate.

2 문맥 속에서 상호 관련된 어구에 주목한다.
(Pay attention to contextually related expressions.)

① 먼저 단문으로 구성된 아래 예문을 통해 문맥 속에서 상호 관련된 어구를 찾는 연습을 해 보자. 색으로 표시한 부분은 의미상 서로 관련이 있는 부분이므로, 쉽게 추론할 수 있다.

1. Her ability to exude confidence made her an inspiring leader, even when she was only pretending to be self-assured.

2. The professor's rigorous and methodical approach to research was much more structured than his casual way of thinking about problems.

3. His actions were guided by a deep sense of altruism, although he often simply wanted to help others.

4. The company's strategy was rooted in an extensive analysis of the market, even if it all started with simple observations.

5. Despite his eloquent and rhetorical speech, his message was simply a call to encourage action.

6. She had a natural ability to empathize with others, always able to feel what they were going through.

7. He was constantly seeking solace in nature, finding comfort in its peaceful surroundings.

8. The team's success was rooted in their collaboration, where they always worked together to achieve their goals.

9. Her arguments were based on logic, always making sense of even the most complicated ideas.

10. His strategic decisions were informed by careful planning, where every move was thought out in advance.

② 문단을 통해 더 연습해 보자.

1. Despite his considerable fame, the scientist maintained a sense of humility that allowed him to constantly seek new perspectives. His ability to remain open-minded meant he was never satisfied with just a superficial understanding. Instead, he was driven by an unyielding desire for deeper knowledge, always seeking to unearth the fundamental truths behind the mysteries of the universe. This perpetual quest for discovery not only earned him respect in the academic community but also served as a reminder that true genius lies not in knowing everything but in embracing the pursuit of understanding. Whether he was engaged in debates with colleagues or formulating new hypotheses, his unwavering commitment to exploration was a testament to his intellectual integrity and his belief in the value of unrelenting inquiry.

2. The leader's strategic approach was marked by careful strategizing, planning not just for the immediate future but for every conceivable outcome. His ability to anticipate challenges and shape his responses with precise tactics made him a master of foresight. Each decision he made was driven by a deep understanding of both the environment and the people around him. He viewed obstacles as opportunities for growth and used his acute insight into human nature to foster collaboration among diverse groups. His leadership was not merely about giving orders but about cultivating an atmosphere of mutual respect, where every member felt valued. His uncanny ability to read situations and respond with the perfect solution earned him a reputation as a visionary in his field, a leader who could inspire others to see beyond the ordinary and act with extraordinary precision.

3. Her success in the corporate world was largely due to her remarkable intuition, an almost instinctive ability to read people and situations with precision. She could often sense shifts in the market before they became apparent to others, a skill she honed through years of careful observation. Whether negotiating deals or managing teams, she trusted her gut instincts, understanding that sometimes the most valuable insights come from the unconscious mind. Her colleagues often marveled at her knack for making the right decisions at the right time, even when data and analysis seemed to point in a different direction. In a world that often relies on hard facts and figures, her ability to blend intuition with logic gave her an edge. She understood that successful leadership wasn't just about expertise; it was about reading between the lines and responding to what couldn't always be seen.

4. The author's writing was a reflection of his profound perspective on the human condition, revealing a deep empathy for the struggles and triumphs of ordinary people. His novels often explored the delicate balance between individual freedom and societal expectations, addressing the conflicts that arise when personal desires clash with social norms. Through his characters, he explored the complexities of identity, love, and loss, offering readers a window into the most vulnerable aspects of the human experience. His ability to empathize with his characters gave his work a raw, unfiltered honesty that resonated deeply with audiences. It was his profound understanding of human nature, combined with his unique narrative voice, that set his writing apart. Each page invited readers to reflect on their own lives, challenging them to confront the tensions between who they are and who they are expected to be.

5. In the realm of diplomacy, the ambassador was known for his remarkable calm, an ability to remain composed even in the most volatile situations. His poise was the result of years spent mastering the art of navigating difficult conversations, where every word could carry weight and consequence. While others might have succumbed to impatience or frustration, he maintained an unwavering sangfroid, understanding that the key to resolution lay in maintaining control over one's emotions. His diplomatic acumen was reflected in his ability to build consensus among disparate groups, each with conflicting interests. He was a master at reading the room, understanding the subtle cues and underlying tensions that others might miss. Through his measured responses and thoughtful engagement, he turned potential conflicts into opportunities for collaboration, a skill that earned him the admiration of his peers and the trust of his international counterparts.

3 설명 또는 비교의 대상을 찾는다.
(Look for the subject of explanation or comparison.)

비교의 내용을 포함하는 문장에서 그 대상들이 지니는 특성을 통해 동의어 또는 반의어를 찾아내면 모르는 단어의 의미 파악이 가능하다.

또, 원인과 결과의 논리적 관계를 내용으로 하는 문장에서는 양자 중에 어느 하나를 알면 다른 하나를 유추할 수 있다.

① 먼저 단문으로 구성된 아래 예문을 통해 유사어, 동의어 또는 반의어를 찾는 연습을 해 보자. **색**으로 표시한 부분은 의미상 서로 관련이 있는 부분이므로, 쉽게 추론할 수 있다.

1. The team's efforts exceeded even the most ambitious goals, outperforming all prior achievements.

2. The book's success surpassed even the most hopeful predictions, overshadowing earlier works.

3. The experiment's outcome exceeded even the most bold hypotheses, eclipsing past discoveries.

4. The company's growth exceeded even the most optimistic forecasts, outpacing earlier records.

5. The athlete's record surpassed even the most impressive expectations, leaving all prior feats behind.

6. The speech's reception surpassed even the most positive predictions, eclipsing previous presentations.

7. The recipe's simplicity outdid even the most hopeful expectations, outshining traditional methods.

8. The vacation's experience went beyond even the most glowing reviews, overshadowing previous trips.

9. The city's transformation transcended even the most ambitious urban plans, redefining prior landscapes.

10. The teacher's dedication outshone even the highest standards, inspiring more than previous instructors.

11. The startup's innovation outpaced even the most forward-thinking ideas, disrupting past technologies.

12. The child's curiosity outmatched even the most optimistic hopes, surpassing what older generations imagined.

13. The festival's attendance broke through even the boldest predictions, eclipsing all past events.

14. The charity's impact rose above even the most generous donations, transforming previous efforts.

15. The community's unity went far beyond even the most optimistic forecasts, standing apart from earlier divisions.

② 문단을 통해 더 연습해 보자.

1. Despite his natural talent for public speaking, he had always been more refined in his delivery than most of his peers. Where others relied on bold gestures and loud assertions, he preferred a more eloquent, measured approach. His presentations were not only convincing but also focused, never meandering or over-elaborate. Unlike some colleagues, whose words were often hastily spoken, his were carefully selected, delivered with the precision of a seasoned orator. The difference was clear: while many were charismatic, few were as impressive in their ability to engage an audience without resorting to theatricality. His calm demeanor was far more engaging than any attempt at dramatic flair, showing that true influence often lies not in flamboyance, but in the subtlety of well-chosen words. Over time, this made him one of the most respected figures in his field, as others recognized the quiet power of his communication.

2. His understanding of complex mathematical theories was more intricate than the more straightforward calculations most engineers used. While his colleagues were content to apply simple formulas to solve problems, he took a more comprehensive approach, drawing from a vast range of concepts. His ability to break down complicated equations was not only analytical but also creatively inspired, often finding new ways to look at problems others thought unsolvable. Where others focused on the practical aspects of their work, he spent considerable time thinking about the underlying principles. Though his methods were more

complex, they often led to breakthroughs that others couldn't have imagined. Over time, his colleagues came to appreciate his seemingly unconventional thinking, recognizing that innovation doesn't always come from simplicity but often from the deeper exploration of the subject.

3. Her leadership style was far more collaborative than authoritative, always striving to empower others rather than giving orders. While some leaders were content to control every aspect of their team's work, she encouraged a more open approach, where each member had a voice. Her decision-making was often more deliberative than impulsive, considering multiple perspectives before acting. This made her both a more patient and more effective leader than many of her contemporaries, who sometimes rushed to make quick decisions. In contrast to the usual top-down hierarchy, she believed in a flatter structure, where the flow of ideas was just as important as the flow of authority. It was this balance of listening and acting that ultimately made her a respected figure in the organization, as others valued her ability to combine empathy with strategy.

4. The artist's use of color was far more subtle than bold, creating depth through nuance rather than through contrast. While other painters used bright, vibrant hues to attract attention, he preferred to work with softer tones, emphasizing the harmony between shades. His style was more mindful than spontaneous, every brushstroke placed with intention, crafting an atmosphere rather than merely depicting a scene. Unlike artists who preferred to paint in broad strokes, his details were more delicate, bringing a quiet beauty to his works. The elegance of his technique was not in the overt drama of his paintings but in the silence between colors, the subtle interplay of light and shadow. His work resonated more deeply than that of many of his contemporaries, as it invited viewers to pause and reflect.

5. In the debate on environmental policies, his approach was more holistic than narrow-minded, addressing the issue from a global perspective rather than focusing solely on local concerns. While other policymakers were inclined to prioritize immediate solutions, he often advocated for long-term, sustainable practices that would benefit future generations. His arguments were more systematic than reactive, carefully laying out the connections between ecological and economic factors. Unlike others who focused on specific aspects of environmental conservation, his approach was more interconnected, highlighting

the interdependence of human and natural systems. His ability to see beyond the immediate needs made his perspective more visionary, enabling him to propose solutions that could have a lasting impact. Though some dismissed his ideas as too idealistic, his ability to weave together complex elements of sustainability made him a trailblazer in the field.

4 논리적으로 접근한다.
(Approach logically.)

원인과 결과의 논리적 관계를 내용으로 하는 문장에서는 두 가지 내용 중 어느 한 가지 내용을 알면 나머지는 몰라도 유추할 수 있다.

① 먼저 단문으로 구성된 아래 예문을 통해 논리적으로 추론하는 연습을 해 보자. **색**으로 표시한 부분은 의미상 서로 관련이 있는 부분이므로, 쉽게 추론할 수 있다.

---

1. The dissolution of alliances often leads to the fragmentation of political power across regions.

2. Excessive stress over prolonged periods can precipitate dysfunction in the body's immune system.

3. The concentration of wealth in the hands of a few has contributed to the exacerbation of social inequality.

4. Imposing strict restrictions on free speech frequently results in the suppression of creativity and innovation.

5. A lack of vigilance in maintaining cybersecurity can lead to the compromise of sensitive data.

6. The erosion of trust often leads to the disintegration of relationships, leaving them beyond repair.

7. Prolonged neglect of a garden results in the withering of even the hardiest plants.

8. Uncontrolled pollution can trigger the degradation of entire ecosystems, rendering them uninhabitable.

9. Continuous pressure on fragile materials inevitably causes their fracture under strain.

10. A slow accumulation of stress can culminate in the collapse of mental and emotional stability.

② 문단을 통해 더 연습해 보자.

1. The decline of ancient empires was frequently tied to the decay of their societal structures. As leaders became increasingly corrupt, systems of governance began to fail. This corruption often triggered a deterioration of public trust, leading to unrest. Economies crumbled under the weight of inefficiency, which resulted in the eventual collapse of trade networks. Over time, these factors contributed to the disintegration of once-thriving civilizations, leaving behind remnants of a glorious past. Historians often point to these patterns of erosion in governance and culture as universal indicators of societal fragility.

2. Unchecked deforestation often results in the degradation of natural habitats. When forests are cleared, the loss of biodiversity becomes inevitable, as species lose their homes. This gradual erosion of ecosystems leads to the diminishment of ecological stability, making regions more susceptible to natural disasters. Furthermore, the disruption of carbon cycles exacerbates climate change, contributing to the acceleration of global warming. The long-term impact of these actions can be seen in the deterioration of air and water quality, which directly affects human health and livelihoods.

3. In urban areas, the congestion of traffic frequently leads to the gridlock of essential transportation networks. This overload of infrastructure often causes the paralysis of daily activities, leaving commuters stranded. Over time, this strain on public systems contributes to their deterioration, making cities less livable. Efforts to reduce crowding by expanding roads or introducing new transit options often fail due to the over-burdening of existing resources. The imbalance between population growth and infrastructure development remains a persistent challenge for urban planners.

4. The exhaustion of natural resources often leads to the depletion of economic opportunities in affected regions. When forests, mines, or fisheries are overused, the draining of these reserves creates scarcity that forces communities to adapt. Over time, this reduction in available resources results in the erosion of traditional ways of life, as industries dependent on these resources begin to falter. The long-term impoverishment of such areas often stems from a lack of sustainable practices, which, if implemented earlier, could have prevented such decline.

5. **The fragmentation of political alliances** is often linked to the disintegration of shared goals and mutual trust. As disagreements deepen, **the division among member states** leads to the weakening of collective bargaining power. **This fracturing of alliances** makes it difficult to address global challenges, ultimately resulting in the breakdown of coordinated efforts. Without unified strategies, nations risk an escalation of conflicts and a deterioration of international stability, which can have far-reaching consequences.

2

어려운 부분을 쉽게 파악하는 방법

다음과 같은 원칙을 잘 알고 있으면 어려운 문장들도 쉽게 파악할 수 있다.

1. 영어는 같은 말을 반복하지 않고 다른 표현으로 바꿔 서술하는 특성이 있으므로, 그러한 특징을 잘 이용하여 모르는 부분을 추론한다.
   (Using the characteristic of English to avoid repetition of the same words enables you to infer unknown parts.)

2. 영어는 강조나 명료한 정보 전달을 위해 재술구조를 가지고 있다.
   (For emphasis or clear communication of information, English adopts rephrasing structures.)

1 같은 말을 반복하지 않고 다른 표현으로 바꿔 서술하는 영어의 특성

위 두 가지 특징 중 첫 번째 특징, 즉 영어는 같은 말을 반복하지 않고 다른 표현으로 바꿔 쓰는 경향이 있다는 점을 먼저 살펴 보자.

① 단문들을 통해 먼저 연습해 보자.

1. The newly published author received praise from her peers and accolades from critics.

2. The orchestra played a symphony that moved the audience, followed by an overture that left them spellbound.

3. He was offered an opportunity to lead the project, a chance he eagerly seized.

4. Their discussion of the topic turned into a debate that revealed differing viewpoints.

5. The explorer endured hardships during his journey, triumphing over formidable challenges.

6. The scientist proposed a hypothesis to explain the anomaly, but her theory was met with skepticism by her colleagues.

7. His articulation of the issue was as eloquent as his defense of the proposed solution was persuasive.

8. The architect's design emphasized functionality, while her vision introduced an artistic elegance to the structure.

9. The diplomat's argument was clear and concise, yet her reasoning revealed a deeper, more nuanced understanding of the conflict.

10. Their celebration of the achievement was heartfelt, but their commemoration of those who contributed was even more poignant.

② 문단별로 연습해 보자.

1. The artist's vision for the project was both ambitious and captivating, merging creativity with a unique sense of purpose. Her design was not only visually striking but also functionally sound, marrying aesthetics with practicality. The careful conception of each detail revealed her meticulous attention to both form and function, while her approach to the project demonstrated a mastery of balancing the two. As the work progressed, her ability to transform abstract ideas into concrete results was a testament to her ingenuity and forward-thinking. Though many in the field praised the innovation she brought to the project, others highlighted the more traditional elements she incorporated, which anchored her work in classic design principles. Ultimately, her work was a synthesis of old and new, blending the best aspects of both to create something wholly original.

2. The economic policies of the government had led to a steady decline in industrial productivity, an inevitable decrease in the workforce, and a growing sense of disenchantment among the citizens. While the ruling party continued to tout their success in other areas, the failure of their economic plans became more apparent with each passing month. The prosperity of the previous decade seemed like a distant memory, replaced by the harsh reality of rising unemployment and stagnant wages. As the gap between the wealthy and the working class grew, the inequality within society deepened, prompting calls for reform. The government's refusal to address these issues only fueled the growing discontent among the people. As a result, many began to question the long-term viability of the policies and the future of their nation's economic health.

3. The novel's narrative was compelling, with the author weaving together themes of fate and destiny, exploring how the two often intertwine in the lives of the characters. The protagonist's journey was fraught with struggles, yet it was equally marked by moments of triumph and redemption, highlighting the complexities of the human condition. The plot was layered with subtle twists that kept readers on edge, while the story itself remained focused on the central conflict, never losing sight of its emotional depth. The interplay of characterization and symbolism added a rich dimension to the narrative, offering deeper insights into the themes of love, loss, and personal growth. While some critics praised the book for its evocative writing, others noted its occasional lack of clarity, particularly in its more ambiguous passages.

4. The company's strategy for growth was both aggressive and well-planned, aiming for expansion into new markets and the diversification of its product offerings. Their focus on innovation set them apart from competitors, who were often more focused on traditional business models. As the company pursued its aggressive growth, it faced the challenge of balancing risk with stability, constantly adjusting their approach in response to changing market conditions. The CEO's leadership was praised for its vision, a clear indication of how the company would navigate future challenges. However, some critics noted that the relentless drive for profit sometimes overshadowed the company's commitment to ethical practices. Despite these concerns, the firm continued to thrive, steadily increasing its market share and strengthening its position in the industry.

5. The exploration of space has always been driven by humanity's curiosity about the unknowable universe. As technology advanced, so too did our understanding of the cosmos, revealing more than we ever anticipated. Space missions, whether manned or robotic, are not only about gathering knowledge but also about pushing the boundaries of what is physically possible. While many viewed the mission to Mars as a challenge, others saw it as an opportunity for discovery. The vastness of space offers an endless series of questions, each more complex than the last, yet each new answer brings us closer to solving the mysteries of the universe. The political and financial hurdles of space exploration are not insignificant, but the reward of advancing human understanding far outweighs these challenges.

2 재술 구조

강조나 명료한 정보 전달을 위해 영어는 재술구조를 가지고 있는데 재술의 형태는 부분 재술과 전체 재술의 두 유형이 있다. 이런 재술구조가 어려운 부분의 추론에 중요한 단서가 된다.

① 먼저 단문을 통해 연습해 보자.

1. The project was ambitious, requiring exceptional skill and dedication.

2. She was reluctant, or at least hesitant, to take the offer.

3. The decision was controversial, sparking debates across the community.

4. The story hinges on the concept of altruism, the selfless concern for the well-being of others.

5. The philosopher grappled with nihilism: a belief in the meaninglessness of existence.

6. His speech championed stoicism: the endurance of hardship without complaint.

7. The emotion he described was melancholy: a profound sense of sadness that comes without clear cause.

8. He sought transcendence: a state of being that rises above ordinary limitations.

9. The weather was unpredictable: one moment it was sunny, and the next it rained heavily.

10. Her speech was inspiring. It gave everyone hope and motivation to pursue their dreams.

11. His argument was compelling: it was logical, persuasive, and grounded in evidence.

12. The building is historic, as it dates back to the 18th century and has housed many prominent figures.

② 문단을 통해 연습해 보자.

1. The crisis shook global economies to their core. Financial institutions, which had been long considered stable, suddenly teetered on the brink of collapse. Investors, gripped by panic—an overwhelming, irrational fear—pulled out of stocks at an unprecedented rate, triggering a chain reaction of failures. Governments, scrambling to stabilize the situation, injected capital into major corporations to prevent further erosion of the economy. This move, however, only served to delay the inevitable. The collapse left millions of people unemployed, with businesses shuttering left and right. It became evident that a decades-old economic framework based on unchecked growth was no longer viable in the face of modern challenges.

2. The artist's vision, a radical departure from traditional techniques, captivated critics and audiences alike. His work, which blurred the lines between abstract and figurative, was hailed as revolutionary—a bold, innovative challenge to conventional norms. His ability to convey complex emotions through simple, yet powerful, brush strokes was unparalleled. Many found the paintings—masterful compositions of vibrant colors and sharp contrasts—to evoke deep, often unsettling feelings. Yet, others dismissed his approach as eccentric. Despite the divided opinions, the impact of his work on the art world was undeniable, ushering in a new era of creative exploration.

3. The experiment was fraught with ethical dilemmas. The subjects, who were deliberately placed in stressful situations, exhibited a range of reactions, from intense fear to calmness, even indifference. Some researchers were disturbed by the methodology—a set of practices designed to push participants to their limits—but others argued that such an approach was necessary for gaining deeper insights into human nature. The findings, though controversial, had significant implications for psychology, suggesting that under extreme duress, humans could display behaviors previously thought to be outside the realm of possibility. The ethical concerns—the question of whether the experiment was justified—remained a point of contention long after the study had concluded.

4. The government's response was met with mixed reactions. Some hailed the measures—the sweeping legislative changes—as a necessary step in restoring stability, while others criticized them as reactive. The interventions—financial

assistance to struggling businesses and citizens—were designed to provide immediate relief, but they also raised concerns about long-term sustainability. Critics argued that these measures failed to address the root causes: the systemic flaws in the economy that had led to the crisis in the first place. Despite the controversy, it was clear that the response was essential in averting a total collapse.

5. The debate, a heated discussion about the ethical implications of artificial intelligence, raged on for hours. The proponents who believed that AI could solve some of humanity's most pressing problems argued that the technology—an advanced system capable of mimicking human intelligence—would revolutionize industries ranging from healthcare to transportation. On the other side, critics who feared the consequences of unchecked technological advancement warned that AI could lead to unforeseen consequences, including widespread job loss and the erosion of privacy. Despite the disagreements—the sharp divisions between the two camps— one thing was certain: the advent of artificial intelligence had irrevocably changed the landscape of technological innovation.

3

속독의 원칙

(The Rudiments of Speed Reading in English)

1 속독의 원칙 1: 주제를 빨리 파악한다.

속독에서 가장 중요한 원칙은 글의 주제를 빨리 파악하는 것이다. 반복되거나 동의어로 표현되는 말이 키워드이며 이것이 주제 파악의 중요한 실마리이다.
(The primary principle of speed reading is to grasp what a piece of writing is about. Repeated words or expressions in synonyms serve as the key words, guiding you in identifying the topic.)

① 단문을 통해 먼저 연습해 보자.

1. The forest was dense, so thick with trees that sunlight barely penetrated the canopy.

2. Her laughter was infectious, so contagious that everyone in the room began to chuckle along with her.

3. The storm raged fiercely, so violent that even the strongest trees swayed and cracked.

4. The city was bustling, so lively that the streets were constantly filled with people and noise.

5. The mountain trail was treacherous, so dangerous that climbers were warned to proceed with extreme caution.

② 문단들을 통해 연습해 보자.

1. The desert stretched as far as the eye could see, an endless expanse of sand and stone under the relentless sun. The heat was oppressively hot, so scorching that the soles of shoes melted if one stood still for too long. Even the shade offered little respite; the rocks themselves radiated with heat, as if they had absorbed the scorching sun's energy over countless hours. The plants that managed to survive in this arid landscape were few and far between, their dry, brittle leaves a testament to the harsh conditions. The wind occasionally swept through, carrying with it particles of sand so fine they felt like fire against the skin, yet even this movement brought no relief from the dry and arid atmosphere. Survival in such a place required remarkable adaptation, and the creatures here were uniquely suited for it.

2. The library was a haven of quiet, an oasis of stillness in an otherwise chaotic world. The quiet was not merely the absence of noise but a profound and almost sacred silence. It felt as though the room itself demanded stillness from everyone who entered, as though any sound would disturb the harmony of the place. Students sat at long wooden tables, their pens scratching faintly against paper, the only sound in this deeply quietude-filled space. The peaceful air encouraged concentration, while the hushed tones of the librarians reinforced the serenity. Even those who did not read or study felt compelled to remain silent, as if the room's aura of peacefulness and quietude was too strong to resist. It was this profound stillness that made the library so beloved—a retreat from the world's noise.

3. The storm arrived with no warning, transforming a calm evening into a scene of chaos. Rain fell in a torrent, each drop merging with others to create a relentless deluge that flooded streets in minutes. The downpour was so heavy, so violent, that visibility was reduced to mere feet, and even the sturdiest umbrellas were no match for its fury. The wind screamed like a living thing, its anger evident in the way it rattled windows and tore branches from trees. Lightning split the sky, illuminating the scene with its intensity, while thunder roared in response, echoing with the storm's raw power. Those caught in the open struggled to find shelter, battling the torrential rain and the raging winds. This was no ordinary storm; its violence and fury left everyone in awe of nature's strength.

4. Her generosity was boundless, a reflection of her kind and genuine spirit. She was always sincere, never offering help out of obligation but because she truly cared. This deep sincerity shone through her actions, making her warmth and kindness unmistakable. If a friend was in need, she would give freely, her generosity knowing no limits. Her benevolence extended even to strangers, as she believed in spreading goodness wherever she could. This innate kindness set her apart, making her someone people instinctively trusted. Her actions spoke louder than words, and her sincere benevolence inspired others to follow her example. Her presence brought warmth to every space she entered, and her goodness left a lasting impression on everyone who crossed her path.

5. The painting captivated everyone who saw it, its beauty so stunning that it stopped them in their tracks. The colors were rich and vibrant, glowing with an intensity that seemed almost unreal. Each brushstroke revealed the artist's extraordinary skill, their genius evident in every detail. Viewers marveled at the composition, noting how even the smallest elements contributed to the stunning overall effect. The light in the painting was particularly remarkable, casting a golden glow that felt alive. This vibrant and intense radiance transformed the canvas into something beyond ordinary art. The artist's work was so extraordinary, so genius, that it left an indelible impression. Critics hailed it as a masterpiece, while casual viewers stood in silent awe, appreciating its profound beauty. This was not just a painting but a testament to the power of human creativity.

2 속독의 원칙 2: 문맥의 길잡이가 되는 안내어에 주목한다.
(The second principle for speed is to pay attention to guide words in the text.)

1. also, so, too, as well 과 같은 유사한 내용을 소개하는 표현들에 주의한다.

2. although, however, but, yet, whereas 와 같이 반대되는 내용을 소개하는 표현들에 주의한다.

3. especially, particularly와 같이 강조하는 내용을 소개하는 표현들에 주의한다.

4. in other words, as it were, or 와 같은 재술 표현들과 그와 유사한 역할을 하는 em dash (—), colon (:), semicolon (;), and comma (,)와 같은 문장 부호에 주의한다.

① 각각의 표현별로 예문들을 살펴 보자.

1. also, so, too, as well 과 같은 유사한 내용을 소개하는 표현들이 들어 있는 문장의 경우.

1. The proposal not only addresses fiscal concerns but also introduces reforms to bolster. environmental sustainability.

2. His commitment to the project was unparalleled; so, too, was his ability to inspire the team under pressure.

3. The architect's design was both innovative and practical, qualities the client appreciated as well.

4. Not only did the research validate their hypothesis, but it also opened new avenues for future inquiry.

5. The ambassador's speech reflected diplomacy and wisdom, traits that defined her career, too.

2 although, however, but, yet, whereas 와 같이 반대되는 표현들이 들어 있는 문장의 경우.

1. **Although** the theory seemed plausible, subsequent experiments failed to produce consistent results.

2. The team excelled in creativity; **however,** their execution of the project lacked precision.

3. She admired his eloquence, **but** questioned the substance of his arguments.

4. **Whereas** traditional approaches rely on extensive testing, the new method prioritizes predictive modeling.

5. **Although** the policy was well-intentioned, its implementation faced significant logistical hurdles.

3 especially, particularly와 같이 강조하는 표현들이 들어 있는 문장의 경우.

1. The symposium attracted scholars from diverse disciplines, **especially** those focused on emerging technologies.

2. Her contributions to the field were remarkable, **particularly** her groundbreaking work on neural networks.

3. The gardens were stunning, **especially** in spring when the cherry blossoms were in full bloom.

4. The critique was scathing, **particularly** in its assessment of the author's lack of originality.

5. His leadership skills shone through in challenging situations, **especially** during the crisis.

4 in other words, as it were, or 와 같은 재술 표현들과 그와 유사한 역할을 하는 em dash (—), colon (:), semicolon (;), and comma (,)와 같은 문장 부호들이 들어 있는 문장의 경우.

---

1. The data reveals a troubling trend; in other words, the system is fundamentally flawed.

2. He was, as it were, the linchpin holding the entire operation together.

3. The phenomenon can be described as both fascinating or utterly perplexing, depending on one's perspective.

4. The report emphasized a single point—the urgent need for action to mitigate the crisis.

5. The project required meticulous planning; careful execution was equally critical.

---

② 문단들을 통해 연습해 보자.

1 also, so, too, as well 과 같은 유사한 내용을 소개하는 표현들이 들어 있는 문장의 경우.

　　The complexity of modern urban planning demands a multifaceted approach that prioritizes both sustainability and accessibility. In recent years, cities have not only embraced green technologies but also reimagined public spaces to foster community engagement. Architects and urban developers recognize that the inclusion of green spaces is crucial for maintaining ecological balance while ensuring that urban environments remain livable. Their efforts are not limited to environmental concerns; the integration of modern infrastructure, such as renewable energy sources, is so vital to the future of these cities that it has become a standard in most new developments. Urbanization can lead to the disconnection of individuals from nature, but forward-thinking cities aim to rectify this by incorporating elements of biophilic design, which connects people to the natural world through architectural choices. These efforts are not just about aesthetics; they are meant to enhance the well-being of residents. The role of public transport in urban planning is equally crucial, as cities focus on providing comprehensive and efficient systems for all, as well as reducing car dependence. In the quest for a balanced future, these interconnected objectives not only improve the cityscape but promote a healthier, more sustainable lifestyle for generations to come.

2 although, however, but, yet, whereas 와 같이 반대되는 표현들이 들어 있는 문장의 경우.

In the realm of technological innovation, the emergence of artificial intelligence has generated widespread excitement within scientific and corporate communities. **Although** many see AI as the key to unlocking unprecedented efficiencies, there remains significant skepticism about its broader implications. Critics argue that, while AI can optimize existing processes, it, **however**, lacks the capacity for true creativity or emotional intelligence, rendering it fundamentally incapable of replacing human decision-making in complex scenarios. These concerns raise important questions about the ethical use of AI, particularly as it becomes more integrated into sectors such as healthcare and finance. Some experts advocate for its cautious deployment, stressing the need for rigorous oversight to prevent unintended consequences. **But** supporters of AI argue that it can revolutionize industries by reducing human error and accelerating problem-solving at a scale previously unimaginable. The divide is clear: **whereas** skeptics emphasize the potential risks, proponents highlight the transformative possibilities of AI in tackling global challenges. As we navigate this technological revolution, it is essential to strike a balance, acknowledging both the opportunities and the dangers inherent in such powerful tools. Only through careful consideration and collaboration can we harness AI's potential while safeguarding against its risks.

3 especially, particularly와 같이 강조하는 표현들이 들어 있는 문장의 경우.

In literature, the complexity of human emotion has always been a central theme explored by authors across genres. Writers strive to capture the nuances of human experience, conveying not only the surface-level emotions but also the deeper, often conflicting feelings that define our existence. **Especially** in the works of modern writers, there is a concerted effort to delve into the intricacies of identity, exploring how personal and societal forces shape an individual's sense of self. In this context, narratives often focus on themes such as alienation, self-discovery, and the search for meaning, all of which resonate deeply with contemporary readers. The power of storytelling lies in its ability to evoke empathy, allowing readers to confront their own emotions through the lives of characters. **Particularly** in psychological dramas, authors employ complex narrative structures to mirror the fragmented nature of human consciousness, drawing readers into a web of conflicting thoughts and feelings. This approach not only challenges the boundaries of traditional storytelling but also invites readers to engage with the text on a profound emotional level. It is this ability to resonate deeply with the human experience that has allowed literature to remain a powerful medium for exploring the complexities of life.

4 in other words, as it were, or 와 같은 재술 표현들과 그와 유사한 역할을 하는 em dash (—), colon (:), semicolon (;), and comma (,)와 같은 문장 부호들이 들어 있는 문장의 경우.

The global economy is in the midst of a significant transformation. Industries once thought impervious to technological change are now being upended by advances in automation, artificial intelligence, and digitalization. In other words, the very foundation of the labor market is shifting, with jobs that were once secure now vulnerable to technological disruption. The rise of AI, for example, has led to the automation of tasks traditionally performed by humans, resulting in both increased efficiency and job displacement. This shift has prompted widespread debates about the future of work and the ethical implications of automation. As it were, the very notion of a stable career is being redefined, as more workers find themselves navigating an increasingly precarious job market. Some argue that technology will create new jobs, while others warn of the dangers of widespread unemployment. The debate centers on whether these changes will ultimately benefit or harm society. Or perhaps the answer lies in finding ways to integrate technology in a manner that enhances human potential, rather than diminishes it. The future of work is uncertain, but one thing is clear change is inevitable. With proper foresight and planning, society can adapt to these transformations while minimizing their negative impacts.

3 **속독의 원칙 3**: 앞의 내용에 기반하여 뒤에 올 내용을 예측하며 읽으면 읽기 속도를 높일 수 있다.

(When reading, you can increase your reading speed by predicting the content that will follow based on what has been read so far.)

① 먼저 단문을 통해 연습해 보자.

1. She claims to be fearless, yet whenever confronted with uncertainty, she RECOILS from challenges.

2. The council of experts agrees that poverty is the root of inequality, But some still deny the undeniable effects of systemic injustice.

3. A true leader values humility over pride, whereas an impostor hides behind arrogance to mask their insecurities.

4. Success is often built upon persistence, but the failure to adapt can lead to the eventual collapse of even the most promising ventures.

5. Though his reputation precedes him, his actions frequently contradict the image he wishes to project.

② 문단을 통해 연습해 보자.

1. Many believe that by exerting control over every aspect of their lives, they can create a perfect existence. This notion is widespread in modern culture, where we are constantly encouraged to meticulously plan and micromanage every decision, believing that control equals success. However, the truth is often more complex. As much as we try to dictate our circumstances, life has a way of introducing unpredictability. While control gives a sense of security, the inability to embrace uncertainty often results in anxiety and dissatisfaction. People who hold onto the idea of perfect control may find themselves more stressed than those who are comfortable with the unknown. True success, in this sense, is not about maintaining a rigid grasp over every detail; it's about being flexible and adaptive in the face of change. Those who understand this are able to pivot when things don't go according to plan, knowing that the path to fulfillment is often winding, not linear. Therefore, while striving for control might give an initial sense of power, it is the ability to relinquish it when necessary, that leads to long-term growth and peace.

2. Ambition is often hailed as the driving force behind achievement and success. From a young age, we are told to set lofty goals, work relentlessly towards them, and never settle for mediocrity. This mindset has produced some of the most innovative and successful individuals in history. Yet, ambition can also be a double-edged sword. When unchecked, it can lead to burnout, disillusionment, and even self-doubt. As ambition drives individuals to reach greater heights, it simultaneously fuels a constant fear of failure. Success becomes an elusive goal, one that seems always just out of reach. Those who are solely driven by ambition may find themselves in a never-ending cycle of striving, but never truly experiencing contentment. What begins as a healthy drive to improve becomes an insatiable hunger for validation and external recognition. In contrast, those who balance ambition with reflection and contentment are often the ones who achieve true success. The key is not simply to push forward relentlessly, but to understand when to pause, reassess, and appreciate the progress made. Ambition is necessary, but so too is the ability to enjoy the present moment and find peace with what has already been accomplished.

3. Perfectionism is often seen as a virtue, especially in environments that value excellence and high standards. We are taught from an early age that striving for perfection is the ultimate way to ensure success. Whether it's in school, work, or personal life, the pursuit of flawlessness can seem like the surest path to fulfillment. However, perfectionism often leads to frustration and disappointment. In reality, perfection is unattainable, and the relentless pursuit of it can result in self-criticism and feelings of inadequacy. The perfectionist is often paralyzed by the fear of making mistakes, leading to procrastination or overworking. Ironically, it is in this very attempt to avoid imperfection that true growth and progress are stifled. People who embrace imperfection, on the other hand, are more likely to take risks, make mistakes, and ultimately learn from them. It's the acceptance of failure as part of the process that fosters resilience and innovation. Perfectionism may seem like a noble pursuit, but it is the acceptance of imperfection that creates space for creativity and growth. Understanding this paradox can transform the way we approach our work, our goals, and even our relationships, allowing us to move forward without the burden of unattainable standards.

4. In today's digital age, we are more connected than ever before, yet many feel increasingly isolated. Social media platforms, while designed to bring people together, often create a facade of connection that masks the deeper loneliness

many experiences. We share our lives with others online, but rarely do we connect in a meaningful, authentic way. This paradox is particularly evident in the professional world, where networking and self-promotion are often seen as the key to success. Yet, the more we focus on building our personal brand, the less we may actually engage with others on a human level. In isolation, people may convince themselves that they are working towards greater personal or professional achievements, yet they are losing the very connections that make those achievements meaningful. True fulfillment comes not from isolated success, but from shared experiences and collaborative efforts. People who prioritize relationships and human connection, rather than simply seeking validation through digital means, tend to find more lasting happiness. The challenge is learning how to balance the convenience of online communication with the deep value of face-to-face interaction, and to recognize that the price of isolation is often higher than it seems.

5. In a world that constantly rewards visible success, many individuals fall into the trap of seeking validation from others. This desire for approval can be a powerful motivator, driving people to achieve great things. However, the pursuit of external validation often leads to a hollow sense of accomplishment. When success is defined by others' opinions, it becomes difficult to know what truly matters. The constant need for praise and recognition can overshadow intrinsic satisfaction and personal growth. People who rely on external validation are often left feeling empty, as they chase one accolade after another, only to find that the rewards never bring lasting happiness. In contrast, those who focus on internal validation—finding fulfillment in their own sense of purpose and accomplishment—tend to experience a more sustainable form of success. It's not about ignoring others' opinions entirely, but about learning to prioritize self-worth over external recognition. When we validate ourselves, we become less dependent on the approval of others and more connected to our own values and goals. True success, then, is not about winning approval from the outside world, but about aligning our actions with our deepest beliefs and feeling fulfilled in our own achievements.

PART 03

장문 독해 지문

장문 독해 지문들은 일반영어와 문학 (소설, 시, 희곡)에서 엄선하여 뽑은 글들입니다. 본문 아래에 영영사전에서 뽑은 단어의 의미와 예문들이 있습니다. 처음에 읽으실 때에는 가능하면 단어를 찾지 말고 본문의 논리에서 추론을 하며 읽기 바랍니다. 두 번째 읽을 때에는 각주에 있는 단어들을 참고하여 읽어보고, 전체적인 내용을 간략하게 요약하는 연습을 해 보시기 바랍니다. 그리고 각주에 있는 예문들은 본문의 내용과 마찬가지로 중요한 문장들이 므로, 가능하면 외우는 것이 좋습니다. 이 책에서 제공하는 지문들을 통해, 영어로 글을 제대로 읽는 방법을 익히고 더 나아가 영어로 글을 쓰는 것에 대해 자신감을 얻을 수 있기를 바랍니다.

일반영어

 What Suffering Does

Over the past few weeks, I've **found myself**[1] in a bunch of conversations in which the unspoken **assumption**[2] was that the main goal of life is to maximize happiness. That's normal. When people plan for the future, they often talk about all the good times and good experiences they hope to have. We live in a culture **awash in talk about happiness**[3]. In one three-month period last year, more than 1,000 books were released on Amazon on that subject.

But notice this phenomenon. When people remember the past, they don't only talk about happiness. It is often the ordeals that seem most significant. People **shoot for**[4] happiness but feel **formed**[5] through suffering.

---

1. find yourself somewhere or find yourself doing something: to realize that you are in a place or doing something without really intending or planning to
   - ex Later that evening **I found myself back at Jason's apartment**.
   - **I found myself agreeing with** everything she said.
2. assumption: A thing that is accepted as true or as certain to happen, without proof
   - ex I made **the assumption that** he was coming, so I was surprised when he didn't show up.
3. awash: overflowing with or as if with water
   - ex He was **awash in a sea of confusion**.
4. shoot for something: to try to achieve a particular thing
5. form: to influence the development of something
   - ex **Her character was largely formed by** the loss of her family in the war.

Now, of course, it should be said that there is nothing **intrinsically**[6] **ennobling**[7] about suffering. Just as failure is sometimes just failure (and not your **path**[8] to becoming the next Steve Jobs) suffering is sometimes just destructive, to be exited as quickly as possible.

But some people are clearly ennobled by it. Think of the way Franklin Roosevelt came back deeper and more **empathetic**[9] after being struck with polio. Often, physical or **social suffering**[10] can give people an outsider's perspective, an **attuned**[11] awareness of what other outsiders are enduring.

But the big thing that suffering does is it takes you outside of precisely that logic that the happiness mentality encourages. Happiness wants you to think about maximizing your benefits. Difficulty and suffering sends you on a different course.

First, suffering drags you deeper into yourself. The theologian Paul Tillich wrote that people who endure suffering are taken beneath the routines of life and find they are not who they believed themselves to be. The agony involved in, say, composing a great piece of music or the grief of having lost a loved one smashes through what they thought was the bottom floor of their personality, revealing an area below, and then it smashes through that floor revealing another area.

Then, suffering gives people a more accurate sense of their own limitations, what they can control and cannot control. When people are thrust down into

---

6 intrinsic: occurring as a natural part of something
 the **intrinsic brightness of a star**
 Creativity is **intrinsic to human nature.**
7 ennoble: to make (someone or something) better or more worthy of admiration
 Her skill and talent **ennoble her profession**.
8 path: the way that someone takes to achieve something
 The company is **on the path to prosperity.**
9 empathetic: able to understand how someone feels because you can imagine what it is like to be them
10 social suffering: the human consequences of war, famine, depression, disease, torture
11 attuned: familiar with something and able to deal with it in a sensitive way
 The company needs people **who are attuned to today's youth culture.**

these deeper zones, they are forced to confront the fact they can't determine what goes on there. **Try as they might**[12], they just can't tell themselves to stop feeling pain, or to stop missing the one who has died or gone. And even when tranquillity begins to come back, or in those moments when grief eases, it is not clear where the relief comes from. The healing process, too, feels as though it's part of some natural or divine process beyond individual control.

People in this circumstance often have the sense that they are swept up in some larger **providence**[13]. Abraham Lincoln suffered through the pain of conducting a civil war, and he came out of that with the Second Inaugural. He emerged with this sense that there were deep currents of agony and redemption sweeping not just through him but through the nation as a whole, and that he was just an instrument for transcendent tasks.

It's at this point that people in the midst of difficulty begin to feel a call. They are not masters of the situation, but neither are they helpless. They can't determine the course of their pain, but they can participate in responding to it. They often feel an overwhelming moral responsibility to respond well to it. People who seek this proper **rejoinder**[14] to ordeal sense that they are at a deeper level than the level of happiness and individual utility. They don't say, "Well, I'm feeling a lot of pain over the loss of my child. I should try to **balance my hedonic account**[15] by going to a lot of parties and **whooping it up**"[16].

---

12 **Try as they might**: no matter how hard they try
13 **providence**: 섭리, a powerful force that some people believe causes everything that happens to us
14 **rejoinder**: a reply or response to a question or remark, esp a quick witty one; retort
15 1) **hedonic**: 쾌락적인, of, relating to, or marked by pleasure
   2) **balance**: to adjust (an account or budget) so that the amount of money available is more than or equal to the amount of money that has been spent
   ex The legislature is still trying to **balance the state's budget**.
16 **whoop it up**: to celebrate and have fun in a noisy way
   ex My pals and I **whooped it up** at the local bar after the concert. The band whooped it up for the sold-out crowd.

The right response to this sort of pain is not pleasure. It's holiness. I don't even mean that in a purely religious sense. It means seeing life as a moral drama, placing the hard experiences in a moral context and trying to **redeem**[17] something bad by turning it into something sacred. Parents who've lost a child start foundations. Lincoln sacrificed himself for **the Union**[18].

Prisoners in the concentration camp with psychologist Viktor Frankl rededicated themselves to **living up to the hopes and expectations**[19] of their loved ones, even though those loved ones might themselves already be dead.

Recovering from suffering is not like recovering from a disease. Many people don't come out healed; they come out different. They crash through the logic of individual **utility**[20] and behave paradoxically. Instead of **recoiling**[21] from the sorts of loving commitments that almost always involve suffering, they throw themselves more deeply into them. Even while experiencing the worst and most **lacerating**[22] consequences, some people **double down on vulnerability**[23]. They hurl themselves deeper and gratefully into their art, loved ones and commitments.

The suffering involved in their tasks becomes a **fearful**[24] gift and very different than that equal and other gift, happiness, conventionally define.

---

17 redeem: to make (something that is bad, unpleasant, etc.) better or more acceptable
   The restaurant's excellent service is **not enough to redeem** [=compensate for] the mediocre food.
18 the Union: 북부연합, the group of northern states that supported the federal government during the American Civil War
19 live up to something: to be as good as what was expected or promised
   The breathtakingly beautiful scenery **certainly lived up to expectations.**
20 utility: the quality or state of being useful
   Some experts question **the utility [=usefulness] of the procedure.**
   a plan without much **practical/economic utility**
21 recoil: to move quickly back from someone or something frightening or unpleasant
   She felt him **recoil from her.**
22 lacerate: to cut or tear (someone's flesh) deeply or roughly
   The broken glass **lacerated his feet.**
   Her cruel remarks **lacerated his feelings.**
   his **lacerating [=extremely harsh] attacks** on his critics
23 double down: To double or significantly increase a risk, investment, or other commitment
   He'd bet three thousand and **double down** to six thousand, all of it hanging on the turn of the next card.
   He decided to **double down** and escalate the war.
24 fearful: (informal/old-fashioned) used for emphasizing how bad someone or something is
   She's a **fearful gossip.**
   a **fearful mess**/muddle

The bluster imbalance

Maybe women are not sufficiently **full of themselves**[1]. But let's not coach them to be full of something else, either.

Read the **rash**[2] of corporate self-help books and articles lately unleashed upon the world's white-collar women—such as "The Confidence Code" and "Lean In"—and you'll learn that there is a **yawning**[3] "confidence gap" between the sexes.

Among the alarming symptoms and evidence: We women, even the most successful of us, **are riddled with**[4] self-doubt. We **second-guess**[5] our next moves constantly and "**ruminate**"[6] over past failures. We withhold our opinions in big meetings, while less-informed men freely bluster and **bloviate**[7], **one-upping**[8] and interrupting each other. Even in anonymous political opinion polls, women are more likely than men to say I don't know when pressed for a view on something about which we actually know quite a bit.

When we do express opinions, we too often apologize for or prematurely **disclaim**[9] them ("I'm not sure about this, but ….") or **intonate**[10] them as questions rather than statements. We don't throw our **bonnets into the ring**[11] for promotions and raises for which we're surely qualified, whereas men toss in their

---

1 If you are **full of yourself**, you think of yourself more than you should.
   ex She is certainly **very full of herself**.
2 rash: a series of usually unpleasant things or events that happen in a short period of time
   ex There has been **a rash of robberies** in the city this summer.
3 yawning: very large or wide open
   ex There was a **yawning** [=gaping] **hole** in the wall.
        There is a **yawning gap** between rich and poor.
4 riddle: to fill (something) with something that is bad or unpleasant usually used as (be) riddled with
   ex The book is **riddled with mistakes**.
5 second-guess: o criticize or question the actions or decisions of someone
   ex Don't **second-guess** the umpire.
6 ruminate: to think carefully and deeply about something
   ex He **ruminated over/about the implications** of their decision.
7 bloviate: to discourse at length in a pompous or boastful manner
8 one-up: to get an advantage over (someone)
   ex They're always trying to **one-up each other** by buying the latest gadgets.
9 disclaim: to say that you do not have (something, such as knowledge, responsibility, etc.)
   ex The government **disclaimed** [=disavowed] any knowledge of his activities.
10 intonate: to utter with a particular tone or modulation of voice
11 throw your hat into the ring: to announce publicly that you will take part in something such as a competition or an election

cowboy hats even when their own credentials appear comically deficient.

The self-assurance deficit reinforces the glass ceiling because confidence seems to help people perform better on certain tasks—and, perhaps more important, swagger leads others to perceive us as more competent. One study that asked business school students about imaginary historical people and events (like a "Queen Shaddock" and a "Galileo Lovano") found that those who **feigned**[12] familiarity with the fictional figures also achieved the highest social status among their peers.

These are familiar, **broad-brush**[13] gender stereotypes, of course, often **underpinned**[14] by tiny lab experiments conducted on **callow**[15] university students or by corporate surveys administered with little outside scrutiny. But many of them **ring true to me**[16]—both as a young woman with brilliant and accomplished but perpetually self-doubting girlfriends and as an opinion journalist. (Op-ed pages are often criticized for their dearth of female voices, but the gender imbalance is because men are much more likely to submit **unsolicited**[17] guest columns and to accept direct invitations to write.)

So sure, whether because of biology or socialization, women are **underselling**[18] themselves, and **could stand to be**[19] a little more self-promotional.

Still, it's not clear to me why this so-called "confidence gap" has been framed

---

12 feign: to pretend to have a particular feeling
13 broad-brush: very general and without many details
   a **broad-brush approach to the problem**
14 underpin: support, justify, or form the basis for
   A language course **should be underpinned by** a sound theoretical basis.
15 callow: young and not experienced in life
16 ring: to seem to have a specified quality or character
   Her explanation didn't ring true. = Her explanation rang false. His apology rang hollow. [=his apology did not sound sincere]
17 unsolicited: given or received without being requested
   That comment **was unsolicited and rude.**
18 undersell: to think or say that someone or something is less important, valuable, effective, etc. than they really are
19 stand: used to say that someone or something should have or do something or would be helped by something usually used after could
   You look like you **could stand some sleep**. [=you look very tired; you look like you need some sleep]
   That bush **could stand to be trimmed**. [=that bush needs to be trimmed]

exclusively as a women's problem or why the optimal solution is for women to ape the men with whom they compete.

Those very same studies that show women to be underconfident often show men to be overconfident. "The Confidence Code" cites one Columbia Business School study documenting that men typically rate their performance 30 percent better than it actually is. Likewise, a survey released last week by YouGov found that, when asked to compare their own intelligence to that of the "average American," about a quarter of men declared themselves "much more intelligent," vs. just 15 percent of women. **Lake Wobegon**[20], it seems, is **brimming**[21] with testosterone.

In short, men seem much more willing to be **blowhards**[22] than women are—during dinner parties, at the office, on anonymous phone surveys and in the nation's fine op-ed pages. And as long as both employers and peers continue to **conflate**[23] bluster with **aptitude**[24] and to reward bombast with respect and job promotions, the only way women can successfully compete with men is to be not just more confident but overconfident in everything they do, too.

Like thrift, bluffing may be a good strategy for individuals who want to get ahead but destructive to society at large. An **arms race**[25] in **B.S.ing**[26] seems unlikely to lead to better-run companies, at least, and it certainly isn't creating

---

20 Lake Wobegon: Lake Wobegon is a fictional town in the U.S. state of Minnesota, said to have been the boyhood home of Garrison Keillor, who reports the News from Lake Wobegon on the radio show A Prairie Home Companion. The Lake Wobegon effect, a natural human tendency to overestimate one's capabilities, is named after the town. The characterization of the fictional location, where "all the women are strong, all the men are good looking, and all the children are above average," has been used to describe a real and pervasive human tendency to overestimate one's achievements and capabilities in relation to others.
참고 워비곤 호수 효과는 다른 사람들보다 재능이나 실력이 뛰어나다고 자신을 과대평가하는 현상을 의미한다.
21 brim: to be full of something
　ex I handed him a cup **brimming with coffee**.
　　　Rob was **brimming with enthusiasm**.
22 blowhard: someone who talks too much about themselves or the things they have achieved
23 conflate: mix together
24 aptitude: a natural ability to do something or to learn something
　ex The new test is supposed to measure **the aptitudes of the students**.
25 arms race: attempts by different groups of people to gain an advantage over one another, especially in developing technology
　ex **the technological arms race** between network engineers and the hackers who challenge them
26 B.S.ing: bullshitting
1) bullshit: to tell someone something that is stupid or not true
　ex Don't **bullshit** me. Tell me the truth!
　　　He tried to **bullshit** his way through the interview. [=to fool the people who were interviewing him by saying things that were not true]

more informed political discourse. (Ever watch cable news shows or presidential debates? You'll notice the words I don't know are generally **frowned upon**[27].) I realize it's easier to teach women to increase their **swagger**[28] than to tell grown men to temper theirs. So maybe the solution involves trying to change Americans' perceptions of bluster rather than their skillfulness at wielding it. Rather than advocating that an entire class of people start **faking it 'til they make it**[29], maybe we should be coaching voters, students, bosses and viewers at home how to be a bit more skeptical of the loudest guy (or gal) in the room.

---

27 frown on someone/something: to not approve of something
   *Personal phone calls **are frowned on** at work.*
28 swagger: a way of walking or behaving that shows you have a lot of confidence
   *He **has a swagger** that annoys some of his teammates.*
29 "Fake it 'til you make it" (also called "act as if") is a common catchphrase that means to imitate confidence so that as the confidence produces success, it will generate real confidence.

Three Myths About the Brain

In the early 19th century, a French **neurophysiologist**[1] named Pierre Flourens conducted a series of innovative experiments. He successively removed larger and larger portions of brain tissue from a range of animals, including pigeons, chickens and frogs, and observed how their behavior was affected.

His findings were clear and reasonably consistent. "One can remove," he wrote in 1824, "from the front, or the back, or the top or the side, a certain portion of the **cerebral lobes**[2], without destroying their function." For mental **faculties**[3] to work properly, it seemed, just a "small part of the lobe" sufficed.

Thus the foundation was laid for a popular myth: that we use only a small portion—10 percent is the figure most often cited—of our brain. An early **incarnation**[4] of the idea can be found in the work of another 19th-century scientist, Charles-Édouard Brown-Séquard, who in 1876 wrote of the powers of the human brain that very few people develop "very much, and perhaps nobody quite fully."

But Flourens was wrong, in part because his methods for assessing mental capacity were crude and his animal subjects were poor models for human brain

---

1 **neurophysiologist**: 신경생리학자
2 **cerebral lobes**: 대뇌엽(大腦葉)
3 **faculty**: a natural physical or mental ability that most people have
   ex *It was sad to see that **his mental faculties** [=his ability to think clearly] had begun to fail.*
   *She needs to learn to develop **her critical faculties**. [=her ability to make judgments about what is good or true]*
4 **incarnation**: a person or thing that is an extremely strong example of a particular quality
   ex *The Greeks saw these tribes as **the incarnation of evil**.*
   In an earlier incarnation [=an earlier phase of her life] she was a rock musician.
   *The TV and movie **incarnations** [=versions] of the story differ significantly.*

function. Today the neuroscience community uniformly rejects the notion, as it has for decades, that our brain's potential is largely **untapped**[5].

The myth persists, however. The movie "Lucy," about a woman who acquires superhuman abilities by tapping the full potential of her brain, is only the latest and most prominent expression of this idea.

Myths about the brain typically arise in this fashion: An intriguing experimental result generates a plausible if speculative interpretation (a small part of the lobe seems sufficient) that is later overextended or distorted (we use only 10 percent of our brain). The **caricature**[6] ultimately infiltrates pop culture and takes on a life of its own, quite independent from the facts that spawned it.

Another such myth is the idea that the left and right hemispheres of the brain are fundamentally different. The "left brain" is **supposedly**[7] logical and detail-oriented, whereas the "right brain" is the seat of passion and creativity. This caricature developed initially out of the observation, dating from the 1860s, that damage to the left hemisphere of the brain can have drastically different effects on language and motor control than does damage to the right hemisphere.

But while these and other, more subtle, asymmetries certainly exist, **far too much has been made of**[8] the idea of distinct left-and right-brain function. The fact is that the two sides of the brain are more similar to each other than they

---

5　untapped: not being used yet, but existing in large amounts that could bring profits or benefits
　　　The oil reserves in this area **remain largely untapped**.
6　caricature: someone or something that is very exaggerated in a funny or foolish way
　　　His performance in the film was **a caricature of a hard-boiled detective**.
　　　The interview made her into **a caricature of a struggling artist**.
7　supposedly: according to what someone has said or what is generally believed to be true or real
8　make much of: to treat (something) as very important
　　　She tends to **make far too much of** her problems.
　　　You shouldn't **make too much of what he said**; he was only joking.

are different, and both sides participate in most tasks, especially complex ones like acts of creativity and **feats**[9] of logic.

In recent years, a new myth about the brain has started to emerge. This is the myth of **mirror neurons**[10], or the idea that a certain class of brain cells discovered in the **macaque monkey**[11] is the key to understanding the human mind.

Mirror neurons are activated both when a macaque monkey generates its own actions, such as reaching for a piece of fruit, and when it observes others who are performing the same action themselves. Some scientists have argued that these cells are responsible for the ability of monkeys to understand other monkeys' actions, by simulating the action in their own brains. It has also been claimed that humans have their own mirror system (most likely true), which not only allows us to understand actions but also **underlies**[12] a wide range of our mental skills—language, imitation, empathy—as well as disorders, such as autism, in which the system is said to be dysfunctional.

The mirror neuron claim has escaped the lab and is starting to **find its way into popular culture**[13]. You might hear it said, for example, that watching a World Cup match is an intense experience because our mirror neurons allow us to experience the game as if we were on the field itself, simulating every kick and pass.

---

9 **feat**: an act or achievement that shows courage, strength, or skill
   ex a performer known for her **astonishing acrobatic feats**
       an **exceptional feat of the human intellect**
10 **mirror neuron**: 미러 뉴런 (거울 신경세포: 거울신경세포란 다른 사람이 어떤 동작을 실행하는 것을 관찰할 때나 자신이 그 동작을 실행할 때에도 활성화되는 신경세포를 말한다. 마치 거울에 비친 것처럼 활성화된다고 하여 붙여진 이름)
11 **macaque monkey**: 짧은 꼬리 원숭이 (아시아와 아프리카 지역에 주로 서식함. 에이즈 연구 등의 연구용 동물로 사용되기도 함)
12 **underlie**: to form the basis or foundation of (an idea, a process, etc.)
   ex We discussed the principles that **underlay their methods**.
       A theme of revenge **underlies much of her writing**.
13 참고 동사 + one's way + 전치사 (또는 부사)의 문장 구조
   ex She **talked her way out of trouble**. [=she got herself out of trouble by talking].
       She has **worked her way into the movie industry** through hard work.
       He **clawed his way to the top**.

But as with older myths, this speculation has lost its connection with the data. We now recognize that physical movements themselves don't uniquely determine our understanding of them. After all, we can understand actions that we can't ourselves perform (flying, **slithering**[14]) and a single movement can be understood in many ways (tipping a carafe can be pouring or filling or emptying). Further research shows that dysfunction of the motor system, for example in **cerebral palsy**[15], stroke or Lou Gehrig's disease, does not **preclude**[16] the ability to understand actions (or enjoy World Cup matches). Accordingly, more recently developed theories of mirror neuron function emphasize their role in motor control instead of understanding actions.

So please, **take heed**[17]. **An ounce of**[18] myth prevention now may save a pound of neuroscientific nonsense later.

---

14 slither: to move by sliding your entire body back and forth
   The snake **slithered** through the garden.
   She **slithered** quietly into the room.
   He **slithered** his hand around her waist.
15 cerebral palsy: 뇌성마비
16 preclude: to prevent (something) from happening
   She suffered an injury that **precluded** the possibility of an athletic career.
   Bad weather **precluded** any further attempts to reach the summit.
17 heed: attention or notice often used with pay or take
   She **pays no heed** to the concerns of others.
   He failed to **take heed of our advice**. = He failed to pay heed to our advice. [=he failed to follow our advice]
18 ounce: a very small amount of something
   If you **had an ounce of** common sense, you wouldn't try it.
   He doesn't have an ounce of decency.
   That story **doesn't have an ounce of truth** in it. [=that story is completely untrue]

The distorting reality of 'false balance' in the media

False equivalence[1] in the media—giving equal **weight**[2] to unsupported or even **discredited**[3] claims for the sake of appearing impartial—is not unusual. But a major media organization taking meaningful steps to **do something**[4] about it is.

Earlier this month, the BBC's governing body issued a report assessing the BBC's impartiality in covering scientific topics. When it comes to an issue like climate change, the report concluded, not all viewpoints share the same amount of scientific **substance**[5]. Giving equal time and weight to a wide range of arguments without regard to their credibility risks creating a "false balance" in the public debate.

This is a lesson for all media on **both sides of the Atlantic**[6]—and not just when it comes to science coverage. There are many sides to almost every story, but that doesn't mean they are automatically equal.

Unfortunately, too much of the media has become increasingly fixated on finding "balance," even if it means presenting **fiction**[7] **on par with**[8] fact. If media outlets wanted to present an accurate account of the climate change "debate," for instance, they would have to **follow comedian John Oliver's lead**[9] and host a

---

1 **False equivalence**: 기계적 균형 (=false balance),
the media phenomenon of presenting two sides of an argument equally in disregard of the merit or evidence on a subject
2 **weight**: the power to influence the opinions of other people
   - ex Her opinion **carries a lot of weight with me**. [=her opinion is very important to me]
3 **discredit**: to cause (someone or something) to seem dishonest or untrue
   - ex The prosecution **discredited** the witness by showing that she had lied in the past.
   Many of his theories have been thoroughly **discredited**.
4 **do something**: to take action in order to deal with a situation
5 **substance**: the quality of being true or believable
   - ex These rumors **have no substance**. = These rumors are without substance. [=these rumors are not true]
   The results of the study **give substance to their theory**.
6 **both sides of the Atlantic**: 미국과 영국
   - 참고 On one side of the Atlantic Ocean is USA, on the other side is Britain and Europe. 'Both sides of the Atlantic' mean both USA and Europe.
7 **fiction**: a report, story, or explanation that is not true
   - ex His alibi was **pure fiction**.
8 **on (a) par with**: at the same level or standard as (someone or something else)
   - ex The new version of the software is **on a par with** the old one. His new book is **on par with** his best sellers.
9 **follow someone's lead**: to do the same thing that someone else has done
   - ex He **followed her lead** and voted in favor of the proposal.

"statistically representative" **face-off**[10] with three climate change deniers up against 97 scientists armed with proof. Instead, they contort themselves to find "balance", and we're left with segments like "Is the climate change threat exaggerated?"—presented on the always reliable Fox News—which promised to "weigh the evidence on both sides of the divisive topic." It's no wonder that only 60 percent of Americans know that most scientists agree that global warming is occurring—and almost 30 percent aren't sure if there is any scientific consensus.

It's not just right-wing **megaphones**[11] that **subscribe to**[12] this kind of journalism. As Media Matters has documented, when reporting on the 2013 United Nations' Intergovernmental Panel on Climate Change fifth assessment report, mainstream outlets like the Wall Street Journal and The Post gave, on average, the three percent of doubters "over five times the amount of representation [they have] in the scientific community." The result, as Bill McKibben has said, is "a massive failure of journalism to communicate the idea to the public that the most dangerous thing that ever happened in the world is in the process of happening." (Indeed, the Los Angeles Times is unusual for its policy of not publishing letters to the editor that deny man's role in climate change.)

As political scientists Thomas Mann and Norm Ornstein have written, "A balanced treatment of an unbalanced phenomenon distorts reality." And this isn't just true

---

10 face-off: a conflict or fight
   *a diplomatic **face-off** between Communist and non-Communist nations*
11 megaphone: 자기 주장만 부각시키는 사람이나 매체
12 subscribe to something: to agree with an idea
   *He **subscribes to the view** that children benefit from being independent.*

when it comes to science coverage—the media has a similar tendency to issue unfiltered "**he said, she said**"[13] accounts of political issues. The result is that every controversy seems to be **reduced to**[14] **a binary debate**[15] between two equal sides. In 2013, when congressional Republicans shut down the government over a health-care law that had been passed in Congress and upheld in the Supreme Court, many in the media continued to pretend that both sides were equally at fault.

My Nation colleague Eric Alterman once wrote that no matter how "outlandish, illogical, or simply untrue," an argument may be, too many editors and journalists bind themselves to an outdated commitment to the ideal of objectivity. This approach has real consequences on the public's understanding of society's most pressing challenges—including the effects of global warming.

Gallup's 2014 poll on the environment found that 42 percent of Americans believe that "the seriousness of global warming is generally exaggerated in the news." Blinded by the **veil**[16] of false equivalence, we believe global warming is happening, but that it won't seriously affect us. As a result, we are not holding our elected leaders accountable for acting to curb the threat of climate change, which only grows more dangerous over time.

Ultimately, forcing balance where there is none is not journalistically ethical. It's not part of the proud and essential tradition of truth telling and evaluation, either.

---

13 he said, she said: 주장이 엇갈리는
   참고 Conflicting reports from two or more parties on an issue, usually involving a situation between a man and a woman with no other witnesses.
14 reduce: to describe (something) in a way that includes only some of the facts and details+ to
   ex You're **reducing religion to a list of do's and don'ts**.
   Her argument **can be reduced to** a few essential points.
15 a binary debate: 일대일의 논쟁
16 veil: something that covers or hides something else
   ex The **veil of secrecy** was lifted. [=the secret was made known]

At best, it's lazy. At worst, it's an **abdication**[17] of the media's responsibility.

Rather than uncritically repeating talking points, isn't it time for the media to take the BBC's bold advice and exercise editorial judgment? Because if the scale tips in favor of the truth, that's not imbalanced reporting. That's journalism.

---

17 abdicate: to fail to do what is required by (a duty or responsibility)
　　*The government **abdicated** [=abandoned] its responsibility to provide a good education to all citizens.*

05 Dangerous Divisiveness

For an increasing number of Americans, the **tenor**[1] of politics has reached a near-religious **pitch**[2], in which people on opposing ends of the ideological **scale**[3] take on theological properties: good or evil, angels or demons, here to either save our way of life or destroy it.

According to a report released last week by the Pew Research Center for the People and the Press: "Republicans and Democrats are more divided along ideological lines—and partisan **antipathy**[4] is deeper and more extensive—than at any point in the last two decades."

The report continued:

"The overall share of Americans who express consistently conservative or consistently liberal opinions has doubled over the past two decades from 10 percent to 21 percent. And ideological thinking is now much more **closely aligned with**[5] partisanship than in the past. As a result, ideological overlap between the two parties has diminished: Today, 92 percent of Republicans are to the right of the **median**[6] Democrat, and 94 percent of Democrats are to the left of the median Republican."

---

1 **tenor**: the general or basic quality or meaning of something
   ex I was surprised by the angry **tenor** [=tone] of her letter.
   The tenor of his remarks is clear.
2 **pitch**: a state of intense feeling
   ex Tensions between the two groups have **risen to a high/feverish pitch**. [=have become very intense]
3 **scale**: a range of levels of something from lowest to highest
   ex He is at the **top of the pay scale** for his position.
   Primates are high **up on the evolutionary scale**.
4 **antipathy**: a strong feeling of dislike
   ex There has always been strong **antipathy** between the two groups.
5 **align**: to organize activities or systems so that they match or fit well together
   ex We have closely **aligned our research and development work with** our business needs.
6 **median**: having a value that is in the middle of a series of values arranged from smallest to largest
   ex What is the **median price** of homes in this area?

This is not to suggest that there is absolute **parity**[7] in our polarization. As the report makes clear, while 27 percent of Democrats see the Republican Party as a threat to the nation's well-being, 36 percent of Republicans see the Democratic Party as a threat. Conservatives were also more likely to say that it was important to live in places where people shared their political views. Additionally, conservatives were more likely to say they would be unhappy if a close relative married a Democrat than were liberals to say they would be unhappy to have a Republican in-law.

This phenomenon coincides, to a certain degree, with the rise of **talk radio**[8] and the **stridently**[9] ideological cable news—profit-driven **provocateurs**[10] whose livelihoods **ride on**[11] their abilities to rouse **rabble**[12], stir passions and **diabolize**[13] opponents.

And many of their listeners, viewers and readers become the **apostles**[14] of passion, enforcing rigid **binary**[15] ideologies that accommodate little subtlety. Any seeming **equivocation**[16] is deemed evidence of **apostasy**[17]. This, in itself, is dangerous.

Our politics are now strung with tripwires of hypersensitivities and **micro-aggressions**[18]. Every position is assumed to have a sinister **subtext**[19], made all the more complicated by the fact that some actually do have such subtexts.

---

7 parity: the state of being equal
8 talk radio: 라디오 시사 토크 쇼
   참고 radio programs in which the hosts discuss subjects with people who telephone them during the program
9 strident: expressing opinions or criticism in a very forceful and often annoying or unpleasant way
   예 **strident** critics/slogans
10 provocateur: 선동가, a person who provokes trouble, causes dissension, or the like
11 ride on something: to depend on something for success
   예 I feel as though **my whole future is riding on this interview.**
12 rabble: a noisy or violent crowd of people
13 diabolize: to cause to be devilish or evil
14 apostle: someone who has a strong belief in an idea and tries to get other people to support it
   예 Ghandi was **a great apostle of non-violence**.
15 binary: consisting of two parts
16 equivocate: to use unclear language especially to deceive or mislead someone
   예 The applicant seemed to be **equivocating** when we asked him about his last job.
   참고 The candidate spoke without **equivocation** about her tax plan.
17 apostasy: 배신 abandonment of one's religious faith, a political party, one's principles, or a cause
18 micro-aggressions: 은연중에 나타나는 모욕적 발언
   참고 Micro-aggressions are quiet, often unintended slights racist or sexist that make a person feel underestimated on the basis of their color or gender.
19 subtext: an idea in a book, movie, etc. that is not clearly stated but can be understood
   예 The drama **has an interesting political subtext**.

The phenomenon, more recently, is **epitomized**[20] by views about President Obama, which, depending on which **silo**[21] one is in, either read as blind allegiance or blind hatred. This robs him of the glory of his legitimate achievements and artificially shields his missteps.

To be fair, his presidency, in many ways, has been **hamstrung**[22] by opposition. In the wake of his **ascension**[23] came the rise of **the Tea Party**[24], the incredible assertion by the Senate minority leader, Mitch McConnell, that conservatives' top priority should be to keep Obama from being re-elected (that didn't work out so well), the stunning assault on voter rights, the influx of conservative billionaires like the Koch brothers into the political arena, blatant **gerrymandering**[25] after the last census and the unprecedented levels of obstruction by Republicans in Congress.

Still, there are real and legitimate debates to be had about the size and role of government, how to grow and expand the economy, how to help the least fortunate in the short and long term, how to position America militarily in the world as the last remaining superpower, how to protect—or expand the recognition of—the right of the individual, especially when those individuals are members of minority groups, while respecting the democratic desires of the majority of our citizens.

---

20 epitomize: to be a perfect example or representation of (something)
   ex He **epitomizes laziness.**
   This student's struggles **epitomize the trouble with our schools.**
21 silo: 자기만의 공간
   참고 a system, process, department, etc. that operates in isolation from others
22 hamstring: to damage or ruin the force or effectiveness of (something or someone)
   ex The mayor tried to **hamstring** our efforts by cutting the budget.
23 ascension: the process of moving to a higher level or position
   ex the story of a young man's rapid political ascension
24 The Tea Party movement is an American political movement known for advocating a reduction in the U.S. national debt and federal budget deficit by reducing U.S. government spending and taxes.
25 gerrymandering: 게리맨더링 (어느 한 정당 혹은 특정 후보에게 유리하도록 선거구를 획정하는 것)

We must wrestle with these each in its own turn.

There are some moral issues on which there can be no ambiguity. For instance, people cannot be treated differently because of the way they were born, developed or identify; women must have access to the full range of reproductive options; and something must be done about the continued carnage of gun violence in this country.

There are other areas, however—the continued existence of the detention center at Guantnamo Bay, the use of drones, government surveillance—that require critical, nonpartisan examination, regardless of who is in charge, in part because many of these policies overlap Republican and Democratic administrations.

We must continuously audit our **allegiances**[26], not only to **keep adversaries at bay**[27], but also to keep allies, and to understand that our friends and our rivals aren't necessarily discrete and oppositional on every issue. Loyalties too freely given and too uncritically maintained become **fertile ground**[28] for—and, in fact, issue **license**[29] for—the corruption of conscience and the betrayal of principle.

---

26 allegiance: strong loyalty to a person, group, idea, or country
27 keep/hold something at bay: to prevent something serious, dangerous, or unpleasant from affecting you
   Doctors recommend Vitamin C **for keeping colds at bay.**
28 fertile ground for something: producing a large amount of something
   Conditions at the time provided **fertile ground for** revolutionary movements.
29 license: official permission for someone to do something

일반영어 06 — Teaching Is Not a Business

TODAY'S education reformers believe that schools are broken and that business can supply the remedy. Some place their faith in the idea of competition. Others embrace **disruptive innovation**[1], mainly through online learning. Both camps share the belief that the solution resides in the **impersonal**[2], whether it's the invisible hand of the market or the transformative power of technology.

Neither strategy has lived up to its **hype**[3], and with good reason. It's impossible to improve education by **doing an end run around**[4] inherently complicated and **messy**[5] human relationships. All youngsters need to believe that they have a **stake**[6] in the future, a goal worth striving for, if they're going to make it in school. They need a **champion**[7], someone who believes in them, and that's where teachers enter the **picture**[8]. The most effective approaches foster bonds of caring between teachers and their students.

---

1. **disruptive innovation**: 파괴적 혁신
   참고 The process of developing new products or services to replace existing technologies and gain a competitive advantage.
2. If you're **impersonal**, you're neutral you're not showing your feelings or your preference.
3. **hype**: extravagant claims about a person or product
   ex *The **hype surrounding these investments*** is not supported by the data.
   *After months of promotional **hype***, the band finally released their new album.
4. **do an end run around**: 편법으로 해결하려고 하다
   ex They tried to ***do an end run around*** the law but they failed.
5. **messy**: complicated, difficult, and unpleasant to deal with
   ex Politics has always been a ***messy*** business.
   a ***messy*** divorce/relationship
6. **stake**: an interest or degree of involvement in something
   ex We all ***have a stake in*** the health of our economy. [=the health of our economy affects us all]
   He ***has a huge stake in*** making the peace process work.
7. **champion**: someone who fights or speaks publicly in support of a person, belief, cause, etc.
   ex She was a lawyer and a ***champion*** of children's rights.
8. **picture**: a general situation
   ex *The overall economic **picture*** is improving.
   Marriage never ***entered the picture*** [=was never considered] until now.

Marketplace **mantras**[9] dominate policy discussions. **High-stakes**[10] reading and math tests are treated as the single **metric**[11] of success, the counterpart to the business bottom line. Teachers whose students do poorly on those tests get pink slips, while those whose students excel receive merit pay, much as businesses pay bonuses to their star performers and fire the **laggards**[12]. Just as companies shut stores that aren't meeting their sales quotas, opening new ones in more promising territory, failing schools are closed and so-called **turnaround model schools**[13], with new teachers and administrators, take their place.

This approach might sound plausible in a think tank, but in practice it has been a **flop**[14]. Firing teachers, rather than giving them the coaching they need, undermines morale. In some cases it may well discourage undergraduates from pursuing careers in teaching, and with a looming teacher shortage as baby boomers retire, that's a **recipe**[15] for disaster. Merit pay invites rivalries among teachers, when what's needed is collaboration. Closing schools treats everyone there as guilty of causing low test scores, ignoring the difficult lives of the children in these schools—"no excuses," say the reformers, as if poverty were an excuse.

---

9   mantra: a word or phrase that is repeated often or that expresses someone's basic beliefs
    His **mantra** is, All I need is within me now.
10 high-stakes: used to describe a situation that has a lot of risk and in which someone is likely to either get or lose an advantage, a lot of money, etc.:
    The company has made some **high-stakes investments** in an attempt to transform itself into a multi-brand empire.
11 metric: a standard of measurement
    No **metric** exists that can be applied directly to happiness.
12 laggard: a person or thing that does not go or move as quickly as others
    The company has been a **laggard** in developing new products.
13 turnaround model schools: 구조조정 시범 학교
    1) turnaround: an important change in a situation that causes it to improve
    an **economic turnaround**
14 flop: a complete failure
    The movie was a **total flop**.
15 recipe: a way of doing something that will produce a particular result+ for
    He says he has an infallible **recipe** for success.
    She's planning to do the plumbing herself. That's **a recipe for disaster.** [=that will result in disaster]

Business does have something to teach educators, but it's neither **the saving power of competition**[16] nor **flashy**[17] ideas like disruptive innovation. Instead, what works are **time-tested**[18] strategies.

"Improve constantly and forever the system of production and service": That's the **gospel**[19] the management guru W. Edwards Deming preached for half a century. After World War II, Japanese firms embraced the "**plan, do, check, act**"[20] approach, and many Fortune 500 companies profited from paying attention. Meanwhile, the Harvard Business School historian and Pulitzer Prize-winner Alfred D. Chandler Jr. demonstrated that firms prospered by developing "organizational capabilities," putting effective systems in place and encouraging learning inside the organization. Building such a culture took time, Chandler emphasized, and could be derailed by executives seduced by **faddishness**[21].

Every successful educational initiative of which I'm aware aims at strengthening personal bonds by building strong **systems of support**[22] in the schools. The best preschools create intimate worlds where students become explorers and attentive adults are close at hand.

An extensive study of Chicago's public schools, Organizing Schools for Improvement, identified 100 elementary schools that had substantially improved and 100 that had not. The presence or absence of social trust among students, teachers, parents and school leaders was a key explanation.

---

16 the saving power of competition: 경쟁 만능주의
　1) the saving power of ~: ~라는 유일한 해결책 (원래는 종교적 의미를 담고 있음)
　　ex This was the greatest testimony to **the saving power of God**.
17 flashy: very fashionable or expensive in a way that is deliberately intended to impress people
18 time-tested: done or used for a long time and proved to be effective
　　ex These **time-tested methods** have worked for farmers for hundreds of years.
19 gospel: something that is believed to be definitely true
　　ex These myths are accepted/taken as **gospel** [=believed to be true] by many teenagers.
　　I didn't do it, and that's **the gospel truth**. [=the absolute truth; a completely true statement]
20 plan, do, check, act: PDCA(Plan(계획)-Do(실행)-Check(평가)-Act(개선))
　사업 활동에서 생산 및 품질 등을 관리하는 방법이다. 4단계를 반복하여 업무를 지속적으로 개선한다. 월터 슈하트(Walter A. Shewhart), 에드워즈 데밍(W. Edwards Deming) 등에 의해 유명해졌다.
21 faddish: very fashionable for a short time, but not destined to last
22 support system: a network of people who provide an individual with practical or emotional support

Over the past 25 years, YouthBuild has given solid work experience and classroom tutoring to hundreds of thousands of high school dropouts. Seventy-one percent of those youngsters, on whom the schools have given up, earn a **G.E.D**[23].—close to the national high school graduation rate. The YouthBuild students say they're motivated to get an education because their teachers "**have our backs**[24]."

The same message—that the personal touch is crucial—comes from community college students who have participated in the City University of New York's anti-dropout initiative, which has doubled graduation rates.

Even as these programs, and many others with a similar philosophy, have proven their worth, public schools have been spending billions of dollars on technology which they envision as the wave of the future. Despite the hyped claims, the results have been disappointing. "The data is pretty weak," said Tom Vander Ark, the former executive director for education at the Bill and Melinda Gates Foundation and an investor in educational technology companies. "When it comes to showing results, we better **put up or shut up**[25]."

While technology can be put to good use by talented teachers, they, and not the futurists, must take the lead. The process of teaching and learning is an intimate act that neither computers nor markets can hope to replicate. Small wonder, then, that the business model hasn't worked in reforming the schools—there is simply no substitute for the personal element.

---

23 G.E.D: 일종의 검정고시
   참고 General Educational Development (GED) tests are a group of four subject tests which, when passed, certify that the test taker has American or Canadian high school-level academic skills.
24 watch someone's back or have someone's back: to protect someone who is doing something that is dangerous or risky
   예문 The police officer's partner always **watches his back**.
   Don't worry, I've **got your back**.
25 put up or shut up: used for telling someone that they should either deal with something or stop talking about doing it

07 Inequality Is a Drag

For more than three decades, almost everyone who matters in American politics has agreed that higher taxes on the rich and increased aid to the poor have hurt economic growth.

Liberals have generally viewed this as a **trade-off**[1] worth making, arguing that it's worth accepting some price in the form of lower G.D.P. to help fellow citizens in need. Conservatives, on the other hand, have advocated trickle-down economics, insisting that the best policy is to cut taxes on the rich, slash aid to the poor and count on **a rising tide to raise all boats**[2].

But there's now growing evidence for a new view—namely, that the whole premise of this debate is wrong, that there isn't actually any trade-off between equity and inefficiency. Why? It's true that market economies need a certain amount of inequality to function. But American inequality has become so extreme that it's **inflicting**[3] a lot of economic damage. And this, **in turn**[4], implies that redistribution—that is, taxing the rich and helping the poor—**may well**[5] raise, not lower, the economy's growth rate.

You might be tempted to dismiss this notion as **wishful thinking**[6], a sort of

---

1 **trade-off**: something that you do not want but must accept in order to have something that you want
 ex The job pays well. The biggest **trade-off** is that you have to work long hours.
2 **A rising tide lifts all boats**: used to describe the idea that when an economy is performing well, all people will benefit from it.
3 **inflict**: to cause someone to experience or be affected by (something unpleasant or harmful)
 ex These insects are capable of **inflicting a painful sting**.
4 **in turn**: as a result
 ex I supported him and expected that he, **in turn**, would support me.
5 **may well**: used for saying that something is fairly likely to be true or is fairly likely to happen
 ex What you say **may well be true**.
6 **wishful thinking**: (막연한) 희망사항
 ex The idea that the enemy will immediately surrender is nothing more than **wishful thinking**.

liberal **equivalent**[7] of the right-wing fantasy that cutting taxes on the rich actually increases revenue. In fact, however, there is solid evidence, coming from places like the International Monetary Fund, that high inequality is a drag on growth, and that redistribution can be good for the economy.

Earlier this week, the new view about inequality and growth got a boost from Standard & Poor's, the rating agency, which put out a report supporting the view that high inequality is a drag on growth. The agency was summarizing other people's work, not doing research of its own, and you don't need to take its judgment as **gospel**[8] (remember its **ludicrous**[9] **downgrade of United States debt**[10]). What S.& P.'s **imprimatur**[11] shows, however, is just how mainstream the new view of inequality has become. There is, at this point, no reason to believe that comforting **the comfortable**[12] and afflicting **the afflicted**[13] is good for growth, and good reason to believe the opposite.

Specifically, if you look systematically at the international evidence on inequality, **redistribution**[14], and growth—which is what researchers at the I.M.F. did—you find that lower levels of inequality are associated with faster, not slower, growth. Furthermore, income redistribution at the levels typical of advanced countries (with the United States doing much less than average) is "**robustly**[15] associated with higher and more durable growth." That is, there's no

---

7 equivalent: someone or something that has the same size, value, importance, or meaning as someone or something else
　　It is a Chinese word for which English has no (exact) **equivalent**.
　　His newspaper column is **the journalistic equivalent of candy**.
8 gospel: something that is believed to be definitely true
　　These myths are accepted/taken as **gospel** [=believed to be true] by many teenagers.
9 ludicrous: very foolish
10 downgrade of United States debt: 미국 국채의 신용등급 강등(2011년 8월 5일 S&P가 재정적자의 우려를 들어 미국의 국가신용등급을 'AAA'에서 'AA+'로 한 단계 강등한 것을 말함.)
11 imprimatur: official approval
　　He gave the book **his imprimatur**.
12 the comfortable: 고소득층
　　1) comfortable: having or providing enough money for everything you need to live well
　　　They enjoy a **comfortable** lifestyle.
13 the afflicted: 저소득층
　　1) afflict: to cause pain or suffering to (someone or something)
　　　The disease **afflicts** an estimated two million people every year.
14 redistribution: 소득 재분배
15 robustly: strongly; closely

evidence that making the rich richer enriches the nation as a whole, but there's strong evidence of benefits from making the poor less poor.

But how is that possible? Doesn't taxing the rich and helping the poor reduce the **incentive**[16] to make money? Well, yes, but incentives aren't the only thing that matters for economic growth. Opportunity is also crucial. And extreme inequality deprives many people of the opportunity to fulfill their potential.

Think about it. Do talented children in low-income American families have the same chance to make use of their talent—to get the right education, to pursue the right **career path**[17]—as those born higher up the ladder? Of course not. Moreover, this isn't just unfair, it's expensive. Extreme inequality means a waste of human resources.

And government programs that reduce inequality can make the nation as a whole richer, by reducing that waste.

Consider, for example, what we know about food stamps, **perennially**[18] targeted by conservatives who claim that they reduce the incentive to work. The historical evidence does indeed suggest that making food stamps available somewhat reduces work effort, especially by single mothers. But it also suggests that Americans who had access to food stamps when they were children grew up to be healthier and more productive than those who didn't, which means that

---

16 **incentive**: something that makes you want to do something or to work harder, because you know that you will benefit by doing this
- ex Many farmers have little **incentive** to invest in costly conservation measures.
  The promise of a job will **give Mary an incentive to pass the exam**.
17 **career path**: 진로
- 참고 A **career path** refers to the careers available to you after you complete certain studies and entry-level jobs within a company
- ex I don't know **what future career path might suit me** but I'm told I relate well to people.
  She **followed an unusual career path**, in that she retrained relatively late in life.
18 **perennial**: always existing, or never seeming to change
- ex Money is a **perennial** source of disagreement among couples.

they made a bigger economic contribution. The purpose of the food stamp program was to reduce misery, but it's a good guess that the program was also good for American economic growth.

The same thing, I'd argue, will end up being true of Obamacare. **Subsidized insurance**[19] will induce some people to reduce the number of hours they work, but it will also mean higher productivity from Americans who are finally getting the health care they need, not to mention making better use of their skills because they can change jobs without the fear of losing coverage. Over all, health reform will probably make us richer as well as more secure.

Will the new view of inequality change our political debate? It should. Being nice to the wealthy and cruel to the poor is not, it turns out, the key to economic growth. On the contrary, making our economy fairer would also make it richer. Goodbye, trickle-down; hello, **trickle-up**[20].

---

19 subsidized insurance: 국가로부터 지원을 받는 의료보험
20 trickle-up effect: 분수 효과론
   참고 The trickle-up effect or fountain effect is an economic theory used to describe the flow of wealth from the poor to the affluent; it is opposite to the trickle-down effect. It states that benefiting the poor directly (for example through micro loans) will boost the productivity of society as a whole and thus those benefits will, in effect, "trickle up" to benefits for the wealthy.

일반영어 08 **Relax, your kids will be fine**

IN 1693 the philosopher John Locke warned that children should not be given too much "unwholesome fruit" to eat. Three centuries later, misguided ideas about child-rearing are still **rife**[1]. Many parents **fret**[2] that their offspring will die unless ceaselessly watched. In America the law can be equally **paranoid**[3]. In South Carolina this month Debra Harrell was jailed for letting her nine-year-old daughter play in a park **unsupervised**[4]. The child, who had a mobile phone and had not been harmed in any way, was briefly taken into custody of the social services.

Ms Harrell's **draconian**[5] punishment reflects the rich world's **angst**[6] about parenting. By most objective measures, modern parents are far more **conscientious**[7] than previous generations. Since 1965 labour-saving devices such as washing machines and ready meals have freed eight hours a week for the average American couple, but slightly more than all of that time has been **swallowed up**[8] by childcare.

Dads are far more hands-on than their fathers were, and working mothers spend more time nurturing their **sprogs**[9] than the housewives of the 1960s did. This works for both sides: children need love and stimulation; and for the

---

1 **rife**: very common and often bad or unpleasant
   ex Speculation about who would be fired **ran rife** for weeks.
2 **fret**: to worry or be concerned
   ex It turned out that it was nothing to **fret about/over**.
3 **paranoid**: worrying that people do not like you and are trying to harm you, although you have no proof of this
   ex They're obviously **paranoid** about somebody copying their products.
4 **unsupervised**: not watched and directed by someone who has authority
   ex The kids were **left unsupervised** while their parents were out.
   Unsupervised visits are not allowed at the prison.
5 **draconian**: very severe or cruel
6 **angst**: a feeling of anxiety about your life or situation
   ex a film about **teenage angst**
7 **conscientious**: very careful about doing what you are supposed to do; concerned with doing something correctly
   ex She has always been a very **conscientious worker**.
   He was **conscientious about** following the doctor's orders.
8 **swallow up**: to use a lot of something such as money, time, or effort
   ex Campaigning **swallows up a lot of time** without guaranteeing success.
9 **sprog**: a child (British, informal)

parents, reading to a child or playing ball games in the garden is more fulfilling than washing dishes.

There are two **blots**[10] in this **picture**[11], connected to class. One is at the lower end. Even if poor parents spend more time with their children than they once did, they spend less than rich parents do—and they struggle to provide enough support, especially in the crucial early years. America is a **laggard**[12] here; its government spends abundantly on school-age kids but much less than other rich countries on the first two or three years of life. As this newspaper has pointed out before, if America did more to help poor parents with young children, it would yield huge returns.

The second problem, less easy to prove, occurs at the other end of the income scale, and may even apply to otherwise rational Economist readers: well-educated, rich parents try to do too much. Safety is part of it: they fear that if they are not constantly vigilant their children may break their necks or eat a cupcake that has fallen on the floor. Over-coaching is another symptom. Parents fear that unless they drive their offspring to Mandarin classes, violin lessons and fencing practice six times a week, they will not get into the right university. The streets of Palo Alto and Chelsea are **clogged**[13] with people-carriers hauling children from one educational event to another.

The fear about safety is the least rational. Despite the impression you get from watching crime dramas, children in rich countries are **mind-bogglingly**[14]

---

10 blot: a drop of liquid, especially ink, on the surface of something
   The table was **covered in blots of ink.**
11 picture: a general situation
   The overall **economic picture** is improving.
   Marriage never entered the picture [=was never considered] until now.
12 laggard: a person or organization that is slow to do something or slow to make progress
13 clog: to block something such as a pipe, tube, or passage, or to become blocked, so that nothing can get through
   The drain's **clogged again.**
   The streams are **clogged with ice in winter.**
14 mind-boggling: very large, unusual, or complicated and not easy to imagine
   athletes who earn a **mind-boggling** amount of money

safe, so long as they look both ways before crossing the road. Kids in the 1950s —that golden era so often **evoked**[15] by conservative politicians—were in fact five times likelier to die before the age of five. Yet their parents thought nothing of letting them roam free. In those days, most American children walked or biked to school; now barely 10% do, prevented by **jittery**[16] parents. Children learn how to handle risks by taking a few, such as climbing trees or taking the train, even if that means scraped knees and seeing the occasional **weirdo**[17]. Freedom is **exhilarating**[18]. It also fosters self-reliance.

The other popular parental fear—that your children might not get into an Ivy League college—is more rational. Academic success matters more than ever before. But beyond a certain point, parenting makes less difference than many parents imagine. Studies in Minnesota and Sweden, for example, found that identical twins grew up equally intelligent whether they were raised together or apart. A study in Colorado found that children adopted and raised by **brainy**[19] parents ended up no brainier than those adopted by average parents. Genes appear to matter more than upbringing in the jobs market, too. In a big study of Korean children adopted in America, those raised by the richest families grew up to earn no more than those adopted by the poorest families.

This does not mean that parenting is irrelevant. The families who adopt children are carefully screened, so they tend to be warm, capable and middle-class. But

---

15 evoke: to bring a particular emotion, idea, or memory into your mind
   ex The recent flood **evoked** memories of the great flood of 1972.
16 jittery: feeling nervous and upset, and sometimes being unable to keep still because of this
17 weirdo: a strange or unusual person
   ex He's **such a weirdo.**
18 exhilarating: making you feel extremely happy, excited, and full of energy
19 brainy: very intelligent

the twin and adoption studies indicate that any child given a loving home and adequate stimulation is likely to fulfil her potential. Put another way, better-off parents can afford to relax a bit. Your kids will be fine if you hover over them less and let them **frolic**[20] in the sun from time to time. You may be happier, too, if you spend the extra time indulging your own hobbies—or sleeping. And if you are less stressed, your children will appreciate it, even if you still make them eat their fruit and vegetables.

20 frolic: to play and move about happily

Harvard Alums Still Say They "Went to College in Boston"

Until recently, I **was of the belief that**[1] no Harvard graduates actually responded to inquiries about their alma mater with "I went to college in Boston," nor Yalies with "New Haven," Princetonians with "New Jersey," or Stanford alumni with "the Bay area." I assumed this conversational **maneuver**[2] was such an embarrassing cliché that it had become obsolete, the **province**[3] of fictional characters like The Great Gatsby's Nick Carraway, who informs readers, "I graduated from New Haven in 1915."

Then I solicited the opinions of my Slate colleagues, many of whom have degrees from universities that rank highly on U.S. News and World Report's annual list. I discovered that many of them had personally heard this **wink**[4] of a **noncommittal**[5] response, and, more alarmingly, some of them had uttered some version of it themselves.

Having thus learned that this is **still a thing**[6], I must urge all Yale, Princeton, and Harvard students and alumni—and anyone else tempted to use a geographical euphemism to describe their **august**[7] alma mater—to please stop doing this. **Cease and desist**[8]. **Cut it out**[9]. I'm sure you are a kind and smart person, but this verbal habit makes you look like a **patronizing**[10], self-serious jerk.

---

1 **be of the belief that**: hold the opinion that; think
   ex *I am firmly of the belief that* we need to improve our product.
2 **maneuver**: a clever plan or action that you use to get something you want
   ex *With a quick maneuver*, she avoided an accident.
   Through *a series of legal maneuvers*, the defense lawyer kept her client out of jail.
   참고 She *maneuvered her car into the tiny garage*.
3 **province**: a subject or area of interest that a person knows about or is involved in usually singular
   ex It's a legal question that *is outside my province*.
   That subject is *the special province of this magazine*.
4 **wink**: a hint or signal given by winking
5 **noncommittal**: not telling or showing what you think about something
   ex She would only *give noncommittal answers about* her plans.
6 **still a thing**: used when the subject is declining in popularity or has lost appeal
   ex Record players are *still a thing?*
7 **august**: having a formal and impressive quality
   ex We visited their *august* mansion and expansive grounds.
   The family claims *an august lineage*.
8 **cease and desist**: to stop and to not resume an action
9 **cut it/that out**: used for telling someone to stop doing something that you do not like
   ex *Will you cut it out* I'm trying to sleep here!
10 **patronizing**: behaving or speaking in a way that shows you think you are more intelligent or important than someone

Sure, there are times when you're telling a story about your college years and your undergraduate city of residence comes up **organically**[11]. E.g., "I went to college in Boston, which is why I'm a Red Sox fan." This is fine—you certainly don't need to be telling people about the fancy, famous school you attended when it's not relevant to what you're talking about. But there is never any reason to answer the direct question "Where did you go to college?" with an **evasive**[12] half-truth.

Elite alumni's main justification for this habit is that some people act weird and make uncomfortable or hostile comments when they learn you went to Harvard, Yale, or Princeton. Indeed, Harvardians frequently refer to telling people you went to Harvard as "**dropping the H-bomb**[13]," which is perhaps the most **cringeworthily**[14] **hyperbolic**[15] expression in the English language. The **unwieldy**[16] conversational power of the H-bomb is a recurring topic of analysis in the Harvard Crimson. See, for instance, this 2002 piece by MSNBC reporter Irin Carmon with the excellent subtitle "Does it help or hinder the **mack**[17]?" (The **gender politics**[18] of the H-bomb are complicated.) Princetonians, similarly, talk about the "P-bomb", a term that implies that the two syllables in "Princeton" can **derail**[19] small talk and **obliterate**[20] **nascent**[21] social connections **in one fell swoop**[22].

Certainly, some small number of people—insecure people who perhaps have not

---

11 organic: happening or developing in a natural and continuous process
　　 The business has expanded through **organic growth**, rather than by taking over other companies.
12 evasive: not honest or direct　　 She gave an **evasive answer**.
13 to drop the h-bomb: telling someone that you go (went) to Harvard.
　1) drop a bomb or drop the bomb: to do or say something that is very shocking and unexpected
　　 She **dropped a bomb** with her resignation. [=her resignation was a complete surprise]
14 cringeworthy: Causing feelings of embarrassment or awkwardness:
　　 The play's cast was excellent, but the dialogue was **unforgivably cringeworthy**.
15 hyperbolic: exaggerated
　1) hyperbole: language that describes something as better or worse than it really is
　　 In describing his accomplishments, **he's somewhat given to hyperbole**. [=he tends to exaggerate his accomplishments]
16 unwieldy: difficult to handle, control, or deal with because of being large, heavy, or complex
　　 The system is **outdated and unwieldy**.
17 mack: flirting
　1) mack: To hit on, flirt with, or seduce a female by using verbal or sometimes physical means of persuasion.
18 gender politics: 남녀 사이의 역학관계, debate about the roles and relations of men and women
19 derail: to prevent something from continuing in the way that it was planned
　　 The incident threatened to **derail her career**.
20 obliterate: to destroy (something) completely so that nothing is left
21 nascent: beginning to exist; recently formed or developed
　　 The actress is now focusing on her **nascent** singing career.
22 in/at one fell swoop: with one sudden action, or on one single occasion

yet learned that Ivy League schools confer degrees on plenty of idiots every year —may react inelegantly upon hearing that you went to Harvard, Yale, or Princeton. But it is not your job to anticipate and preemptively manage another person's emotional response to your biography. If you tell people you went to Harvard and they respond by **freaking out**[23], that **reflects poorly on them**[24].

If, on the other hand, you refuse to tell someone you went to Harvard, that reflects poorly on you—it implies that, on some level, you buy into the overblown mythos of Harvard and the presumption of Ivy League superiority. To fear the effects of the word "Harvard" is to take Harvard way too seriously. Once you understand that Harvard is just a college, and that getting into Harvard probably had more to do with your socioeconomic background and the luck of the draw than with your merits **vis-à-vis**[25] people who didn't get into (or, more likely, just didn't apply to) Harvard, the **cagey**[26] "college in Boston" response starts to sound very, very silly.

Or look at it this way: Saying you "went to college in Boston" or "went to college in New Haven" functions as an elitist **dog whistle**[27]. There are people who pick up on the hint, people who, like you perhaps, spend a lot of time around **snotty**[28] people who went to prestigious schools. But if your **interlocutor**[29] understands the dog whistle, he will probably be offended that you have judged

---

23 if you **are freaked out** or if something **freaks you out**, you become so angry, surprised, excited, or frightened that you cannot control yourself
 ex *Meeting my dad again after all these years **really freaked me out**.*
24 **reflect on** someone/something: to give people a particular opinion of someone or something
 ex *The affair **reflected very badly on the government**.*
 *We hope her success will **reflect well on the school**.*
25 **vis-à-vis**: compared to or relating to someone or something
 ex *Our students' scores are quite good **vis--vis the national averages**.*
26 **cagey**: not saying much about something, because you do not want people to know very much
 ex *He **was very cagey about** his reasons for leaving.*
27 A **dog whistle** is a type of whistle that emits sound in the ultrasonic range, which people cannot hear but other animals can, including dogs and domestic cats, and is used in their training.
28 **snotty**: a snotty person thinks they are better or more important than other people
29 **interlocutor**: a person who is having a conversation with you

him incapable of gracefully handling the news about where you went to school. And if your interlocutor doesn't understand the dog whistle, he will simply wonder why you are being so evasive and weird—and then, if he does eventually find out you went to Yale, he will be offended that you have judged him incapable of gracefully handling that fact. Either way, you'll look like a **shmuck** [30].

---

[30] shmuck: Schmuck or shmuck in American English is a pejorative meaning one who is stupid or foolish; or an obnoxious, contemptible or detestable person.

10 The Structures of Growth

Most of us are trying to get better at something. And when we think about our future progress, we tend to imagine we will improve **linearly**[1]. We'll work hard at mastering some skill; we'll steadily get better and better.

But, as the Canadian writer Scott H. Young points out in a recent blog post, progress in most domains is not linear. In some spheres, like learning a language or **taking up running**[2], improvement is. You make a lot of progress when you first begin the activity, but, as you get better, it gets harder and harder to improve.

Logarithmic[3] activities require a certain sort of mind-set, Young writes. During the early high-growth phase, when everything is coming easily, you have to make sure you maintain your disciplined habits, or else you will fall backward. Then later, during the slow-growth phase, you have to break some of your habits. To move from good to great, you have to break out of certain **routines**[4] that have become **calcified**[5] and are now holding you back.

For example, when Tiger Woods was first competing at golf, he had to stick to his arduous practice routine even though success seemed to come ridiculously

---

1 **linear**: going from one thing to the next thing in a direct and logical way
   ex Students' reading does not always progress **in a linear fashion**.
2 **take up**: to start doing something regularly as a habit, job, or interest
   ex Chris has **taken up jogging**.
3 **logarithmic growth**: 처음에는 성장 속도가 빠르다가 나중에 둔화되는 성장
4 **routine**: a regular way of doing things in a particular order
   ex Grandma gets upset if we **change her routine**.
   A brisk walk is part **of her morning routine.**
5 **calcify**: to make or become inflexible and unchanging.

easy. But then, when he hit a plateau, he had to reinvent his swing to reach that final **tippy-top**[6] level.

In other domains, growth is **exponential**[7]. In these activities, you have to work for weeks or even years at mastering the fundamentals, and you barely see any return. But then, after you have put in your 10,000 hours of effort, suddenly you develop a natural ease and your progress multiplies quickly.

Mastering an academic discipline is an exponential domain. You have to learn the basics over years of graduate school before you **internalize**[8] the structures of the field and can begin to play creatively with the concepts. Ice hockey is an exponential activity (it takes years just to skate well enough).

Many people quit exponential activities in the early phases. You've got to be **bullheaded**[9] to work hard while getting no glory. But then when you are in the later fast-progress stage, you've got to be open-minded to turn your hard-earned skill into **poetry**[10]. Vincent van Gogh had to spend years learning the basics of drawing, but then, when he'd achieved mastery, he had to let loose and create art.

I could think of some other growth structures. In some domains progress comes like a stairway. There's a period of stagnation, followed by a step upward, followed by a period of stagnation, followed by another step. In other domains,

---

6   tippy-top: 최고의
7   exponential growth: 처음에는 속도가 완만하다가 나중에 빨라지는 성장
    1) exponential: very fast; increasingly rapid
        The business has experienced several years of **exponential growth**.
        Prices have increased at an **exponential rate.**
8   internalize: to make (something, such as an idea or an attitude) an important part of the kind of person you are
        They have **internalized** their parents' values.
9   bullheaded: very stubborn in a foolish or annoying way
10 poetry: someone or something of great beauty, emotion, or imagination, or the quality of beauty, emotion, or imagination
        Their chocolate cakes are pure **poetry**!
        Her dancing is **pure poetry**.
        He is **poetry in motion** when he catches and throws the ball.

progress comes like waves repetitively **lapping the shore**[11]. You go over some material and the wave leaves a residue of knowledge; then you go over the same material again and the next wave leaves a bit more residue.

Yet other domains follow a valley-shaped curve. You have to go down initially before you can go up. The experience of immigrating to a new country can be like this; you have to start at the bottom as you learn a new society before you can make your way upward. Moral progress is like this, too. You have to go down and explore your own failures before you can conquer them. You have to taste humiliation before you can aspire toward excellence.

Thinking about growth structures reminds you that really successful people often have the ability to completely flip their mental **dispositions**[12]. In many fields, it pays to be rigid and disciplined at first, but then flexible and playful as you get better. If you go into politics, you have to make the transition from campaigning, which is an instantly gratifying activity, to governing, which is an exponential activity, requiring experience, patience and **hard-earned**[13] wisdom.

This way of thinking also makes it clear that skill acquisition is a deeply moral activity. You don't only need knowledge about what to do; you have to train yourself to defeat your natural desires. In the fast growth phase of a logarithmic activity, you have to fight the urge to self-celebrate and relax. In the later

---

11 if water **laps** something or laps against something, it moves against it gently with a soft sound
　ex The waves **lapped gently against the rocks.**
12 disposition: a tendency to act or think in a particular way
　ex Her **disposition** was to always think negatively.
13 hard-earned: earned or achieved only after a lot of effort
　ex **hard-earned** money

phase, when everyone is singing your praises, you have to fight self-satisfaction.

It does seem clear that our society celebrates fast-payoff **instrumental**[14] activities, like sports and rock stardom, while undervaluing exponential activities, like being a statesman or craftsman. Kids increasingly flock to logarithmic sports, like soccer, over exponential sports, like baseball.

Finally, this focus on growth structures takes your eyes off yourself. The crucial thing is not what **traits**[15] you **intrinsically**[16] possess. The crucial questions are: What is the structure of your domain? Where are you now on the progress curve? How are you interacting with the structures of the field?

The crucial answers to those questions are not found in the mirror. They are found by seeing yourself from a distance as part of a landscape. That's a more pleasing and healthier perspective in any case.

---

14 instrumental: very important in helping or causing something to happen or be done often + in
 He was **instrumental** in organizing the club. = He played an instrumental part/role in organizing the club.
 Her influence was **instrumental** in bringing the painting to the museum.
15 trait: a quality that makes one person or thing different from another
 Humility is an **admirable trait**. [=quality]
16 intrinsic: belonging to the essential nature of a thing
 the **intrinsic** brightness of a star
 Creativity is **intrinsic** to human nature.

Diet Lures and Diet Lies

My home is like any other, **chockablock**[1] with stuff that I wouldn't want the world to see: trashy books, **cheesy**[2] clothes, a **cache**[3] of scented candles so enormous you might think I'm prepping for some **epically**[4] smelly **apocalypse**[5].

But the most embarrassing thing by far is in a kitchen cupboard, near the Tabasco. It's a green and white bottle of pills—supplements, to use the proper marketing lingo—that are supposed to make me effortlessly slim.

I **know better**[6]. We all do.

Garcinia Cambogia[7] is what the label says, and the pills contain the powdered extract of an exotic fruit for which **quasi-mystical**[8] claims are made. It blocks fat absorption, or at least it might. It suppresses appetite, or so a few people have reported. It regulates **emotional eating**[9], in unproven theory.

I stumbled across a mention of it on the Internet perhaps 18 months ago, and the mention was coupled with an **endorsement**[10] **of sorts**[11] by Dr. Mehmet Oz. And I thought: Who knows? What could it hurt? Minutes later I was typing in my credit-card number, hitting "send" and joining—or, rather, rejoining—the millions of Americans duped annually into this manner of ridiculousness.

---

1 **chockablock**: very full usually + with
   ex *The shelves are* **chockablock with books**.
2 **cheesy**: lacking style or good taste
3 **cache**: a quantity of things that have been hidden, especially weapons
   ex *a huge cache of illegal guns and home-made explosives*
4 **epically**: Epically is defined as something which is done in an epic way, meaning in a lengthy, grand or important way.
5 **apocalypse**: a great disaster
   ex *His book tells of* **an environmental apocalypse**.
       fears of **a nuclear apocalypse** [=a disaster caused by nuclear weapons]
6 **know better**: to know that what someone else says or thinks is wrong
   ex *Everyone thought it was an innocent mistake,* **but I knew better**.
7 **Garcinia Cambogia**: 가르시니아 캄보지아 (남아시아에서 서식하는 나무인 가르시니아종의 과일)
8 **quasi-mystical**:
   1) **quasi-**: in some way or sense but not in a true, direct, or complete way
   ex *The descriptions contain a fantastic amount of* **quasi-scientific detail**.
9 **emotional eating**: 스트레스로 인한 폭식
10 **endorsement**: an occasion when someone famous says in an advertisement that they like a product
    ex *Many retired athletes are able to make a lot of money by doing* **product endorsements**.
11 **of sorts** or **of a sort**: of a type that is not exactly the same as the actual thing, or is not as good as the actual thing
    ex *She's* **an artist of sorts**.

We talk a whole lot these days about the **perfidies**[12] of the fast-food industry, the snack-food industry, the soft-drink industry. There are books **aplenty**[13], documentaries **galore**[14]. And that's terrific. That's progress.

But we should take care that our intensifying alarm over all of the aggressively marketed junk that makes us fatter doesn't **crowd out**[15] **a measure of**[16] sustained **pique**[17] at all of the aggressively marketed pills, products and plans that fail to make us any thinner, despite their **lavish**[18] promises and the money we **plunk down**[19]. We should save some room for them.

They show no signs of going away anytime soon. Worse yet, they belong to, and are complemented by, a **brimming**[20] culture of micro theories and **boutique**[21] science that seeks explanations for excess pounds in equations well beyond the sturdy **maxim**[22] of calories in, calories out.

Yes, that maxim oversimplifies. Yes, we learn more all the time about the **asterisks**[23] to it and about which kinds of calories set you up to be hungrier (and to continue eating) or not.

---

12 perfidy: deliberately betraying a trust
13 aplenty: in a large number or amount
14 galore: in large numbers or amounts
　　The store promises bargains **galore** [=promises that there will be many bargains] during its weekend sale.
15 crowd out: to push, move, or force (something or someone) out of a place or situation by filling its space
　　She worries that junk food is **crowding fruits and vegetables out of her children's diet.**
16 measure: an amount of a particular quality that is neither large nor small
　　The system gives people **a measure of protection against pollution.**
17 pique: an annoyed feeling that you show when you think someone has insulted you or been rude to you
　　He slammed the door **in a fit of pique.**
18 lavish: given in large amounts　　She has **drawn/gained lavish praise** [=a great amount of praise] for her charitable works.
19 plunk down: to pay a particular amount of money for something, especially when it is expensive
　　When I **plunk down** $3000 for a computer, I expect it to work right.
20 brim: to be full of something
　　I handed him a cup **brimming with coffee.** / Rob was **brimming with enthusiasm.**
21 boutique: 소규모로 특화된, of, designating, or characteristic of a small, exclusive producer or business
　　one of California's **best boutique wineries.**
22 maxim: a well-known phrase that expresses a general truth about life or a rule about behavior
　　My mother's **favorite maxim** [=saying] was Don't count your chickens before they hatch. [=don't assume that things will happen the way you expect them to happen]
23 asterisk: the symbol *.
　　In a piece of writing, an asterisk is used after a word or phrase to show that more information is given in a footnote.

But consult the most respected physicians in the field of weight loss and they'll tell you that the maxim remains as relevant as ever. And the **vogue**[24] for painstakingly tailored eating **regimens**[25] and dieting techniques is to some extent a distraction from that, a dangerous one, because it promotes the idea that basic nature and fundamental biology can somehow be **gamed**[26], cheated, transcended.

"In terms of diet, **the general laws of thermodynamics**[27] hold," Rudolph Leibel, an obesity expert at the Columbia University Medical Center, told me. "The issue of—'If I eat a diet of all watermelons as opposed to a diet of hamburgers with the same number of calories, will I be able to lose more weight on the watermelons?'—that's a **specious**[28] argument. We're dealing with chemistry and physics, not imagination.

But how imaginative we get! How creatively we edit the **smorgasbord**[29] of possibility, intent on a formula superior to all others. This person **forswears**[30] gluten. That person exiles starch. There are **plutocrats**[31] who are **eating like cavemen**[32]. There are disciples of the lifestyle **guru**[33] Timothy Ferriss[34] who are weighing their poop.

---

24 **vogue**: something (such as a way of dressing or behaving) that is fashionable or popular in a particular time and place
[count] ex His art seems to be **enjoying a vogue** these days.
[noncount] Short skirts are **in vogue** right now. = Short skirts are (all) the vogue right now.
When did Thai food **come into vogue**?
That style **went/fell out of vogue** years ago.
25 **regimen**: a plan or set of rules about food, exercise, etc., to make someone become or stay healthy
ex a daily training/exercise **regimen**
26 **game**: to take dishonest advantage of; cheat ex **game** the tax system
27 **the general laws of thermodynamics**: 열역학의 일반 법칙들
28 **specious**: seeming to be true but in fact wrong ex a specious argument
29 **smorgasbord**: a large mixture of many different things
ex We were presented **with a smorgasbord [=variety] of options.**
30 **forswear**: to promise to give up (something) or to stop doing (something)
ex She **forswore** her allegiance to the old regime. / He **foreswore** cigarettes/smoking as his New Year's resolution.
31 **plutocrat**: a person who has power because of great wealth
32 **eating like cavemen**: 팔레오 다이어트
참고 Paleo Diet is also called the Caveman Diet or the Stone Age diet, it's basically a high-protein, high-fiber eating plan that promises you can lose weight without cutting calories.
33 **guru**: a person who has a lot of experience in or knowledge about a particular subject
ex She's a self-proclaimed **financial guru**. / **Fitness gurus** call it the hottest new exercise trend of the year.
34 Timothy Ferriss (born July 20, 1977) is an American author, entrepreneur, angel investor, and public speaker.

Enhanced education and growing **sophistication**[35] haven't done away with fads. There's still too much **favor to be curried**[36] and money to be made by **trumpeting**[37] them.

Cue[38] Oz. A distinguished **cardiothoracic surgeon**[39], he has traded time in the hospital for time on TV, where he revisits no topic more incessantly than (**supposedly**[40]) **ingenious**[41] ways to slim down. With a shameless vocabulary of "magic," "miracle" and "revolutionary," he has showcased or outright **validated**[42] HCG hormone shots, green coffee bean supplements, raspberry ketone supplements and more. He told viewers: "I'm going to show you how you can get fat to eat itself right out of your body."

The sum of these **exhortations**[43] "just violates science," said Leibel. "It'd be like if we went to NASA and they were using astrological charts to try to figure out how to get a rocket to **Europa**[44]. It's at that level."

On Oz's website, under the Weight Loss Directory, there are subcategories including "Rapid Belly Melt" and "Mega Metabolism Boosters." Garcinia Cambogia is celebrated **ad nauseam**[45].

---

35 sophistication: the quality of knowing and understanding a lot about a complicated subject
   - computer users with a high degree of **sophistication**
36 curry favor (with someone): to try to make someone like you or give you something
   - Big tax cuts are often proposed to **curry favor with voters**.
37 trumpet: to praise (something) loudly and publicly especially in a way that is annoying
   - He likes to **trumpet** his own achievements.
38 cue: to give (someone) a signal to do something during a performance
   - **Cue the band.**
   - **Cue the lights/sound.** [=give a signal to the person running the lights/sound]
39 cardiothoracic surgery: 흉부외과
40 supposedly: as some people believe or say, although you may not agree with this
   - The house is **supposedly** haunted.
   - **Supposedly** the process causes no environmental damage.
41 ingenious: an ingenious plan, piece of equipment, etc. uses new and clever ideas
   - an **ingenious** device for opening bottles
42 validate: to officially prove that something is true or correct
   - The evidence does seem to **validate** his claim.
43 exhort: to try to persuade someone to do something
44 Europa: 목성의 위성 가운데 네 번째로 큰 위성
45 ad nauseam: if you do or say something ad nauseam, you repeat it so many times that it annoys other people

And a person can start to wonder. A person can **cave**[46]. I did, even though the "**starch blocker**[47]" tablets that I took in college did nothing and decades of trendy diets have confirmed one and only one **magic bullet**[48]: a mix of restrained eating and regular exercise.

The Garcinia Cambogia is still in the cabinet because it's half full. I **wised up**[49] after a futile week of two pills daily. If I wise up **all the way**[50], I'll throw the bottle out.

---

46 cave: to suddenly stop opposing something, especially because people have persuaded you
   ex She finally **caved in** and gave the press the interview they wanted.
47 starch blocker: 탄수화물 차단제
48 magic bullet: something that solves a difficult problem easily
   ex There is **no magic bullet** to fix our educational system.
49 wise up: to start to think and act in a more intelligent way
   ex They could lose everything they have if they don't **wise up**. [=smarten up]
50 if you do something all the way, you put all your effort into doing it
   참고 if you say that you go or travel all the way somewhere, you emphasize that it is a long way
   ex We'll have **to go all the way back to get the list**.

12 The Mental Virtues

We all know what **makes for**¹ good character in soldiers. We've seen the movies about heroes who display courage, loyalty and coolness under fire. But what about somebody who sits in front of a keyboard all day? Is it possible to display and cultivate character if you are just an information age **office jockey**², alone with a memo or your computer?

Of course it is. Even if you are alone in your office, you are thinking. Thinking well under a **barrage**³ of information may be a different sort of moral challenge than fighting well under a **hail**⁴ of bullets, but it's a character challenge nonetheless.

In their 2007 book, "Intellectual Virtues," Robert C. Roberts of Baylor University and W. Jay Wood of Wheaton College list some of the **cerebral**⁵ virtues. We can all grade ourselves on how good we are at each of them.

First, there is love of learning. Some people are just more ardently curious than others, either by cultivation or by nature.

Second, there is courage. The obvious form of intellectual courage is the willingness to hold unpopular views. But the **subtler**⁶ form is knowing how much

---

1 make for something: to help to make something possible
   The new computers **make for much greater productivity**.
2 office jockey: a person whose job involves working at a desk (=desk jockey)
   1) jockey: someone who operates or works with a specified vehicle, device, object, or material
      a **bus jockey** [=a bus driver]
      computer jockeys
3 barrage: a great amount of something that comes quickly and continuously+ of
   The reporters overwhelmed her with **a barrage of questions.**
   a barrage [=flood] of phone calls
4 hail: a large number of small hard objects (such as bullets or stones) flying or falling together
   They were gunned down **in a hail of bullets.**
   often used figuratively
   The court's decision was **met with a hail of criticism**. [=was strongly criticized by many people]
5 cerebral: related to the mind rather than to feelings; intellectual and not emotional
   He's a very **cerebral comedian**.
   The novel was a little too **cerebral [=highbrow]** for me.
6 subtle: not obvious, and therefore difficult to notice
   a **subtle** scent of lilacs
   I detected a **subtle** change in his attitude toward us.

risk to take in jumping to conclusions. The reckless thinker takes a few pieces of information and leaps to some **faraway**[7] conspiracy theory. The perfectionist, on the other hand, is unwilling to **put anything out there**[8] except under ideal conditions for fear that she could be wrong. Intellectual courage is self-regulation, Roberts and Wood argue, knowing when to be daring and when to be cautious. The philosopher Thomas Kuhn pointed out that scientists often simply ignore facts that don't fit with their existing paradigms, but an intellectually courageous person is willing to look at things that are surprisingly hard to look at.

Third, there is firmness. You don't want to be a person who surrenders his beliefs at the slightest **whiff**[9] of opposition. On the other hand, you don't want to hold dogmatically to a belief against all evidence. The median point between **flaccidity**[10] and rigidity is the virtue of firmness. The firm believer can build a **steady**[11] worldview on **solid timbers**[12] but still delight in new information. She can gracefully adjust the strength of her conviction to the strength of the evidence. Firmness is a quality of mental **agility**[13].

Fourth, there is humility, which is not letting your own desire for status **get in the way of**[14] accuracy. The humble person fights against vanity and self-importance. He's not writing those sentences people write to make themselves seem smart; he's not thinking of himself much at all. The humble researcher

---

7 faraway: very distant
8 put something out there: 의견을 당당하게 밝히다, throw in an idea into a conversation
   ex Even though the book didn't quite feel finished, it was time to be done with it and **put it out there**.
9 whiff: a slight amount or sign of something
   ex a **whiff** of danger
10 flaccid: lacking strength or force; weak
   ex **flaccid** leadership
      a **flaccid** response
11 steady: dependable or reliable
   ex She has been a **steady** friend to me.
      He's a very **steady** worker.
12 solid timbers: solid foundation
13 agile: able to think quickly, solve problems, and have new ideas
   ex an **agile** mind
14 get in the way of something: to prevent something from happening
   ex I never let unimportant details **get in the way of** a good plan.

doesn't become arrogant toward his subject, assuming he has mastered it. Such a person is open to learning from anyone at any stage in life.

Fifth, there is **autonomy**[15]. **You don't want**[16] to be a person who slavishly adopts whatever opinion your teacher or some author gives you. On the other hand, you don't want to reject all guidance from people who **know what they are talking about**[17]. Autonomy is the median of knowing when to bow to authority and when not to, when to follow a role model and when not to, when to adhere to tradition and when not to.

Finally, there is generosity. This virtue starts with the willingness to share knowledge and give others credit. But it also means hearing others as they would like to be heard, looking for what each person has to teach and not looking to triumphantly **pounce upon**[18] their errors.

We all probably excel at some of these virtues and are deficient in others. But I'm struck by how much of the mainstream literature on decision-making treats the mind as some **disembodied**[19] organ that can be programed like a computer.

In fact, the mind **is embedded in**[20] human nature, and very often thinking well means **pushing against the grain of our nature**[21]—against vanity, against laziness, against the desire for certainty, against the desire to avoid painful truths. Good

---

15 autonomy: the power to make your own decisions
   New regulations have severely restricted **the autonomy of doctors.**
16 you want/don't want to do something: used for advising or warning someone that they should/should not do something
   You want to be careful, I think you've drunk too much.
   You don't want to go there alone.
17 know what you are talking about: to understand a subject because of your experience:
   He **doesn't know what he's talking about;** he's never even been to Africa.
18 pounce: to react in a very sudden way, especially by criticizing someone
   White House aides **pounced on the remark**.
19 disembodied: separated from the body
20 embed: to make something a fixed and important part of something else
   Traces of earlier ways of life **are embedded in** modern society.
   Those values **are embedded in our culture** [=that are established as part of our culture]
21 To be/go against the grain is to be different or to act in a way that is different from what is normal or usual.
   It takes courage to **go against the grain** and stand up for what you believe in.
   If something goes against your grain, it does not seem right or natural to you.
   It goes against his grain to question the boss's judgment.

thinking isn't just adopting the right technique. It's a moral **enterprise**[22] and requires good character, the ability to go against our lesser impulses for the sake of our higher ones.

Montaigne once wrote that "We can be knowledgeable with other men's knowledge, but we can't be wise with other men's wisdom." That's because wisdom isn't a body of information. It's the moral quality of knowing how to handle your own limitations. Warren Buffett made a similar point in his own sphere, "Investing is not a game where the guy with the 160 I.Q. beats the guy with the 130 I.Q. Once you have ordinary intelligence, what you need is the temperament to control the urges that get other people into trouble."

Character tests are pervasive even in modern everyday life. It's possible to be heroic if you're just sitting alone in your office. It just doesn't make for a good movie.

---

22 enterprise: the ability or desire to do dangerous or difficult things or to solve problems in new ways
ex She **showed great enterprise** [=initiative] as a young reporter.
He was criticized for **his lack of enterprise** in dealing with the crisis.

13 Is American democracy headed to extinction?

Behind **dysfunctional**¹ government, is democracy itself in decay?

It took only 250 years for democracy to **disintegrate**² in ancient Athens. A wholly new form of government was invented there in which the people ruled themselves. That **constitution**³ proved marvelously effective. Athens grew in wealth and capacity, fought off the Persian challenge, established itself as the leading power in **the known world**⁴ and produced treasures of architecture, philosophy and art that **bedazzle**⁵ to this day. But when privilege, corruption and mismanagement **took hold**⁶, the lights went out.

It would be 2,000 years before democracy was reinvented in the U.S. Constitution, now as **representative democracy**⁷. Again, government by popular consent proved **ingenious**⁸. The United States grew into the world's leading power—economically, culturally and militarily. In Europe, democracies overtook authoritarian monarchies and fascist and communist dictatorships. In recent decades, democracy's spread has made the remaining autocracies a minority.

The second democratic experiment is approaching 250 years. It has been as successful as the first. But the lesson from Athens is that success does not **breed**⁹

---

1. dysfunctional: not working normally
2. disintegrate: stop working effectively and fails completely
3. constitution: the form or structure of something, or the way in which it is organized
   - We plan to change **the constitution of the council** so that it includes more members of the public.
4. the known world: 당시 그리스인들이 알고 있던 세계
   1) known: included in the knowledge that all people considered as one group have
   - There is **no known cure for the disease**. [=there is no cure that anyone knows about, although a cure may exist that has not yet been discovered]
5. bedazzle: to thrill or excite (someone) very much
   - Fans were **bedazzled** by movie stars.
6. take hold: to become stronger and difficult to stop
   - They were fortunate to escape before the fire **took hold.**
7. representative democracy: 대의 민주주의
8. ingenious: very smart or clever
   - She was **ingenious** at finding ways to work more quickly.
9. breed: to cause or lead to (something)
   - Despair often **breeds** violence.

success. Democracy is not the **default**[10]. It is a form of government that must be created with determination and that will disintegrate unless nurtured. In the United States and Britain, democracy is disintegrating when it should be nurtured by leadership. If the lights go out in the model democracies, they will not stay on elsewhere.

It's not enough for governments to simply be democratic; they must deliver or decay. In Britain, government is increasingly ineffectual. The constitutional scholar Anthony King has described it as declining from "order" to "mess" in less than 30 years. During 10 years of New Labor rule, that **proposition**[11] was tested and confirmed. In 1997 a new government was voted in with a **mandate**[12] and determination to **turn the tide on**[13] Thatcherite inequality. It was given all the parliamentary power a democratic government could dream of and benefited from 10 years of steady economic growth. But a strong government was defeated by a weak system of **governance**[14]. It delivered nothing of what it intended and left Britain more unequal than where the previous regime had left off.

The next government, a center-right coalition, has proved itself equally unable. It was supposed to repair damage from the economic crisis but has responded with inaction on the causes of crisis, in a **monopolistic**[15] financial-services sector, and with a **brand**[16] of austerity that protects the privileged at the expense of the poor.

---

10 **default**: used to describe something that happens or is done when nothing else has been done or can be done usually used in the phrase by default
   ex *No one else wanted the job, so he became the club's president **by default**.*
11 **proposition**: a statement to be proved, explained, or discussed
   ex *Her theory rejects the basic **proposition** that humans evolved from apes.*
12 **mandate**: the power to act that voters give to their elected leaders
   ex *He won the election so convincingly that he believed he had been given a **mandate** for reform.*
13 **tide**: the way in which something is changing or developing
   ex *We tried to **gauge the tide of public opinion**. [=to find out how public opinion was changing]*
   *The team was on a losing streak, but **then the tide turned** [=their luck changed] and they went on to win the championship.*
14 **governance**: the way in which an organization is managed at the highest level, and the systems for doing this:
   ex *a company with a reputation for **good governance***
   *We have tried to strengthen the position of shareholders **in the governance of the corporation**.*
15 **monopolistic**: 독점적인, used to describe the actions of a company that is able to control the supply and price of a particular product or service
   ex *If they used their **monopolistic** power to bully rivals, then they should be called to account for conduct that is prohibited.*
16 **brand**: a particular kind or type of something
   ex *I don't like **his brand of humor**.*

Again, what has **transpired**[17] is inability rather than ill will. Both these governments **came up against**[18] concentrations of economic power that have become politically unmanageable.

Meanwhile, the health of the U.S. system is even worse than it looks. The three branches of government are designed to deliver through checks and balances. But balance has become **gridlock**[19], and the United States is not getting the governance it needs. Here, the link between inequality and inability is on sharp display. Power has been sucked out of the constitutional system and **usurped**[20] by actors such as **PACs**[21], think tanks, media and lobbying organizations.

In the age of mega-expensive politics, candidates depend on sponsors to fund permanent campaigns. When money is allowed to **transgress**[22] from markets, where it belongs, to politics, where it has no business, those who control it gain power to decide who the successful candidates will be—those they wish to fund— and what they can decide once they are in office. Rich supporters get two **swings**[23] at influencing politics, one as voters and one as donors. Others have only the vote, a power that diminishes as political inflation deflates its value. It is a misunderstanding to think that candidates chase money. It is money that chases candidates.

In Athens, democracy disintegrated when the rich grew super-rich, refused to

---

17 transpire: to happen
   • They wouldn't say **what had transpired** [=taken place] at the meeting.
18 come up against something: to have to deal with something difficult or unpleasant
   • In the first week, **we came up against** a pretty tricky problem.
19 gridlock: a situation in which no progress can be made [noncount]
   • Disagreements about funding have caused **legislative gridlock** in Congress.
20 usurp: to take and keep (something, such as power) in a forceful or violent way and especially without the right to do so
   • Some people have accused city council members of trying to **usurp** the mayor's power.
21 PAC: 정치 후원회 (=political action committee) a group that is formed to give money to the political campaigns of people who are likely to make decisions that would benefit the group's interests
   • The governor received over $3 million in campaign contributions from **political action committees**.
22 transgress: go beyond the limits of (what is morally, socially, or legally acceptable):
   • She had **transgressed** an unwritten social law.
23 swing: freedom of action
   • The children have free **swing** in deciding what color to paint their room.

play by the rules and undermined the established system of government. That is the point that the United States and Britain have reached.

Nearly a century ago, when capitalist democracy was in a crisis not unlike the present one, Supreme Court Justice Louis Brandeis warned: "We may have democracy, or we may have wealth concentrated in the hands of a few, but we can't have both." Democracy **weathered**[24] that storm for two reasons: It is not inequality **as such**[25] that destroys democracy but the more recent combination of inequality and transgression. Furthermore, democracy was then able to learn from crisis. The New Deal **tempered**[26] economic **free-for-all**[27], primarily through the 1933 Banking Act, and gave the smallfolk new **social securities**[28].

The lesson from Athens is that success breeds complacency. People, notably those in privilege, stopped caring, and democracy was neglected. Six years after the global economic crisis, the signs from the model democracies are that those in privilege are unable to care and that our systems are unable to learn. The crisis started in out-of-control financial services industries in the United States and Britain, but control has not been **reasserted**[29]. Economic inequality has followed through to political inequality, and democratic government is **bereft of**[30] power and capacity. Brandeis was not wrong; he was ahead of his time.

---

24 **weather**: to manage a difficult experience without being seriously harmed
   ex He **has weathered two corruption scandals** already.
25 **as such**: by, of, or in itself used to indicate that something is being considered by itself and not along with other things
   ex There's nothing wrong with gambling **as such** [=per se], but it's best to do it in moderation.
26 **temper**: to make something less strong or extreme, especially by adding something that has the opposite effect
   ex The hot sunny days **were tempered by** a light breeze.
27 **free-for-all**: an uncontrolled situation in which people are competing with each other to gain as much as they can for themselves
28 **social security**: public provision for the economic, and sometimes social, welfare of the aged, unemployed, etc, esp through pensions and other monetary assistance
29 **reassert**: to make other people accept or respect (something that has been in doubt)
   ex He tried to **reassert his authority/leadership/power/control**.
30 **bereft of**: not having (something that is needed, wanted, or expected)
   ex They appear to **be completely bereft of new ideas**. [=to be completely without new ideas]
   He **was bereft of all hope**.

일반영어 14   Hello, Stranger

If you've ever been on a subway or public bus, you know the rules. Don't make eye contact, stay as far away from other people as the space allows, and **for the love of God**[1], don't talk to anyone. But what if the rules are wrong?

The behavioral scientists Nicholas Epley and Juliana Schroeder approached commuters in a Chicago area train station and asked them to break the rules. In return for a $5 Starbucks gift card, these commuters agreed to participate in a simple experiment during their train ride. One group was asked to talk to the stranger who sat down next to them on the train that morning. Other people were told to follow standard commuter **norms**[2], **keeping to themselves**[3]. By the end of the train ride, commuters who talked to a stranger reported having a more positive experience than those who had sat in solitude.

If the idea of talking to a random seatmate fills you with dread, **you're not alone**[4]. When Dr. Epley and Ms. Schroeder asked other people in the same train station to predict how they would feel after talking to a stranger, the commuters thought their ride would be more pleasant if they sat on their own.

Why are these commuters' predictions and their experiences so **at odds**[5]? Most

---

1   for the love of God: used to give added force to an angry statement
     For the love of God, quiet down! I'm trying to get some sleep here!
2   norms [plural]: standards of proper or acceptable behavior
     Each culture develops **its own social norms.**
     참고 the norm: something (such as a behavior or way of doing something) that is usual or expected
     Smaller families **have become the norm.**
     Women used to stay at home to take care of the children, but **that's no longer the norm.**
3   keep to yourself: to stay alone or with your family rather than spending time with other people
     They were a quiet couple **who kept to themselves.**
4   If you are not alone when you do something, you are not the only person who is doing it.
     She's worried about losing her job, **and she's not alone.** [=other people are also worried about losing their jobs]
     He was not alone in calling for reform. Many people were demanding changes.
5   if things are at odds with each other, they are different or opposite when they should be the same
     This statement is completely **at odds with** what was said last week.
6   snub: to insult someone by ignoring them or being rude to them

people imagined it would be difficult to start a conversation. They estimated that fewer than half of their fellow commuters would want to talk to them. But in fact, not a single person reported having been **snubbed**[6]. And the conversations were **consistently**[7] pleasant.

According to a 2004 study published in Science, commuting is associated with fewer positive emotions than any other common daily activity. By avoiding contact, we're all following a collective **assumption**[8] that turns out to be false. When the middle-aged woman starts playing Candy Crush Saga after she sits down next to the **hipster**[9] scrolling through his iTunes library, they both miss out on an opportunity for **connection**[10].

Individuals and governments pour money into making commutes slightly more bearable by investing in everything from noise-canceling headphones to more spacious seating. But what if the research showed that we would improve our commutes more by investing in **social capital**[11]—interacting with the strangers sitting all around us?

The great thing about strangers is that we tend to put on our happy **face**[12] when we meet them, **reserving**[13] our **crankier**[14] side for the people we know and love. When one of us, Liz, was in graduate school, she noticed that her boyfriend, Benjamin, felt free to act **grumpy**[15] around her. But if he was forced

---

7 **consistent**: continuing to happen or develop in the same way
   ex The pain **has been consistent**. / Your grades have **shown consistent improvement** this school year.
8 **assumption**: something that is believed to be true or probably true but that is not known to be true: something that is assumed
   ex I **made the assumption** that he was coming, so I was surprised when he didn't show up.
   Many scientific **assumptions** about Mars were wrong.
9 **hipster**: a person who follows the latest styles, fashions, etc.
   ex The movie appeals equally to **hipsters** and suburbanites.
10 **connection**: a shared feeling of affection and understanding
   ex We didn't know each other for very long, but we had a real connection.
   They're working hard to make an emotional connection with their adopted children.
11 **social capital**: 사회적 자본 (인간 관계)
   참고 The networks of relationships among people who live and work in a particular society, enabling that society to function effectively.
12 **face**: the expression on someone's face, that shows how they are feeling
   ex Marsha came back in **with a worried face**.
13 **reserve**: to keep (something) for a special or future use
   ex She usually **reserved her best dishes for** very important dinners.
   She spoke **in a tone of voice that she usually reserved for** her students. [=that she usually only used for her students]
14 **cranky**: easily annoyed or angered   ex I've been **cranky** all day because I didn't get enough sleep.
15 **grumpy**: having a bad temper or complaining often
   ex Our neighbor is a **grumpy** old man. / I was feeling **grumpy** after my long flight.

to interact with a stranger or acquaintance, he would **perk right up**[16]. Then his own pleasant behavior would often erase his bad mood.

One of the **perks**[17] of being a behavioral scientist is that when your partner does something annoying, you can bring dozens of couples into the laboratory and **get to the bottom of it**[18]. When Liz tested her hypothesis in a lab experiment, she discovered that most people showed the "Benjamin Effect": They acted more cheerful around someone they had just met than around their own romantic partner, leaving them happier than they expected.

Many of us assume, however, that our **well-being**[19] depends on our closest ties, and not on the **minor characters**[20] in our daily lives. To investigate the validity of this assumption, our student Gillian M. Sandstrom asked people to **keep a running tally of**[21] their social interactions.

She had them carry clickers—one red, one black—in their pockets all day. They clicked the red one whenever they interacted with someone close to them (a "strong tie") and the black one whenever they interacted with someone they didn't know so well (a "weak tie"). She found that introverts and extroverts alike felt happier on days when they had more social interactions.

More surprisingly, interactions with weak ties **correlated at least as highly with happiness**[22] as interactions with strong ties. Even the **bit players**[23] in our lives

---

16 if someone perks up, or if something perks them up, they begin to feel happier or more lively
   Sue **perked up** when she heard the news.
17 perk: a benefit or advantage that you get from a situation
   At 15 I looked forward to **the perks of adult life.**
   One of the perks of being a celebrity is that people often want to give you things.
18 get to the bottom of something: to find out the true cause or explanation of a bad situation
   She was determined to **get to the bottom of what went wrong.**
19 well-being: the state of being happy, healthy, or successful
   Meditation can increase a person's sense of **well-being**.
20 minor character: 단역 배우 (낯선 사람)
21 running tally: (=running total) a total which changes because numbers keep being added to it as something progresses
   He **kept a daily/running tally** [=account] of his expenses.
22 If two things correlate, a change in one thing results in a similar or an opposite change in the other thing.
   In general terms, brain size **correlates with intelligence**. [=a larger brain generally suggests greater intelligence]
   Some studies have shown that **the success of students correlates negatively with** the number of students in a class.
23 bit: a very short performance in a movie, play, etc.
   a **bit** part/role
   bit players

may influence our well-being.

In a recent study, we recruited people on their way into a busy Starbucks with a $5 gift card. We asked some customers to "have a genuine interaction with the cashier," smiling and having a brief conversation. Others were told to be as efficient as possible: Get in, get out, go on with the day. Those who lingered left Starbucks feeling more cheerful. Efficiency, it seems, is **overrated**[24].

Even fleeting glances can make a difference. Many of us have had the experience of **what the Germans call "wie Luft behandeln" ("to be looked at as though air")**[25]. The social norm of avoiding eye contact seems harmless, but it might not be. In an experiment conducted at a large Midwestern university, a college-age woman walked by people on campus and either made eye contact, smiled at them while making eye contact, or directed her gaze "beyond the ear of the passer-by," deliberately avoiding eye contact.

She **was trailed by**[26] another researcher, who surveyed people in her wake. Those who were looked at as though they weren't there reported feeling more disconnected from others.

Simply acknowledging strangers on the street may alleviate their **existential angst**[27]; and being acknowledged by others might do the same for us. (One **caveat**[28]: Another set of studies has shown that people are motivated to flee from

---

24 overrate: to rate, value, or praise (someone or something) too highly
   ex That movie was disappointing and **highly overrated**.
25 what the Germans call wie Luft behandeln (to be looked at as though air): 내 옆의 허공을 응시하는 듯한 상대방의 눈길
26 trail: to walk or move slowly as you follow behind (someone or something)
   ex He **trailed us** as we worked our way up the mountain.
27 existential angst: 실존적 고민
   참고 Existential angst is the anxiety that arises when you feel that life is inherently meaningless, that your existence is only an accident and has no real purpose in the universal/spiritual sense
   ex a film about **teenage angst**
28 caveat: a warning of the limits of a particular agreement or statement
   ex She will be offered radiation treatment **with the caveat that** the method has only around a 30% chance of success.

strangers who stare at them intently.)

The benefits of connecting with others also turn out to be contagious. Dr. Epley and Ms. Schroeder found that when one person took the initiative to speak to another in a waiting room, both people reported having a more positive experience. Far from annoying people by violating their **personal bubbles**[29], reaching out to strangers may improve their day, too.

Rather than **fall back on**[30] our **erroneous**[31] belief in the pleasures of solitude, we could reach out to other people. At least, when we walk down the street, we can refuse to accept a world where people look at one another as though through air. When we talk to strangers, we **stand to gain much**[32] more than the "**me time**[33]" we might lose.

---

29 personal bubbles: personal space
30 fall back on something to use or do something else after other things have failed
　　She always has her teaching experience **to fall back on**.
　　They had to **fall back on their emergency supplies** when the snow storm blocked the road to town.
31 erroneous: not correct
32 stand to do something: to be in a particular situation or state that makes something likely to happen to you
　　Many small companies **stand to lose financially** if the new law is introduced.
33 me time: time that you spend relaxing and doing things that you enjoy rather than time spent doing things for other people
　　Like most parents with young children, **I don't get much me time.**

15 Introspective[1] or Narcissistic?

Some people like to keep a journal. Some people think it's a bad idea.

People who keep a journal often see it as part of the process of self-understanding and personal growth. They don't want insights and events to slip through their minds. They **think with their fingers**[2] and have to write to process experiences and become aware of their feelings.

People who oppose journal-keeping fear it contributes to self-absorption and narcissism. C.S. Lewis, who kept a journal at times, feared that it just aggravated sadness and reinforced **neurosis**[3]. Gen. George Marshall did not keep a diary during World War II because he thought it would lead to "self-deception or hesitation in reaching decisions."

The question is: How do you succeed in being introspective without being self-absorbed?

Psychologists and others have given some thought to this question. The **upshot**[4] of their work is that there seems to be a paradox at the heart of **introspection**[5]. The self is something that can be seen more accurately from a distance than from close up. The more you can **yank**[6] yourself away from your own intimacy with

---

1 **introspective**: tending to examine your own feelings, thoughts, or ideas instead of communicating with other people
   ex *Ben was naturally **introspective** and enjoyed being alone.*
2 **think with their fingers**: 글을 쓰면서 생각을 정리하다
3 **neurosis**: 신경증, an emotional illness in which a person experiences strong feelings of fear or worry
4 **the upshot**: the final result or outcome of a process, discussion, etc.
   ex *The **upshot** is that we'll see him Thursday.*
5 **introspection**: the process of carefully examining your own feelings, thoughts, and ideas
6 **yank**: to pull something or someone suddenly with a lot of force

yourself, the more reliable your self-awareness is likely to be.

The problem is that the mind is vastly deep, complex and **variable**[7]. As Immanuel Kant famously put it, "We can never, even by the strictest examination, **get completely behind**[8] the secret springs of action." At the same time, your self-worth and identity are **at stake**[9] in every judgment you make about yourself.

This combination of **unfathomability**[10] and "at stakeness" is a perfect **breeding ground**[11] for self-deception, rationalization and **motivated reasoning**[12].

When people examine themselves from too close, they often end up **ruminating**[13] or oversimplifying. Rumination is like that middle-of-the-night thinking—when the rest of the world is hidden by darkness and the mind descends into a **spiral**[14] of endless reaction to itself. People have repetitive thoughts, but don't take action. Depressed ruminators end up making themselves more depressed.

---

7 variable: able or likely to change or be changed
　　*The winds were light and **variable**. / The loan has a **variable** interest rate.*
8 get behind: understand
　　The basic meaning of get behind is support. But in practice people often say they can't get behind [an idea, or a proposed course of action] when what they mean is they don't accept it. And sometimes (perhaps by association with get = grasp), when they don't understand it.
9 at stake: used about important issues that are involved in a situation or could be decided by it
　　*Few voters had any idea of the issues **at stake**.*
　　*There are ancient rivalries **at stake**.*
10 unfathomable: impossible to explain or understand
11 breeding ground: a situation or place in which bad things can easily begin to develop
　　*The university was **a breeding ground for political radicals**.*
12 motivated reasoning: 감정에 치우친 판단
　　Motivated reasoning is an emotion-biased decision-making phenomenon studied in cognitive science and social psychology.
13 ruminate: to think carefully and deeply about something
　　*The question got us **ruminating** on the real value of wealth.*
　　*He **ruminated** over/about the implications of their decision.*
14 spiral: a situation in which something continuously increases, decreases, or gets worse usually singular
　　*an **inflationary spiral** [=a continuous increase in prices]*
　　*Gas prices continued their dizzying **upward spiral**. [=gas prices got higher]*
　　*His drug use drove him into a **downward spiral**. [=his condition became worse and worse]*

Oversimplifiers don't really understand themselves, so they just invent an explanation to describe their own desires. People make checklists of what they want in a spouse and then usually marry a person who is nothing like their abstract criteria. Realtors know that the house many people buy often has nothing in common with the house they thought they wanted when they started shopping.

We are better self-perceivers if we can create distance and see the general **contours**[15] of our **emergent**[16] **system**[17] selves—rather than trying to **unpack**[18] **constituent**[19] parts. This can be done in several ways.

First, you can distance yourself by time. A program called **Critical Incident Stress Debriefing**[20] had victims of trauma write down their emotions right after the event. (The idea was they shouldn't **bottle up their feelings**[21].) But people who did so suffered more **post-traumatic stress**[22] and were more depressed in the **ensuing**[23] weeks. Their intimate **reflections**[24] impeded healing and **froze the pain**[25]. But people who write about trauma later on can place a broader perspective on things. Their lives are improved by the **exercise**[26].

---

15 contour: the shape of the outside edge of something   ex *The sculpture reproduces **the smooth contours of the human body**.*
16 emergent: just beginning to exist or be noticed
17 system: a group of related parts that move or work together
   ex *a **system of rivers** / **railroad systems** / a security/telephone/heating **system***
18 unpack: to make (something) easier to understand by breaking it up into smaller parts that can be examined separately
   ex *She's good at **unpacking complex concepts**.*
19 constituent: forming part of a whole   ex *The company can be separated into several **constituent parts/elements**.*
20 Critical Incident Stress Debriefing: 위기 상황 심리 진단 프로그램
   1) debrief: to officially question (someone) about a job that has been done or about an experience
   ex *Police **debriefed** the hostages upon their return. / The pilot **was debriefed** after his flight.*
21 bottle up (something): to keep (a feeling or emotion) inside of you instead of expressing it
   ex *She's **kept** her feelings about the accident **bottled up for too long**.*
   *I know he's angry, but he **bottles it up inside** instead of talking to someone about it.*
22 post-traumatic stress: 외상후 스트레스 장애
23 an ensuing event or activity happens after something else, often as a result of it
   ex *The guards returned fire, and **the ensuing gunfight** lasted all day.*
24 reflection: an opinion that you form or a remark that you make after carefully thinking about something usually plural
   ex *The book features the writer's **reflections** on America and its people.*
25 freeze: to stop moving or making progress
   ex *Their wine glasses **frozen** in mid-air, they all stared at me. / It seemed as though time had **frozen**.*
26 exercise: an activity that has a specified quality or result
   ex *The negotiations have gotten nowhere, and I see no reason to continue with **this pointless exercise**.*
   *Waiting for the letter to come was **an exercise in patience**.*
   *The negotiations turned out to be **an exercise in futility**.* [=the negotiations were not successful or worthwhile]

Second, we can achieve distance from self through language. We're better at giving other people good advice than at giving ourselves good advice, so it's smart, when trying to counsel yourself, to pretend you are somebody else. This can be done a bit even by thinking of yourself in the third person. Work by Ozlem Ayduk and Ethan Kross finds that people who view themselves from a self-distanced perspective are better at **adaptive**[27] self-reflection than people who view themselves from a self-immersed perspective.

Finally, there is **narrative**[28]. Timothy Wilson of the University of Virginia suggests in his book "Strangers to Ourselves" that we shouldn't see ourselves as archaeologists, minutely studying each feeling and trying to dig deep into the unconscious. We should see ourselves as literary critics, putting each incident in the perspective of a longer life story. The narrative form is a more **supple**[29] way of understanding human processes, even unconscious ones, than rationalistic analysis.

---

27 adaptive: changing in order to deal with new situations
28 A narrative is any account of connected events, presented to a reader or listener in a sequence of written or spoken words, or in a sequence of (moving) pictures.
29 supple: soft and able to bend or fold easily

Wilson writes, "The point is that we should not analyze the information [about our feelings] in an overly deliberate, conscious manner, constantly making explicit lists of pluses and minuses. We should let our adaptive unconscious do the job of finding reliable feelings and then trust those feelings, even if we cannot explain them entirely."

Think of one of those **Chuck Close self-portraits**[30]. The face takes up the entire image. You can see every **pore**[31]. Some people try to introspect like that. But others see themselves in broader landscapes, in the context of longer narratives about forgiveness, or redemption or **setback**[32] and **ascent**[33]. Maturity is moving from the close-up to the landscape, focusing less on your own supposed strengths and weaknesses and more on the sea of empathy in which you swim, which is the **medium**[34] necessary for understanding others, one's self, and survival.

---

30 Chuck Close self-portrait: 화가 척 클로스의 자화상
   참고 Chuck Close (born in 1940, Monroe, WA) is renowned for his highly inventive techniques of painting the human face, and is best known for his large-scale, photo-based portrait paintings.
31 pore: 모공, a very small opening on the surface of your skin that liquid comes out through when you sweat
32 setback: a problem that makes progress more difficult or success less likely
   ex Despite some early **setbacks**, they eventually became a successful company.
33 ascent: the process of moving to a higher level or position
34 medium: the thing by which or through which something is done
   ex Money is **a medium [=means] of exchange**.
   English is **an important medium of** international communication.

16 The one fight to have before your wedding

Betrothed[1] women of the world, unite! You have nothing to lose but your husbands' names.

I'm getting married in a few days, and—as I'm told happens with most weddings—lots of exhausting fights over **minuscule**[2] details have broken out along the long, **treacherous**[3] road to the altar. But the biggest **blow-ups**[4], in my case, were over names.

Specifically, women's names. Or lack **thereof**[5].

Here's how it began. My mother was in charge of paper products—invitations, envelopes and seating cards—mostly because she had much stronger preferences about these things than I did. I didn't particularly care if the **paper stock**[6] came from ancient Egyptian papyri **burgled**[7] from an archeological **dig**[8], or from recycled toilet paper or if we had **dead-tree invitations**[9] at all. I'm pretty cool with **Evite.com**[10].

I had but one unyielding, **Bridezillian**[11] demand, championed by my feminist fiance as well: how women's names were **rendered**[12]. Specifically, that they be rendered at all.

I have always hated the tradition of calling married women, in formal

---

1 betrothed: (formal + old-fashioned) engaged to be married
    *She had been **betrothed to** the prince since she was a young girl.*
2 minuscule: 사소한, extremely small in size or amount   *The risk to public health is **minuscule**.*
3 treacherous: very dangerous and difficult to deal with
    *They were not prepared to hike over such **treacherous terrain**.*
    *Discussions about money can lead couples into **treacherous territory**.*
4 blow-up: an angry argument   *The two of them had a big **blowup** about something trivial.*
5 thereof: of the thing that has been mentioned
    *The professor explained the problem and solution **thereof**. [=the problem and the solution of the problem]*
    *The problem is money, **or (a/the) lack thereof**. [=the problem is a lack of money]*
6 paper stock: 종이 재질
7 burgle: to illegally enter (a building) and steal things
    *They were caught **burgling** [=burglarizing] a jewelry store.*
8 dig: a place where scientists try to find buried objects by digging
    archaeological digs
9 dead-tree: made of or pertaining to paper, especially as opposed to a digital alternative
10 Evite.com is a social-planning website for creating, sending, and managing online invitations.
11 Bridezilla: (usually humorous) A woman who, in the course of planning her wedding, exercises or attempts to exercise a high degree of control over all or many minor details of the ceremony and reception.
12 render: to express, show, or perform something in a particular way
    *The power of the ocean **was beautifully rendered in the poem**.*

correspondence, by their husband's full names. You know what I mean: "Mr. and Mrs. Robert Smith," as opposed to some version of "Mr. Robert Smith and Mrs./Ms. Jane Smith." I understand why women often choose to adopt their husbands' surnames upon marriage—for family unity, or avoiding confusion at preschool pickup, or whatever—even if I have personally decided to hang onto my own name. But why must we confiscate married women's first names as well? Even wedded women have their own identities; they are not mere **appendages**[13] of their spouses.

So when it came to planning my own wedding, I decreed that any time we referred to a married couple, we would spell out the woman's full first and last name. My mother initially resisted, saying she was reluctant to mess with tradition, but she ultimately agreed to respect my wishes.

This turned out to be much harder than either of us realized.

When my mother instructed a stationery vendor to begin our wedding invitation with "[Mother's name] and [Father's name] request the pleasure of your company ...," the stationer was **aghast**[14]. In all her years of crafting wedding invitations, she **squawked**[15], not once had she **veered**[16] into such utterly **tacky**[17] territory. My mother called me in a panic, convinced that my requested wording would **subvert**[18] the proper order of the universe.

---

13 **appendage**: something connected or joined to a larger or more important thing
   ex The court system acts as **an appendage to the government**.
14 **aghast**: shocked and upset
15 **squawk**: to complain or protest loudly or with strong feeling
   ex The customers **squawked about** the high prices.
16 **veer**: to change direction quickly or suddenly
   ex The ship **veered away** to the north.
   The story **veers toward** the ridiculous at times.
17 **tacky**: not socially proper or acceptable
18 **subvert**: to secretly try to ruin or destroy a government, political system, etc.
   ex They conspired to **subvert the government**.

I told her to fire the stationer and find another who would accept whatever damn phrasing we chose. Ultimately, she did.

Then it came time to have the invitations addressed, and my mother decided to splurge and hire a calligrapher. She sent the calligrapher an Excel spreadsheet with all our invitees' names and told her to transcribe them exactly as we had them or else suffer the wrath of Bridezilla. The calligrapher agreed.

But guess what form of address was on the envelopes that my married friends received? "Mr. and Mrs. Robert Smith." Even, in at least one case, where the wife had kept her maiden name.

At first I thought we'd just been unlucky in our choice of vendors. Perhaps the calligrapher had made an honest mistake. Then I started looking around online.

The Web, it seems, is also **conspiring**[19] to uphold this awful, antifeminist tradition.

Online addressing guidelines from obscure artisans and well-established stationery companies alike—including Crane & Co. and Hallmark—still generally recommend **excising**[20] a married woman's name. (**The Emily Post Institute**[21] **waffles**[22] somewhat in its recommendations.) Meanwhile there are just as many wedding Web sites and message boards from brides-to-be agonizing over how to get around this dumb tradition without appearing **déclassé**[23].

---

19 conspire: to happen in a way that produces bad or unpleasant results often followed by to + verb
   *My illness and the bad weather **conspired to** ruin my vacation.*
   *Several things **conspired to** force them to change the policy.*
20 excise: to remove (something) by cutting it out
21 The Emily Post Institute was created by etiquette author Emily Post in 1946. She published *Etiquette: The Blue Book of Social Usage* in 1922, which grew her career, resulting in a radio show and newspaper column. Emily Post named consideration, respect and honesty as the tenets of etiquette - the principles upon which all manners are built.
22 waffle: to be unable or unwilling to make a clear decision about what to do often + on
   *Her opponent has accused her of **waffling** on the important issues.*
23 déclassé: fallen or lowered in class, rank, or social position

Of course, the Mr.-and-Mrs.-His-Name tradition is not isolated to wedding invitations. It appears on mailings from alumni organizations, church groups, charities and junk-mail marketers. I've even heard of women's social clubs whose directories list their impressive, professionally accomplished members as "Mrs. Husband's Name."

But it's during the wedding planning process—when a couple is figuring out exactly what it means to form a legal and spiritual union of two separate beings—that the pressure to perpetuate this archaic tradition, of wholly subsuming the wife's identity into her husband's, especially **rankles**[24].

So I urge all you fellow brides-to-be out there: If you choose just one detail to fight over with your family, friends and vendors—and, oh, there are so many less meaningful, more expensive ones to choose from—let it be this one. Call your married female friends by their given names, and then, post-wedding, insist they do the same for you.

---

24 **rankle**: to cause (someone) to feel angry or irritated especially for a long time
  ex The joke about her family **rankled her.**

 문학 지문

 소설

 An American Tragedy by Theodore Dreiser (Chapter 11)

The effect of this adventure on Clyde was such as might have been expected in connection with one so new and strange to such a world as this. In spite of all that deep and urgent curiosity and desire that had eventually led him to that place and caused him to yield, still, because of the moral **precepts**[1] with which he had so long been familiar, and also because of the nervous **esthetic**[2] inhibitions which were characteristic of him, he could not but look back upon all this as decidedly degrading and sinful. His parents were probably right when they

---

1 precept: a rule that says how people should behave
　　[count] the **basic/moral precepts** of a religion
　　[noncount] I was taught **by precept** and **by example**.
2 aesthetic: of or relating to art or beauty
　　There are practical as well as **aesthetic** reasons for planting trees.
　　the statue's **aesthetic** [=artistic] beauty
　　making **aesthetic** improvements to the building
　　aesthetic values/ideals

preached that this was all low and shameful. And yet this whole adventure and the world in which it was laid, once it was all over, was lit with a kind of gross, **pagan**[3] beauty or vulgar charm for him. And until other and more interesting things had partially **effaced**[4] it, he could not help thinking back upon it with considerable interest and pleasure, even.

In addition he kept telling himself that now, having as much money as he was making, he could go and do about as he pleased. He need not go there any more if he did not want to, but he could go to other places that might not be as low, maybe—more refined. He wouldn't want to go with a crowd like that again. He would rather have just one girl somewhere if he could find her—a girl such as those with whom he had seen Sieberling and Doyle associate. And so, despite all of his troublesome thoughts of the night before, he was thus **won quickly over**[5] to this new source of pleasure if not its primary setting. He must find a free pagan girl of his own somewhere if he could, like Doyle, and spend his money on her. And he could scarcely wait until opportunity should provide him with the means of gratifying himself in this way.

But more interesting and more to his purpose at the time was the fact that both Hegglund and Ratterer, in spite of, or possibly because of, a secret sense of superiority which they detected in Clyde, were inclined to look upon him with **no little**[6] interest

---

3   pagan: (old-fashioned + often offensive) a person who is not religious or whose religion is not Christianity, Judaism, or Islam
4   efface: to cause (something) to fade or disappear
    ex coins with dates **effaced** by wear
        a memory **effaced** by time
5   win (someone) over: to persuade someone to support you or agree with you, often when they were opposed to you before:
    ex He's not sure about the idea, but I'm sure **we'll win him over in the end**.
        This is the last chance for the candidates to **win over voters**.
6   no little: a lot
    ex There was **no little** sadness in his voice.

and to court him and to include him among all their thoughts of affairs and pleasures. Indeed, shortly after his first adventure, Ratterer invited him to come to his home, where, as Clyde most quickly came to see, was a life very different from his own. At the Griffiths' all was so solemn and **reserved**[7], the **still**[8] moods of those who feel the pressure of dogma and conviction. In Ratterer's home, the reverse of this was nearly true. The mother and sister with whom he lived, while **not without**[9] some moral although no particular religious convictions, were inclined to view life with a great deal of generosity or, as a moralist would have seen it, **laxity**[10]. There had never been any keen moral or **characterful**[11] direction there at all. And so it was that Ratterer and his sister Louise, who was two years younger than himself, now did about as they pleased, and without thinking very much about it. But his sister **chanced to be**[12] shrewd or individual enough not to wish to cast herself away on just any one.

The interesting part of all this was that Clyde, in spite of a certain **strain**[13] of refinement which caused him to look **askance**[14] at most of this, was still fascinated by the crude picture of life and liberty which it offered. Among such as these, at least, he could go, do, be as he had never gone or done or been before. And particularly was he pleased and enlightened—or rather dubiously liberated—in connection with his nervousness and uncertainty in regard to his

---

7   reserved: not openly expressing feelings or opinions
       She is a very **reserved** young woman.
8   still: lacking motion or activity
       Everyone had left, and **the house was finally still**.
9   not without: some
       The research literature, too, asks these questions, and **not without reason.**
10 laxity: the quality of not being severe or strong enough
       Many people will be appalled at the **laxity** of the country's laws with regards to drugs.
       lax: not careful enough; not strict enough
       The university has been **lax** about/in enforcing these rules.
11 characterful: having interesting or unusual qualities; having character
       a **characterful** old house
12 chance: [no object] formal used to describe something that happens because of luck or chance followed by to + verb
       It **chanced** [=(more commonly) happened] **to** rain that day.
       We **chanced to** arrive at the same time.
13 strain: (literary + somewhat old-fashioned) a usually bad quality that someone or something has usually singular usually + of
       There is **a strain of snobbery** in her.
       There is **a strain of madness** in that family.
14 askance: in a way that shows a lack of trust or approval
       Most scientists **looked askance at** the new discovery. [=most scientists were doubtful about the new discovery]
       Several people **looked at him askance** when he walked into the room. = Several people eyed him askance when he walked into the room.

charm or fascination for girls of his own years. For up to this very time, and in spite of his recent first visit to the erotic temple to which Hegglund and the others had led him, he was still convinced that he had no skill with or charm where girls were concerned. Their mere proximity or approach was sufficient to cause him to recede mentally, to **chill**[15] or **palpitate**[16] nervously, and to lose **what little**[17] natural skill he had for conversation or **poised**[18] banter such as other youths possessed. But now, in his visits to the home of Ratterer, as he soon discovered, he was to have ample opportunity to test whether this shyness and uncertainty could be overcome.

For it was a center for the friends of Ratterer and his sister, who were more or less of one **mood**[19] in regard to life. Dancing, card-playing, love-making rather open and unashamed, went on there. Indeed, up to this time, Clyde would not have imagined that a parent like Mrs. Ratterer could have been as **lackadaisical**[20] or indifferent as she was, apparently, to conduct and morals generally. He would not have imagined that any mother would have **countenanced**[21] the easy **camaraderie**[22] that existed between the sexes in Mrs. Ratterer's home.

---

15 chill: to cause (someone) to feel afraid
   ex Here's a ghost story that will **chill** you.
      Her screams **chilled** me to the bone/marrow.
      a horrible sight that **chilled** my bones/blood
16 palpitate: to beat quickly and strongly and often in a way that is not regular because of excitement, nervousness, etc.
   ex My heart began to **palpitate** when I was announced as the winner.
17 what little: used to emphasize how small an amount there is, how small an amount is possible etc.
   ex We did **what little** we could to help.
      I handed over **what little** money I had left.
18 poised: having or showing a calm, confident manner
   ex a very **poised** young woman
19 mood: an attitude or feeling shared by many people
   ex The **mood** of the country/city was grim.
20 lackadaisical: feeling or showing a lack of interest or enthusiasm
   ex a **lackadaisical** student
      His teachers did not approve of his **lackadaisical** approach to homework.
21 countenance: to accept, support, or approve of (something)
   ex The city would not **countenance** [=permit] a rock concert in the park.
      The leader did not officially **countenance** [=encourage] negotiations with the rebels.
22 camaraderie: a feeling of good friendship among the people in a group
   ex [noncount] There is great **camaraderie** among the teammates.
      [singular] They have developed a real **camaraderie** after working together for so long.

And very soon, because of several cordial invitations which were extended to him by Ratterer, he found himself **part and parcel**[23] of this group—a group which from one point of view—the ideas held by its members, the rather **wretched**[24] English they spoke—he looked down upon. From another point of view—the freedom they possessed, the **zest**[25] **with which they managed to contrive**[26] social activities and exchanges—he was drawn to them. Because, for the first time, these permitted him, if he chose, to have a girl of his own, if only he could summon the courage. And this, owing to the **well-meant**[27] **ministrations**[28] of Ratterer and his sister and their friends, he soon sought to accomplish. Indeed the thing began on the occasion of his first visit to the Ratterers.

Louise Ratterer worked in a **dry-goods store**[29] and often came home a little late for dinner. On this occasion she did not appear until seven, and the eating of the family meal was postponed accordingly. In the meantime, two girl friends of Louise arrived to consult her in connection with something, and finding her delayed, and Ratterer and Clyde there, they made themselves at home, rather impressed and interested by Clyde and his new **finery**[30]. For he, at once girl-hungry and girl-shy, held himself nervously **aloof**[31], a **manifestation**[32] which they mistook for a conviction of superiority on his part. And in consequence, **arrested**[33] by this, they determined to show how really interesting they were—

---

23 part and parcel of: a basic and necessary part of (something)　　Stress was **part and parcel of the job**.
24 wretched: very poor in quality or ability　　What a **wretched performance** that was.
25 zest: lively excitement; a feeling of enjoyment and enthusiasm
26 contrive: to make (something) happen in a clever way or with difficulty　　He **contrived** a meeting with the president. often followed by to + verb
　　She **contrived** [=managed] to make it to the airport in time.
27 well-meant: said or done in order to be helpful, but not always achieving this:
　　[before noun] a **well-meant suggestion**
28 ministrations: (formal + humorous) actions done to help someone
　　She recovered quickly despite the **ministrations** of her doctor.
29 dry-goods store: 잡화점
　　In the United States, dry goods are products such as textiles, ready-to-wear clothing, sundries, and "grocery items (such as tobacco, sugar, flour, and coffee) that do not contain liquid." In US retailing, a dry-goods store carries consumer goods that are distinct from those carried by hardware stores and grocery stores.
30 finery: ornament, decoration; especially : dressy or showy clothing and jewels
31 aloof: not involved with or friendly toward other people
　　She remained **aloof** [=distant] despite their efforts to make friends.
32 manifestation: a sign that shows something clearly usually + of
　　The first **manifestations** of her behavior problems occurred soon after she left home.
　　Her work with the poor was a **manifestation** [=indication] of her compassionate nature.
33 arrest: to attract and hold the attention of (someone or something)
　　My attention was **arrested** [=caught] by a sudden movement.

vamp[34] him—**no less**[35]. And he found their crude briskness and **effrontery**[36] very appealing—**so much so**[37] that he was soon taken by the charms of one, a certain Hortense Briggs, who, like Louise, was nothing more than a crude shop girl in one of the large stores, but pretty and dark and self-appreciative. And yet **from the first**[38], he realized that she was **not a little**[39] coarse and vulgar—a very long way removed from the type of girl he had been imagining in his dreams that he would like to have.

"Oh, hasn't she come in yet?" announced Hortense, on first being admitted by Ratterer and seeing Clyde near one of the front windows, looking out. "Isn't that too bad? Well, we'll just have to wait a little bit if you don't mind"—this last with a **switch**[40] and a **swagger**[41] that plainly said, who would mind having us around? And forthwith (4) she began to **primp**[42] and admire herself before a mirror which **surmounted**[43] an **ocher-colored**[44] mantelpiece that **graced**[45] a fireless **grate**[46] in the dining-room. And her friend, Greta Miller, added: "Oh, dear, yes. I hope you won't make us go before she comes. We didn't come to eat. We thought your dinner would be all over by now."

---

34 **vamp**: act seductively with (someone)
35 **no less**: used to suggest that something is surprising or impressive
　　ex He insists on being driven to the airport, and in a limousine **no less**! [=it is surprising that he insists on being driven in a limousine]
36 **effrontery**: a very confident attitude or way of behaving that is shocking or rude
　　ex He had the **effrontery** to deny doing something that we saw him do.
37 **so much so**: to such a great degree　　ex It was a great project, so much so that it won first prize.
38 **from the first**: from the beginning
39 **not a little**: very; a lot
40 **switch**:
41 **swagger**: a way of walking or behaving that shows you have a lot of confidence
　　ex He has a **swagger** that annoys some of his teammates.
42 **primp**: to try to make yourself more attractive by making small changes to your clothes, hair, etc., especially while looking at yourself in a mirror
　　ex [no object] The girls spent hours **primping** in front of the mirror.
　　[+ object] He **primped** his hair while waiting for his date.
43 **surmount**: to be placed at the top of (something) usually used as (be) surmounted
　　ex a chain-link fence that is **surmounted** [=topped] by barbed wire
44 **ocher-colored**: 황토색
45 **grace**: to decorate or add beauty to (something)
　　ex Several marble statues **grace** the courtyard. / Her face has **graced** [=appeared on] the cover of many magazines.
46 **grate**: a metal frame with bars across it that is used in a fireplace or to cover an opening

"Where do you get that stuff—'**put you out**⁴⁷'?" replied Ratterer cynically. "As though anybody could drive you two outa here if you didn't want to go. Sit down and play the **victrola**⁴⁸ or do anything you like. Dinner'll soon be ready and Louise'll be here any minute." He returned to the dining-room to look at a paper which he had been reading, after pausing to introduce Clyde. And the latter, because of the looks and the airs of these two, felt suddenly as though he had been cast adrift upon a **chartless**⁴⁹ sea in an open boat.

"Oh, don't say eat to me!" exclaimed Greta Miller, who was surveying Clyde calmly as though she were debating with herself whether he was worth-while **game**⁵⁰ or not, and deciding that he was: "With all the ice-cream and cake and pie and sandwiches we'll have to eat yet to-night. We was just going to warn Louise not to fill up too much. Kittie Keane's givin' a birthday party, you know, Tom, and she'll have a big cake an' everythin'. You're comin' down, ain't you, afterwards?" she concluded, with a thought of Clyde and his possible companionship in mind.

"I wasn't thinkin' of it," calmly observed Ratterer. "Me and Clyde was thinkin' of goin' to a show after dinner."

"Oh, how foolish," put in Hortense Briggs, more to attract attention to herself and take it away from Greta than anything else. She was still in front of the mirror, but turned now to cast a **fetching**⁵¹ smile on all, particularly Clyde, for whom she **fancied**⁵² her friend might be **angling**⁵³, "When you could come along

---

47 put out someone or something: to expel someone or something from a premises
   They had to **put out the drunk**.
   The guard **put out the rowdy students**.
48 victrola: 축음기의 일종, a brand of phonograph
49 chartless: not mapped; uncharted or unknown
50 game: animals that are hunted
   wild **game**
   a **game** bird/fish [=a bird or fish that may be legally hunted or caught]
   The police aren't interested in these small-time drug dealers; they're after **much bigger game**.
51 fetching: attractive or pleasing
   a **fetching** smile
   You look very **fetching** in that outfit.
52 fancy: British : to imagine (something)
   I have a hard time **fancying** you as a father.
   often used to express surprise
   Fancy [=imagine] our embarrassment when the police showed up at the door.
   The baby she brought home was the wrong one. **Fancy** that! [=imagine that]
53 angle: to try to get what you want in a clever or indirect way
   She's been **angling** to get a promotion.

and dance. I call that silly."

"Sure, dancing is all you three ever think of—you and Louise," retorted Ratterer. "It's a wonder you don't give yourselves a rest once in a while. I'm on my feet all day an' I like to sit down once in a while." He could be most matter-of-fact at times.

"Oh, don't say sit down to me," commented Greta Miller with a lofty smile and a gliding, dancing motion of her left foot, "with all the dates we got ahead of us this week. Oh, gee!" Her eyes and eyebrows went up and she clasped her hands dramatically before her. "It's just terrible, all the dancin' we gotta do yet, this winter, don't we, Hortense? Thursday night and Friday night and Saturday and Sunday nights." She counted on her fingers most **archly**[54]. "Oh, gee! It is terrible, really." She gave Clyde an appealing, sympathy-seeking smile. "Guess where we were the other night, Tom. Louise and Ralph Thorpe and Hortense and Bert Gettler, me and Willie Bassick—out at Pegrain's on Webster Avenue. Oh, an' you oughta seen the crowd out there. Sam Shaffer and Tillie Burns was there. And we danced until four in the morning. I thought my knees would break. I ain't been so tired in I don't know when."

"Oh, gee!" broke in Hortense, seizing her turn and lifting her arms dramatically. "I thought I never would get to work the next morning. I could just barely see the customers moving around. And, wasn't my mother fussy! Gee! She

---

54 **archly**: in an amused way that suggests you know more about something than someone else does:
ex *She smiled **archly** at him.*
*"I fail to understand what you're suggesting," said Claire **archly**.*

hasn't gotten over it yet. She don't mind so much about Saturdays and Sundays, but all these week nights and when I have to get up the next morning at seven—gee—how she can pick!"

"An' I don't blame her, either," commented Mrs. Ratterer, who was just then entering with a plate of potatoes and some bread. "You two'll get sick and Louise, too, if you don't get more rest. I keep tellin' her she won't be able to keep her place or stand it if she don't get more sleep. But she don't pay no more attention to me than Tom does, and that's just none at all."

"Oh, well, you can't expect a fellow in my line to get in early always, Ma," was all Ratterer said. And Hortense Briggs added: "Gee, I'd die if I had to stay in one night. You gotta have a little fun when you work all day."

What an easy household, thought Clyde. How liberal and indifferent. And the sexy, gay way in which these two girls posed about. And their parents thought nothing of it, evidently. If only he could have a girl as pretty as this Hortense Briggs, with her small, sensuous mouth and her bright hard eyes.

"To bed twice a week early is all I need," announced Greta Miller archly. "My father thinks I'm crazy, but more'n that would do me harm." She laughed jestingly, and Clyde, in spite of the "we was'es" and "I seen's," was most vividly impressed. Here was youth and **geniality**[55] and freedom and love of life.

---

55 genial: cheerful and pleasant
 a **genial** host
 a host with a **genial** manner
 He was **genial** to/toward everyone.

소설 02 **The Age of Innocence** by Edith Wharton

That evening, after Mr. Jackson had taken himself away, and the ladies had retired to their **chintz-curtained**[1] bedroom, Newland Archer **mounted**[2] thoughtfully to his own study. A **vigilant**[3] **hand**[4] had, as usual, kept the fire alive and the lamp trimmed; and the room, with its rows and rows of books, its bronze and steel statuettes of "The Fencers" on the mantelpiece and its many photographs of famous pictures, looked singularly homelike and welcoming.

As he dropped into his armchair near the fire his eyes rested on a large photograph of May Welland, which the young girl had given him in the first days of their romance, and which had now **displaced**[5] all the other portraits on the table. With a new sense of awe he looked at the frank forehead, serious eyes and gay innocent mouth of the young creature whose soul's custodian he was to be. That terrifying product of the social system he belonged to and believed in, the young girl who knew nothing and expected everything, looked back at him like a stranger through May Welland's familiar features; and once more it was **borne in on**[6] him that marriage was not the safe **anchorage**[7] he had been taught to think, but a voyage on uncharted seas

---

1 **chintz**: cotton cloth, usually with patterns of flowers, that has a slightly shiny appearance
2 **mount**: to go up or onto:
   ex He **mounted the platform** and began to speak to the assembled crowd.
3 **vigilant**: always being careful to notice things, especially possible danger:
   ex Following the bomb scare at the airport, the staff have been warned to be **extra vigilant**.
4 **hand**: a person who does physical work or is skilled or experienced in something
   ex How many **extra hands** will we need to help with the harvest?
5 **displace**: to force (people or animals) to leave the area where they live
   ex The war has **displaced** thousands of people.
   The hurricane **displaced** most of the town's residents.
   animals **displaced** by wildfire
6 If something is borne in on/upon you, it is made very clear to you. This is a formal phrase.
   ex **It was borne in on us** by the new evidence that prompt action was very important. [=the new evidence strongly indicated that prompt action was very important]
7 **anchorage**: a place where boats and ships are anchored
   ex [count] a safe/secluded **anchorage**
   [noncount] an area of safe **anchorage**
   참고 **anchorage**: something that provides a strong hold or connection
   ex [noncount] A heavy metal ring provides **anchorage** for the cable.

The case of the Countess Olenska had stirred up old settled convictions and set them drifting dangerously through his mind. His own exclamation: "Women should be free—as free as we are," **struck to the root of** a problem that it was agreed in his world to regard as non-existent. "Nice" women, however **wronged**[8], would never claim the kind of freedom he meant, and generous-minded men like himself were therefore—**in the heat of**[9] argument—the more **chivalrously**[10] ready to concede it to them. Such verbal generosities were in fact only a **humbugging**[11] disguise of the **inexorable**[12] conventions that tied things together and bound people down to the old pattern. But here he was pledged to defend, on the part of his **betrothed's**[13] cousin, conduct that, on his own wife's part, would justify him in **calling down on**[14] her all the thunders of Church and State. Of course the dilemma was purely hypothetical; since he wasn't a **blackguard**[15] Polish nobleman, it was absurd to speculate what his wife's rights would be if he *were*. But Newland Archer was too imaginative not to feel that, in his case and May's, the tie might **gall**[16] for reasons far less gross and palpable. What could he and she really know of each other, since it was his duty, as a "decent" fellow, to conceal his past from her, and hers, as a marriageable girl, to have no past to conceal? What if, for some one of the subtler reasons that would tell with both of them, they should tire of each other, misunderstand or irritate each other? He reviewed his friends' marriages—the

---

8 wronged: treated unfairly or unjustly
 the **wronged** party in the dispute.
9 in the heat of: In the most intense or active stage of some activity or condition.
 One never knows how soldiers will behave in **the heat of battle.**
 In the heat of the moment she accepted his proposal.
10 chivalrous: considerate and courteous to women; gallant.
11 humbug: to cheat or deceive (someone)
 humbug: language or behavior that is false or meant to deceive people
 Their claims are **humbug**.
 She's only 30? **Humbug**!
12 inexorable: continuing without any possibility of being stopped
 the **inexorable** progress of science
13 betrothed: (formal + old-fashioned) the person that someone has promised to marry
 He spent the afternoon with his **betrothed**. [=fiance]
14 call something down on someone: to pray for something bad to happen to someone
15 blackguard: a person, usually a man, who is not honest or fair and has no moral principles
16 gall: to make sore by rubbing; chafe severely:
 The saddle **galled** the horse's back.

supposedly happy ones—and saw none that answered[17], even remotely, to the passionate and tender comradeship which he pictured as his permanent relation with May Welland. He perceived that such a picture **presupposed**[18], on her part, the experience, the versatility, the freedom of judgment, which she had been carefully trained not to possess; and with a **shiver**[19] of **foreboding**[20] he saw his marriage becoming what most of the other marriages about him were: a dull association of material and social interests held together by ignorance on the one side and hypocrisy on the other.

17 answer to (something): to be the same as (something); to be in agreement with (something, such as a description)
   ex *The suspect **answers to** [=answers, matches] the description perfectly.*
18 presuppose: If an idea or situation presupposes something, that thing must be true for the idea or situation to work:
   ex *Investigative journalism **presupposes** some level of investigation.*
   *Prayer **presupposes** a belief in a higher being. [=in order to pray you must believe that a higher being exists]*
19 shiver: a small shaking movement caused by cold or strong emotion
   ex *She felt a **shiver** of delight/pleasure when she opened the gift.*
   *Her performance was so brilliant that it sent **shivers** up (and down) my spine. [=it thrilled or excited me]*
   *The look in his eyes gave me the **shivers**. [=made me very afraid]*
20 foreboding: a feeling that something bad is going to happen
   ex *[noncount] She was filled with a sense of **foreboding**.*
   *[count] It seems that her **forebodings** were justified.*

소설 03 Call of the Wild by Jack London

When Buck earned sixteen hundred dollars in five minutes for John Thornton, he made it possible for his master to pay off certain debts and to journey with his partners into the East after a **fabled**[1] lost mine, the history of which was as old as the history of the country. Many men had sought it; few had found it; and more than a few there were who had never returned from the quest. This lost mine was **steeped**[2] in tragedy and shrouded in mystery. No one knew of the first man. The oldest tradition stopped before it got back to him. From the beginning there had been an ancient and ramshackle cabin. Dying men had sworn to it, and to the mine the site of which it marked, **clinching**[3] their testimony with nuggets that were unlike any known grade of gold in the Northland.

But no living man had looted this treasure house, and the dead were dead; **wherefore**[4] John Thornton and Pete and Hans, with Buck and half a dozen other dogs, faced into the East on an unknown trail to achieve where men and dogs as good as themselves had failed. They sledded seventy miles up the Yukon, swung to the left into the Stewart River, passed the Mayo and the McQuestion, and held

---

1 fabled: used to refer to something or someone who has been made very famous, especially by having many stories written about it, him, or her
   the **fabled** movie director Cecil B. De Mille
2 steeped: used as (be) steeped in to say that there is a lot of something in a place, time, etc.
   an area **steeped in history** [=an area where many important historical events occurred]
   It was a time in the nation's history that **was steeped in bloodshed**. [=a time when there was a lot of bloodshed]
   steep (someone) in (something): to make (someone) know and understand a lot about (something)
   Prior to his trip, he spent a few weeks **steeping himself in** the language. [=learning a lot about the language]
3 clinch: to make (something) certain or final
   I hear he finally **clinched** the deal to buy the land he wanted.
4 wherefore: therefore; consequently
   wherefore: used in the past to mean why
   Wherefore art thou Romeo? [=why are you Romeo?]
   Shakespeare, Romeo and Juliet (159495)
5 thread: to move forward by turning and going through narrow spaces
   [+ object] They had to **thread** their way through the crowd.
   [no object] Waiters **threaded through** the crowd.
6 fare: to do something well or badly
   How did you **fare** [=do] on your exam?
   The team hasn't **fared** [=done] well in recent weeks.

on until the Stewart itself became a streamlet, **threading**[5] the upstanding peaks which marked the backbone of the continent.

Thornton asked little of man or nature. He was unafraid of the wild. With a handful of salt and a rifle he could plunge into the wilderness and **fare**[6] wherever he pleased and as long as he pleased. Being in no haste, Indian fashion, he hunted his dinner in the course of the day's travel; and if he failed to find it, like the Indian, he kept on travelling, secure in the knowledge that sooner or later he would come to it. So, on this great journey into the East, **straight meat**[7] was the **bill of fare**[8], ammunition and tools principally made up the load on the sled, and the time-card was drawn upon the limitless future.

To Buck it was boundless delight, this hunting, fishing, and indefinite wandering through strange places. For weeks at a time they would hold on steadily, day after day; and for weeks upon end they would camp, here and there, the dogs loafing and the men burning holes through frozen **muck**[9] and **gravel**[10] and **washing countless pans of dirt**[11] by the heat of the fire. Sometimes they went hungry, sometimes they feasted riotously, all according to the abundance of game and the fortune of hunting. Summer arrived, and dogs and men packed on their backs, rafted across blue mountain lakes, and descended or ascended unknown rivers in slender boats **whipsawed**[12] from the standing forest.

---

7 straight meat: 사냥한 고기만 먹었다는 의미
   ex We had bread at every meal, which is in itself a luxury after four months of **straight meat**.
   참고 straight: not including any things or parts of a different kind
   ex a **straight** romance novel / The band plays **straight** blues.
8 bill of fare: (somewhat formal + old-fashioned) a list of the things that are served at a restaurant; menu
   ex The **bill of fare** includes several soups.
9 muck: mud, dirt, or a sticky natural substance such as animal waste
   ex There was green **muck** at the bottom of the boat.
        You're treading **muck** into the carpet with your dirty shoes!
10 gravel: small, rounded stones, often mixed with sand:
   ex a **gravel** path
11 wash pans of dirt: 사금을 채취하기 위해 흙을 체로 거르다
12 whipsaw: cut with a whipsaw (= a long saw)
   참고 whipsaw: to move, or to make something move, quickly between two directions
   ex The rope **whipsawed** back and forth.
        Prices on the stock exchange **whipsawed** wildly.

The months came and went, and back and forth they twisted through the uncharted vastness, where no men were and yet where men had been if the Lost Cabin were true. They went across divides in summer blizzards, shivered under the midnight sun on naked mountains between the **timber line**[13] and the eternal snows, dropped into summer valleys amid swarming **gnats**[14] and flies, and in the shadows of glaciers picked strawberries and flowers as ripe and fair as any the Southland could boast. In the fall of the year they penetrated a weird lake country, sad and silent, where **wildfowl**[15] had been, but where then there was no life nor sign of life—only the blowing of chill winds, the forming of ice in sheltered places, and the melancholy rippling of waves on lonely beaches.

And through another winter they wandered on the obliterated trails of men who had gone before. Once, they came upon a path blazed through the forest, an ancient path, and the Lost Cabin seemed very near. But the path began nowhere and ended nowhere, and it remained mystery, as the man who made it and the reason he made it remained mystery. Another time they chanced upon the **time-graven**[16] wreckage of a hunting lodge, and amid the shreds of rotted blankets John Thornton found a long-barrelled **flint-lock**[17]. He knew it for a Hudson Bay Company gun of the young days in the Northwest, when such a gun

---

13 timber line: (in high northern (or southern) latitudes) the line north (or south) of which no trees grow.
14 gnat: 날벌레
15 wildfowl: birds that people shoot for sport, especially ones such as ducks that live near water
16 time-graven: Changed or created by the effects of time, eroded.
　　His **time-graven** face showed the toughness of one who has survived many difficulties.
17 flint-lock: 수발총
　　Flintlock is a general term for any firearm that uses a flint striking ignition mechanism.

was worth its height in beaver skins packed flat, And that was all—no hint as to the man who in an early day had reared the lodge and left the gun among the blankets.

Spring came on once more, and at the end of all their wandering they found, not the Lost Cabin, but a shallow **placer**[18] in a broad valley where the gold showed like yellow butter across the bottom of the **washing-pan**[19]. They sought no farther. Each day they worked earned them thousands of dollars in clean dust and nuggets, and they worked every day. The gold was sacked in moose-hide bags, fifty pounds to the bag, and piled like so much firewood outside the **spruce-bough**[20] lodge. **Like giants**[21] they toiled, days **flashing**[22] **on the heels of days**[23] like dreams as they heaped the treasure up.

There was nothing for the dogs to do, **save**[24] the hauling in of meat **now and again**[25] that Thornton killed, and Buck spent long hours **musing**[26] by the fire. The vision of the short-legged hairy man came to him more frequently, now that there was little work to be done; and often, blinking by the fire, Buck wandered with him in that other world which he remembered.

---

18 **placer**: 사금 퇴적지, a deposit of sand or gravel in the bed of a river or lake, containing particles of valuable minerals
19 **washing-pan**: 사금 채취망
   참고 **pan-washing**: the action or process of separating gold from gravel, etc., by stirring it in water in a pan; the gravel, etc., being washed in this manner.
20 **spruce**: 가문비 나무
21 **like a giant**: of great size, strength, etc.
22 **flash**: to move or pass very quickly
   ex A car **flashed** by.
      An idea **flashed into/through his mind**. [=he suddenly had an idea]
23 **on the heels of**: directly behind, immediately following,
   ex Mom's birthday comes **on the heels of Mother's Day**.
      Hard **on the heels of the flood** there was a tornado.
24 **save**: other than; but or except
   ex We had no hope **save one**.
   참고 **save for**: not including (someone or something); except for (someone or something)
   ex The park was deserted **save for a few joggers**.
25 **now and again**: not often but sometimes ((every) now and then; (every) now and again)
   ex We still see each other **(every) now and then**.
26 **muse**: to think about something carefully or thoroughly usually + about, on, over, or upon
   ex She **mused on** the possibility of changing jobs.

The **salient**[27] thing of this other world seemed fear. When he watched the hairy man sleeping by the fire, head between his knees and hands **clasped**[28] above, Buck saw that he slept restlessly, with many **starts**[29] and awakenings, at which times he would peer fearfully into the darkness and fling more wood upon the fire. Did they walk by the beach of a sea, where the hairy man gathered shellfish and ate them as he gathered, it was with eyes that **roved**[30] everywhere for hidden danger and with legs prepared to run like the wind at its first appearance. Through the forest they crept noiselessly, Buck at the hairy man's heels; and they were alert and vigilant, the pair of them, ears twitching and moving and nostrils **quivering**[31], for the man heard and smelled as keenly as Buck. The hairy man could spring up into the trees and travel ahead as fast as on the ground, swinging by the arms from **limb**[32] to limb, sometimes a dozen feet apart, letting go and catching, never falling, never missing his grip. In fact, he seemed as much at home among the trees as on the ground; and Buck had memories of nights of vigil spent beneath trees wherein the hairy man **roosted**[33], holding on tightly as he slept.

27 salient: very important or noticeable
   the **salient facts** / a **salient** characteristic/feature
28 clasp: to hold (someone or something) tightly with your hands or arms
   He **clasped her hand** gently/firmly.
   She **clasped her son** in her arms.
   She **clasped her hands** tightly in her lap. = Her hands were clasped tightly in her lap. [=she held her hands tightly together in her lap]
29 start: a brief, sudden action or movement
   She **gave a start** [=started, jumped] when he tapped her on the shoulder.
   He woke **with a start**.
30 rove: to go to different places without having a particular purpose or plan
   [no object] We **roved** [=roamed, wandered] around town/Europe.
   [+ object] They **roved** [=roamed, wandered] the streets of the village.
   His eyes **roved** the room [=he looked around the room] in search of her.
31 quiver: to shake because of fear, cold, nervousness, etc. : tremble
   Her lips **quivered** when she heard the bad news.
   often + with
   He was **quivering** with excitement/rage.
32 limb: a large branch of a tree
   They tied a rope to one of **the limbs of the maple tree.**
33 roost: to rest or sleep somewhere
   Pigeons **roost on the building's ledge**.

And closely akin to the visions of the hairy man was the call still sounding in the depths of the forest. It filled him with a great unrest and strange desires. It caused him to feel a vague, sweet gladness, and he was aware of wild yearnings and **stirrings**[34] **for he knew not what**[35]. Sometimes he pursued the call into the forest, looking for it as though it were a tangible thing, barking softly or defiantly, as the mood might **dictate**[36]. He would thrust his nose into the cool wood moss, or into the black soil where long grasses grew, and snort with joy at the fat earth smells; or he would **crouch**[37] for hours, as if in concealment, behind fungus-covered trunks of fallen trees, wide-eyed and wide-eared to all that moved and sounded about him. It might be, lying thus, that he hoped to **surprise**[38] this call he could not understand. But he did not know why he did these various things. He was impelled to do them, and did not **reason**[39] about them at all.

Irresistible impulses seized him. He would be lying in camp, dozing lazily in the heat of the day, when suddenly his head would lift and his ears cock up, intent and listening, and he would spring to his feet and dash away, and on and on, for hours, through the forest aisles and across the open spaces where the **niggerheads**[40] bunched. He loved to run down dry watercourses, and to creep and spy upon the bird life in the woods. For a day at a time he would lie

---

34 **stirring**: causing strong feelings
   ex She **gave a stirring** [=moving] **speech** at the awards banquet. / a **stirring rendition** of the national anthem
   참고 **stir**: to cause (an emotion or reaction)
   ex The bad economic news has **stirred anxiety among investors**. [=has caused investors to worry]
   usually + up
   The bad news has **stirred up a lot of anxiety**. / The story **stirred up some deep emotions within him**.
35 **for he knew not what**: 분명히 무엇인지 알 수는 없어도
   참고 **for he knew not what**: although he did not know what they really were
36 **dictate**: to make (something) necessary
   ex Our choice of activities will likely be **dictated** [=determined, controlled] by the weather.
   His health **dictates** [=requires] that he work at home.
   Tradition **dictates** that the youngest member should go first.
   The basket's function **dictates** its size and shape.
37 **crouch**: (of an animal) to lie on the stomach close to the ground with the legs bent
   ex The lion **crouched** in the tall grass, waiting to attack the gazelle.
38 **surprise**: to find, attack, or meet (someone or something) unexpectedly
   ex A police officer **surprised the burglars**. / The **troops were surprised by** an attack from the north.
39 **reason**: to form (a conclusion or judgment) by thinking logically
   ex He **reasoned that** both statements couldn't be true. / She **reasoned that** something must be wrong.
40 **niggerhead**: any hard black rock or stone
   참고 In several English-speaking countries, **niggerhead** or **nigger head** is a former name for several things thought to resemble the head of a black person (cf. "nigger"). The name is now taboo in normal usage.

in the **underbrush**[41] where he could watch the **partridges**[42] **drumming**[43] and **strutting**[44] up and down. But especially he loved to run in the dim twilight of the summer midnights, listening to the subdued and sleepy murmurs of the forest, reading signs and sounds as man may read a book, and seeking for the mysterious something that called—called, waking or sleeping, at all times, for him to come.

---

41 underbrush: the brush (small trees and bushes and ferns etc.) growing beneath taller trees in a wood or forest. undergrowth, underwood. brush, coppice, copse, thicket, brushwood - a dense growth of bushes.
42 partridge: 꿩
43 drum: to make a sound by hitting a surface over and over again
   [no object] Rain **drummed** [=beat] on the roof.
   Her fingers **drummed** nervously on the table
44 strut: to walk in a confident and proud way
   She **strutted** across the stage.

Anne of Green Gables by Lucy Maud Montgomery

It was not until the next Friday that Marilla heard the story of the flower-wreathed hat. She came home from Mrs. Lynde's and **called Anne to account**[1].

"Anne, Mrs. Rachel says you went to church last Sunday with your hat **rigged out**[2] ridiculous with roses and **buttercups**[3]. What on earth **put you up to**[4] such a **caper**[5]? A pretty-looking object you must have been!"

"Oh, I know pink and yellow aren't **becoming**[6] to me," began Anne.

"Becoming **fiddlesticks**[7]! It was putting flowers on your hat at all, no matter what color they were, that was ridiculous. You are the most **aggravating**[8] child!"

"I don't see why it's any more ridiculous to wear flowers on your hat than on your dress," protested Anne. "Lots of little girls there had bouquets pinned on their dresses. What's the difference?"

Marilla was not to be drawn from the safe concrete into dubious paths of the abstract.

"Don't answer me back like that, Anne. It was very silly of you to do such a thing. Never let me catch you at such a **trick**[9] again. Mrs. Rachel says she thought she would sink through the floor when she saw you come in all rigged

---

1 bring/call/hold (someone) to account: to require (someone) to explain and accept punishment or criticism for bad or wrong behavior
   ex He **was called to account** by his boss for failing to spot the mistake in the company's records.
2 rig out: to dress or be dressed   ex **rigged out smartly**
   참고 rig out: to equip or fit out (with)
   ex His car is **rigged out** with gadgets.
3 buttercup: 미나리아재비 (꽃)
4 put (someone) up to (something): to convince (someone) to do (something stupid or foolish)
   ex His friends **put him up to (playing) the prank**.
      Who **put you up to** this?
5 caper: an illegal or improper activity that is usually seen as amusing or not very serious
   ex She has a long record of small-time **capers** [=crimes] that include everything from shoplifting to fraud.
      a jewelry **caper** [=theft, heist]
6 becoming: causing someone to look attractive : having a flattering or attractive effect
   ex That jacket is very **becoming** on you.
      She's had her hair cut in a **becoming** new style.
7 fiddlesticks: (informal + old-fashioned) used to express mild anger or disagreement
   ex I had nothing to do with it. Oh, **fiddlesticks**! I know you did.
8 aggravating: annoying, irritating
9 trick: something you do to surprise someone and to make other people laugh
   ex I'm getting tired of your silly **tricks**.
      The girls were playing **tricks** on their teacher.

out like that. She couldn't get near enough to tell you to take them off till it was too late. She says people talked about it something dreadful. Of course they would think I had no better sense than to let you go decked out like that."

"Oh, I'm so sorry," said Anne, tears welling into her eyes. "I never thought you'd mind. The roses and buttercups were so sweet and pretty I thought they'd look lovely on my hat. Lots of the little girls had artificial flowers on their hats. I'm afraid I'm going to be a dreadful **trial**[10] to you. Maybe you'd better send me back to the **asylum**[11]. That would be terrible; I don't think I could endure it; most likely I would go into **consumption**[12]; I'm so thin as it is, you see. But that would be better than being a trial to you."

"Nonsense," said Marilla, **vexed**[13] at herself for having made the child cry. "I don't want to send you back to the asylum, I'm sure. All I want is that you should behave like other little girls and not make yourself ridiculous. Don't cry any more. I've got some news for you. Diana Barry came home this afternoon. I'm going up to see if I can borrow a skirt pattern from Mrs. Barry, and if you like you can come with me and get acquainted with Diana."

---

10 trial: something or someone that is difficult to deal with : an annoying or unpleasant thing or person
   I know I was a bit of a **trial** to my parents when I was a teenager.
   Cold winters can be a **trial** for older people.
   The book describes the **trials** and tribulations [=difficult experiences, problems, etc.] of the colony's earliest settlers.
11 asylum: (=orphan asylum) 고아원, a public institution for the care and protection of children without parents
12 consumption: 결핵
   Tuberculosis (TB) is an infectious disease usually caused by Mycobacterium tuberculosis (MTB) bacteria. Tuberculosis generally affects the lungs, but can also affect other parts of the body.[1] Most infections show no symptoms, in which case it is known as latent tuberculosis. It was historically called **consumption** due to the weight loss.
13 vex: to annoy or worry (someone)
   This problem has **vexed** researchers for years. / We were **vexed** by the delay.
14 glisten: to shine with light reflected off a wet surface
   Rain made the streets **glisten**.
   The streets **glistened** in the rain.
   Her eyes **glistened** with tears/emotion.
   a long beach of **glistening** sand
15 hem: to sew down a folded edge of cloth on (something); to give (something) a hem
   hem the dress/skirt/trousers / The curtains need to be **hemmed**.
16 unheeded: heard or noticed but then ignored or not followed
   unheeded warnings
   The panel's recommendations **went unheeded**. [=were ignored]

Anne rose to her feet, with clasped hands, the tears still **glistening**[14] on her cheeks; the dish towel she had been **hemming**[15] slipped **unheeded**[16] to the floor.

"Oh, Marilla, I'm frightened—now that it has come I'm actually frightened. What if she shouldn't like me! It would be the most tragical disappointment of my life."

"Now, don't get into a **fluster**[17]. And I do wish you wouldn't use such long words. It sounds so funny in a little girl. I guess Diana'll like you well enough. It's her mother you've got to **reckon with**[18]. If she doesn't like you it won't matter how much Diana does. If she has heard about your outburst to Mrs. Lynde and going to church with buttercups round your hat I don't know what she'll think of you. You must be polite and well behaved, and don't make any of your startling speeches. For pity's sake, if the child isn't actually trembling!"

Anne WAS trembling. Her face was pale and tense.

"Oh, Marilla, you'd be excited, too, if you were going to meet a little girl you hoped to be your **bosom friend**[19] and whose mother mightn't like you," she said as she hastened to get her hat.

---

17 **fluster**: a state of agitated confusion
  ex They had been talking about it for days, and when they were getting ready to go out they were all in a fluster.
  참고 **fluster**: to put into a state of agitated confusion; upset
  ex The speaker was obviously **flustered** by the interruption.
  "Now don't overexcite yourself, Grandpa," Mrs. Bucket said. "And don't fluster poor Charlie. We must all try to keep very calm."
18 **reckon with** (someone or something): to deal with (someone or something that can cause problems or trouble)
  ex Anyone who tries to change the system will have to **reckon with me**. = Anyone who tries to change the system will have me to reckon with. [=I will oppose/fight anyone who tries to change the system]
19 **bosom friend**: a friend that you like a lot and have a very close relationship with

They went over to Orchard Slope by the short cut across the brook and up the firry hill **grove**[20]. Mrs. Barry came to the kitchen door in answer to Marilla's knock. She was a tall black-eyed, black-haired woman, with a very resolute mouth. She had the reputation of being very strict with her children.

"How do you do, Marilla?" she said cordially. "Come in. And this is the little girl you have adopted, I suppose?"

"Yes, this is Anne Shirley," said Marilla.

"Spelled with an E," **gasped**[21] Anne, who, **tremulous**[22] and excited as she was, was determined there should be no misunderstanding on that important point.

Mrs. Barry, not hearing or not comprehending, merely shook hands and said kindly:

"How are you?"

"I am well in body although considerable **rumpled up**[23] in spirit, thank you ma'am," said Anne gravely. Then aside to Marilla in an audible whisper, "There wasn't anything startling in that, was there, Marilla?"

Diana was sitting on the sofa, reading a book which she dropped when the

---

20 grove: a small group of trees
    a **grove** of oaks
    especially: a group of trees that produce fruit or nuts
    an **orange grove**
    a **pecan grove**
21 gasp: to say (something) with quick, difficult breaths
    He **gasped** (out) a plea for mercy.
    Have mercy! he **gasped**.
22 tremulous: shaking slightly especially because of nervousness, weakness, or illness
    She opened the letter with **tremulous** hands.
    He spoke with a **tremulous** voice.
23 rumple: to cause something to become wrinkled or creased. A noun or pronoun can be used between "rumple" and "up."
    Make sure you don't **rumple up your shirt** before your interview tomorrow!
    Don't toss your clothes in a heap like that—you'll rumple them up!

callers entered. She was a very pretty little girl, with her mother's black eyes and hair, and rosy cheeks, and the merry expression which was her inheritance from her father.

"This is my little girl Diana," said Mrs. Barry. "Diana, you might take Anne out into the garden and show her your flowers. It will be better for you than straining your eyes over that book. She reads entirely too much—" this to Marilla as the little girls went out—"and I can't prevent her, for her father aids and abets her. She's always **poring over**[24] a book. I'm glad she has the prospect of a playmate—perhaps it will take her more out-of-doors."

Outside in the garden, which was full of **mellow**[25] sunset light streaming through the dark old firs to the west of it, stood Anne and Diana, gazing bashfully at each other over a **clump**[26] of gorgeous **tiger lilies**[27].

The Barry garden was a **bowery**[28] wilderness of flowers which would have delighted Anne's heart at any time less fraught with **destiny**[29]. It was encircled by huge old willows and tall firs, beneath which flourished flowers that loved the shade. **Prim**[30], **right-angled**[31] paths neatly bordered with **clamshells**[32], intersected it like moist red ribbons and in the beds between old-fashioned flowers **ran riot**[33]. There were rosy **bleeding-hearts**[34] and great splendid

---

24 **pore over** (something): to read or study (something) very carefully
   ex He **pored over** the map for hours.
25 **mellow**: pleasantly rich, full, or soft : not harsh, bright, or irritating
   ex The painting captures the **mellow** light of a summer evening. / **mellow** music / a **mellow** golden color
26 **clump**: a group of things or people that are close together
   ex There is a **clump** of bushes/trees at the edge of the field. / a **clump** of spectators
27 tiger lily: 참나리
28 **bowery**: a farm or plantation of an early Dutch settler of New York.
29 **destiny**: [noncount]: a power that is believed to control what happens in the future
   ex She felt that **destiny** [=fate] had decided that she would one day be President. / motivated by a sense of **destiny**
30 **prim**: very neat in appearance   ex a **prim** little house
31 A **right-angled bend** is a sharp bend that turns through approximately ninety degrees.
32 **clamshell**: either of a pair of doors (as in an airplane tail) that open out and away from each other
33 if a plant **runs riot**, it grows very quickly
   ex The weeds have **run riot over our poor garden**. [=the weeds in our garden have grown quickly and have taken over the garden]
   참고 1) if your imagination, emotions, thoughts etc **run riot**, you cannot or do not control them
   ex Manufacturers have let their imaginations **run riot** to create new computer games.
   참고 2) if people **run riot**, they behave in a violent, noisy, and uncontrolled way
   ex Some people let their children **run riot**.
34 bleeding-heart: 금낭화

crimson **peonies**[35]; white, fragrant **narcissi**[36] and thorny, sweet Scotch roses; pink and blue and white **columbines**[37] and lilac-tinted **Bouncing Bets**[38]; clumps of **southernwood**[39] and **ribbon grass**[40] and mint; purple **Adam-and-Eve**[41], daffodils, and masses of sweet clover white with its delicate, fragrant, **feathery**[42] sprays; **scarlet lightning**[43] that shot its fiery **lances**[44] over prim white musk-flowers; a garden it was where sunshine lingered and bees hummed, and winds, **beguiled**[45] into loitering, **purred**[46] and rustled.

"Oh, Diana," said Anne at last, clasping her hands and speaking almost in a whisper, "oh, do you think you can like me a little—enough to be my bosom friend?"

Diana laughed. Diana always laughed before she spoke.

"Why, I guess so," she said frankly. "I'm awfully glad you've come to live at Green Gables. It will be jolly to have somebody to play with. There isn't any other girl who lives near enough to play with, and I've no sisters big enough."

"Will you swear to be my friend forever and ever?" demanded Anne eagerly.

Diana looked shocked.

"Why it's dreadfully wicked to swear," she said rebukingly.

"Oh no, not my kind of swearing. There are two kinds, you know."

---

35 peony: 작약
36 Narcissus: 수선화
   참고 All **daffodils** are members of the genus Narcissus. In other words, daffodil is the official common name for ANY of the plants that fall into the genus Narcissus.
37 columbine: 매발톱꽃
38 Bouncing Bets: 비누풀꽃 (soapwort)
39 southernwood: 쌍떡잎 식물
40 ribbon grass: 갈풀
41 Adam-and-Eve: Aplectrum (난초의 일종)
42 feathery: resembling, suggesting, or covered with feathers especially; extremely light
43 scarlet lightning: 애기동자꽃
44 lance: 창처럼 뾰족한 꽃잎, a long, pointed weapon used in the past by knights riding on horses
45 beguile: to attract or interest someone
   예문 Almost everything in the quaint little town **beguiles**, from its architecture to its art to its people.
46 purr: to make a purr or a sound like a purr
   예문 The cat was **purring** contentedly in my lap.
   The cars were **purring** along the highway.
   The engine **purred** smoothly.

"I never heard of but one kind," said Diana doubtfully.

"There really is another. Oh, it isn't wicked at all. It just means vowing and promising solemnly."

"Well, I don't mind doing that," agreed Diana, relieved. "How do you do it?"

"We must join hands—so," said Anne gravely. "It ought to be over running water. We'll just imagine this path is running water. I'll repeat the oath first. I solemnly swear to be faithful to my bosom friend, Diana Barry, as long as the sun and moon shall endure. Now you say it and put my name in."

Diana repeated the "oath" with a laugh fore and aft. Then she said:

"You're a queer girl, Anne. I heard before that you were queer. But I believe I'm going to like you real well."

When Marilla and Anne went home Diana went with them as far as the log bridge. The two little girls walked with their arms about each other. At the brook they parted with many promises to spend the next afternoon together.

"Well, did you find Diana a **kindred**[47] spirit?" asked Marilla as they went up through the garden of Green Gables.

"Oh yes," sighed Anne, blissfully unconscious of any sarcasm on Marilla's

---

47 kindred: alike or similar
   ex *philosophy, political theory, and **kindred** topics*
   *I believe she and I are **kindred** spirits/souls.*

part. "Oh Marilla, I'm the happiest girl on Prince Edward Island this very moment. I assure you I'll say my prayers with a right good-will tonight. Diana and I are going to build a playhouse in Mr. William Bell's birch grove tomorrow. Can I have those broken pieces of china that are out in the woodshed? Diana's birthday is in February and mine is in March. Don't you think that is a very strange coincidence? Diana is going to lend me a book to read. She says it's perfectly splendid and tremendously exciting. She's going to show me a place back in the woods where rice lilies grow. Don't you think Diana has got very soulful eyes? I wish I had soulful eyes. Diana is going to teach me to sing a song called 'Nelly in the Hazel Dell.' She's going to give me a picture to put up in my room; it's a perfectly beautiful picture, she says—a lovely lady in a pale blue silk dress. A sewing-machine agent gave it to her. I wish I had something to give Diana. I'm an inch taller than Diana, but she is ever so much fatter; she says she'd like to be thin because it's so much more graceful, but I'm afraid she only said it to soothe my feelings. We're going to the shore some day to gather shells. We have agreed to call the spring down by the log bridge the Dryad's Bubble. Isn't that a perfectly elegant name? I read a story once about a spring called that. A dryad is sort of a grown-up fairy, I think."

"Well, all I hope is you won't talk Diana to death," said Marilla. "But remember this in all your planning, Anne. You're not going to play all the time nor most of it. You'll have your work to do and it'll have to be done first."

Anne's cup of happiness was full, and Matthew caused it to overflow. He had just got home from a trip to the store at Carmody, and he sheepishly produced a small parcel from his pocket and handed it to Anne, with a **deprecatory**[48] look at Marilla.

"I heard you say you liked chocolate sweeties, so I got you some," he said.

"Humph," sniffed Marilla. "It'll ruin her teeth and stomach. There, there, child, don't look so dismal. You can eat those, since Matthew has gone and got them. He'd better have brought you peppermints. They're wholesomer. Don't sicken yourself eating all them at once now."

"Oh, no, indeed, I won't," said Anne eagerly. "I'll just eat one tonight, Marilla. And I can give Diana half of them, can't I? The other half will taste twice as sweet to me if I give some to her. It's delightful to think I have something to give her."

"I will say it for the child," said Marilla when Anne had gone to her gable, "she isn't stingy. I'm glad, for of all faults I detest stinginess in a child. Dear

---

[48] **deprecatory**: expressing disapproval; disapproving.

me, it's only three weeks since she came, and it seems as if she'd been here always. I can't imagine the place without her. Now, don't be looking I told-you-so, Matthew. That's bad enough in a woman, but it isn't to be endured in a man. I'm perfectly willing to own up that I'm glad I consented to keep the child and that I'm getting fond of her, but don't you **rub it in**[49], Matthew Cuthbert."

---

49 rub it in: to make someone feel worse about something the person already feels embarrassed about:
*I know I shouldn't have paid that much for the poster don't **rub it in**, OK?*

2 시

01 **Love is Not All (Sonnet XXX)** by Edna St. Vincent Millay

Love is not all: it is not meat nor drink
Nor slumber nor a roof against the rain;
Nor yet a floating **spar**[1] to men that sink
And rise and sink and rise and sink again;
Love can not fill the thickened lung with breath,
Nor clean the blood, nor set the fractured bone;
Yet many a man is making friends with death
Even as I speak, for lack of love alone.
It **well may**[2] be that in a difficult hour,
Pinned down by pain and moaning for release,
Or nagged by want **past**[3] resolution's power,
I might be driven to sell your love for peace,
Or trade the memory of this night for food.
It well may be. I do not think I would.

---

1 **spar**: 스파 (배의 구조물)
   a thick pole or similar structure that supports something (such as the sails of a ship or the wing of an aircraft)
2 **well may**: may well을 도치하여 만든 표현
   참고 If you say that something **may well** happen, you mean that it is likely to happen:
   ex She may well not want to travel alone.
3 **past**: beyond or no longer at (a particular point)
   ex The milk is past its expiration date.
   The daffodils are past blooming.
   They tried marriage counseling, but they were already **past the point of reconciling**.

To Science by Edgar Allan Poe

Science! true daughter of Old Time thou art!
    Who alterest all things with thy peering eyes.
Why preyest thou thus upon the poet's heart,
    Vulture, whose wings are dull realities?
How should he love thee? or how deem thee wise,
    Who wouldst not leave him in his wandering
To seek for treasure in the jewelled skies,
    Albeit[1] he soared with an undaunted wing?
Hast thou not dragged **Diana**[2] from her car,
    And driven the **Hamadryad**[3] from the wood
To seek a shelter in some happier star?
    Hast thou not torn the **Naiad**[4] from her flood,
The **Elfin**[5] from the green grass, and from me
The summer dream beneath the **tamarind**[6] tree?

---

1. albeit: even though; although
   She appeared on the show, albeit briefly.
   It was an amazing computer, albeit expensive.
2. Diana: In Roman mythology, Diana was the goddess of hunting, and in later times, the moon and chastity. Cypress trees were sacred to her. She was the daughter of Jupiter and the Titan Latona (or Leto). In Greek mythology, Diana was called Artemis.
3. Hamadryad is a Greek mythological being that lives in trees. It is a particular type of dryad—which, in turn, is a particular type of nymph. Hamadryads are born bonded to a certain tree. Some maintain that a hamadryad is the tree itself, with a normal dryad being simply the indwelling entity, or spirit, of the tree.
4. In Greek mythology, the Naiads are a type of female spirit, or nymph, presiding over fountains, wells, springs, streams, brooks and other bodies of fresh water.
5. Elfin: of, relating to, or produced by an elf
6. Tamarind is a tree. Its partially dried fruit is used to make medicine.

"Under the greenwood tree" by William Shakespeare
(from As You Like It)

Under the greenwood tree
Who loves to lie with me,
And turn his merry note
Unto¹ the sweet bird's throat,
Come hither, come hither, come hither:
      Here shall he see
        No enemy
But winter and rough weather.

Who doth² ambition shun
And loves to live i' the sun,
Seeking the food he eats,
And pleased with what he gets,
Come hither, come hither, come hither:
      Here shall he see
        No enemy
But winter and rough weather.

---

1 **unto**: (old-fashioned) used in the past like to
   ex *I will search unto the ends of the earth for thee.*
      *I will be with you **unto** [=until] the end of time.*
2 **doth**: in the past, the third person singular of the present tense of "do":
   ex *he/she/it **doth** (= he/she/it does)*

04 I Should Not Dare To Leave My Friend by Emily Dickinson

I should not dare to leave my friend,
Because—because if he should die
While I was gone—and I—too late—
Should reach the Heart that wanted me—

If I should disappoint the eyes
That **hunted**[1]—hunted so—to see—
And could not bear to shut until
They "noticed" me—they noticed me—

If I should stab the patient faith
So sure I'd come—so sure I'd come—
It listening—listening—went to sleep—
Telling my **tardy**[2] name—

My Heart would wish it broke before—
Since breaking then—since breaking then—
Were useless as next morning's sun—
Where midnight frosts—had lain!

---

1 hunt: to search for something or someone very carefully and thoroughly
   [no object] She **hunted** around in the closet for a pair of shoes.
   often + for
   The police are **hunting for a killer**.
   He's **hunting for a new apartment**.
   We went to the mall to **hunt for bargains**.
2 tardy: done or happening late
   a **tardy** payment/arrival
   tardy: arriving or doing something late
   tardy students
   She was **tardy** to/for work.
   They were **tardy** in filing the application.

❸ 희곡

The Crucible by Arthur Miller

Proctor goes. Hale stands embarrassed for an instant.

Parris, *quickly*: Will you look at my daughter, sir? *Leads Hale to the bed.* She has tried to leap out the window; we discovered her this morning on the highroad, waving her arms as though she'd fly.

Hale, *narrowing his eyes*: Tries to fly.

Putnam: She cannot bear to hear the' Lord's name, Mr. Hale; that's a sure sign of witchcraft afloat.

Hale, *holding up his hands*: No, no. Now let me instruct you. We cannot **look to**[1] superstition in this. The Devil is precise; the marks of his presence are definite as stone, and I must tell you all that I shall not proceed unless you are prepared to believe me if I should find no bruise of hell upon her.

Parris: It is agreed, sir—it is agreed—we will abide by your judgment.

Hale: Good then. *He goos to the bed, looks down at Betty. To Parris*: Now, sir, what were your first warning of this strange-ness?

---

1 look to
look to (someone): to hope or expect to get help, advice etc. from someone
ex As young children, we **looked to our parents for guidance.**
They're **looking to me** to help improve sales figures.

Parris: Why, sir—I discovered her—*indicating Abigail*—and my niece and ten or twelve of the other girls, dancing in the forest last night.

Hale, *surprised*: You permit dancing?

Parris: No, no, it were secret —

Mrs. Putnam, *unable to wait*: Mr. Parris's slave has knowledge of **conjurin'**[2], sir.

Parris, *to Mrs. Putnam*: We cannot be sure of that, Goody Ann —

Mrs. Putnam, *frightened, very softly*: I know it, sir. I sent my child—she should learn from Tituba who murdered her sisters.

Rebecca horrified: Goody Ann! You sent a child to conjure up the dead?

Mrs. Putnam: Let God blame me, not you, not you, Rebecca! I'll not have you judging me any more! *To Hale*: Is it a natural work to lose seven children before they live a day?

Parris: Sssh!

Rebecca, with great pain, turns her face away. There is a pause.

Hale: Seven dead in childbirth.

Mrs. Putnam, *softly*: Aye. *Her voice breaks; she looks up at him. Silence. Hale is impressed. Parris looks to him. He goes to his books, opens one, turns*

---

2 conjure: to make (something) appear or seem to appear by using magic
 a magician who **conjures live doves** from silk scarves
 usually + up
 In the movie she has the power to **conjure up storms, fires, and earthquakes.**

pages, then reads. All wait, avidly.

Parris, *hushed*: What book is that?

Mrs. Putnam: What's there, sir?

Hale, *with a tasty[3] love of intellectual pursuit*: Here is all the invisible world, caught, defined, and calculated. In these books the Devil stands stripped of all his brute disguises. Here are all your familiar spirits—your **incubi**[4] and **succubi**[5]; your witches that go by land, by air, and by sea; your wizards of the night and of the day. Have no fear now—we shall find him out if he has come among us, and I mean to crush him utterly if he has shown his face! *He starts for the bed.*

Rebecca: Will it hurt the child, sir?

Hale: I cannot tell. If she is truly in the Devil's grip we may have to rip and tear to get her free.

REBECCA: I think I'll go, then. I am too old for this. *She rises.*

Parris, *striving for conviction*: Why, Rebecca, we may open up the **boil**[6] of all our troubles today!

Rebecca: Let us hope for that. I go to God for you, sir.

---

3 **tasty**: very appealing or interesting
   ex a **tasty** [=juicy] bit of gossip
4 An **incubus** is a demon in male form in folklore that seeks to have sexual intercourse with sleeping women
5 A **succubus** is a demon or supernatural entity in folklore, in female form, that appears in dreams to seduce men, usually through sexual activity.
6 **boil**: 종기, a painful, swollen area under the skin that is caused by infection
   It is ironic that Reverend Parris says that the witchcraft investigation might reveal the source of all the community's problems 'Why, Rebecca, we may open up the boil of all our troubles today' because in the end the witchcraft investigation provokes the burning down and destruction of the community.

Man and Superman by George Bernard Shaw

ANA. You mean that it was an immoral impulse.

DON JUAN. Nature, my dear lady, is what you call immoral. I blush for it; but I cannot help it. Nature is a **pandar**[1], Time a **wrecker**[2], and Death a murderer. I have always preferred to **stand up to**[3] those facts and build **institutions**[4] on their recognition. You prefer to **propitiate**[5] the three devils by proclaiming their chastity, their thrift, and their loving kindness; and to base your institutions on these flatteries. Is it any wonder that the institutions do not work smoothly?

THE STATUE. What used the ladies to say, Juan?

DON JUAN. Oh, come! Confidence for confidence. First tell me what you used to say to the ladies.

THE STATUE. I! Oh, I swore that I would be faithful to the death; that I should die if they refused me; that no woman could ever be to me what she was—

ANA. She? Who?

THE STATUE. Whoever it happened to be at the time, my dear. I had certain things I always said. One of them was that even when I was eighty, one white

---

1. pandar: 채홍사, A person who furthers the illicit love affairs of others; a pimp or procurer, especially when male.
2. wrecker: someone or something that destroys something used in combination
   - Lying about your education is **a surefire career-wrecker**.
   - **a home-wrecker** [=someone who has an affair with a married person and causes that person's marriage to fail]
3. stand up to (something): to confront or resist courageously
   - 참고1 stand up to (something): to remain in good condition despite (something)
     - These boots have **stood up to** [=withstood] a lot of abuse.
   - 참고2 stand up to (someone): to refuse to accept bad treatment from (someone)
     - She finally **stood up to the girl** who had been teasing her at school.
4. institution: a custom, practice, or law that is accepted and used by many people
   - Family visits are **a Thanksgiving institution**.
   - She's not interested in **the institution of marriage**.
   - **the institution of slavery**
5. propitiate: to make someone who has been unfriendly or angry with you feel more friendly by doing something to please them; appease

hair of the woman I loved would make me tremble more than the thickest gold tress from the most beautiful young head. Another was that I could not bear the thought of anyone else being the mother of my children.

DON JUAN. [revolted] You old rascal!

THE STATUE. [Stoutly] Not a bit; for I really believed it with all my soul at the moment. I had a heart: not like you. And it was this sincerity that made me successful.

DON JUAN. Sincerity! To be fool enough to believe a **ramping**[6], **stamping**[7], **thumping**[8] lie: that is what you call sincerity! To be so greedy for a woman that you deceive yourself in your eagerness to deceive her: sincerity, you call it!

THE STATUE. Oh, damn your **sophistries**[9]! I was a man in love, not a lawyer. And the women loved me for it, bless them!

DON JUAN. They made you think so. What will you say when I tell you that though I played the lawyer so **callously**[10], they made me think so too? I also had my moments of **infatuation**[11] in which I gushed nonsense and believed it. Sometimes the desire to give pleasure by saying beautiful things so rose in me on the flood of emotion that I said them recklessly. At other times I **argued against**[12] myself with a devilish coldness that drew tears. But I found it just as hard to escape in the one case as in the others. When the lady's instinct was set on me, **there was nothing for it but**[13] lifelong servitude or flight.

---

6 ramp: to increase or to cause (something) to increase in speed, size, etc.
7 stamp: to pound or crush with a heavy instrument
8 thumping: very large, great, etc.
  ex She won the election by a **thumping** [=whopping] 79 percent.
  He told a **thumping** lie.
9 sophistry: 궤변, the use of fallacious arguments, especially with the intention of deceiving.
  ex Trying to argue that I had benefited in any way from the disaster was **pure sophistry**.
10 callously: in a way that is unkind, cruel, and without sympathy or feeling for other people:
  ex She was **callously** indifferent to the suffering of those she made jobless.
  He **callously** uses the people around him.
11 infatuation: a feeling of foolish or very strong love or admiration for someone or something
  ex [noncount] The attraction he felt for her was **just infatuation**, not true love.
  [count] It was **just an infatuation**.
  She had a series of **frivolous infatuations with younger men**.
12 argue against: 1. to state reasons in opposition to something.
  ex My uncle is an ardent liberal and **argues against my mother's conservative beliefs** every time they're together.
  2. To serve as evidence in opposition to something.
  ex Hinton's novel **argues against a simplistic understanding of teenage life in the 1960s**.
13 there's nothing for it but to do something: (British English) used when there is only one thing you can do in a particular situation
  ex **There was nothing for it but to** go back the way we came.

희곡 03 A Streetcar Named Desire by Tennessee Williams

STANLEY [*He hangs up and returns to the table. Blanche fiercely controls herself, drinking quickly from her tumbler of water. He doesn't look at her but reaches in a pocket. Then he speaks slowly and with false amiability.*] Sister Blanche, I've got a little birthday remembrance for you.

BLANCHE: Oh, have you, Stanley? I wasn't expecting any, I—I don't know why Stella wants to observe my birthday! I'd much rather forget it—when you—reach twenty-seven! Well—age is a subject that you'd prefer to—ignore!

STANLEY: Twenty-seven?

BLANCHE [*quickly*]: What is it? Is it for me? [*He is holding a little envelope toward her.*]

STANLEY: Yes, I hope you like it!

BLANCHE: Why, why—Why, it's a—

STANLEY: Ticket! Back to Laurel! On the Greyhound! Tuesday! [*The **Varsouviana**[1] **music steals**[2] in softly and continues playing. Stella rises abruptly and turns her back. Blanche tries to smile. Then she tries to laugh. Then she gives both up and springs from the table and runs into the next room. She*

---

1 Varsouviana
   참고 The ***Varsouviana*** is the polka tune to which Blanche and her young husband, Allan Grey, were dancing when she last saw him alive.
2 steal: to come or go quietly or secretly
   예문 They **stole out of the room**.
   She **stole away silently**.

clutches her throat and then runs into the bathroom. Coughing, gagging sounds are heard.] Well!

STELLA: You didn't need to do that.

STANLEY: Don't forget all that I took off her.

STELLA: You needn't have been so cruel to someone alone as she is.

STANLEY: Delicate piece she is.

STELLA: She is. She was. You didn't know Blanche as a girl. Nobody, nobody, was tender and trusting as she was. But people like you abused her, and forced her to change. [*He crosses into the bedroom, ripping off his shirt, and changes into a brilliant silk bowling shirt. She follows him.*] Do you think you're going bowling now?

STANLEY: Sure.

STELLA: You're not going bowling. [*She catches hold of his shirt*] Why did you do this to her?

STANLEY: I done nothing to no one. Let go of my shirt. You've torn it

STELLA: I want to know why. Tell me why.

STANLEY: When we first met, me and you, you thought I was common. How right you was, baby. I was **common as dirt**[3]. You showed me the snapshot of the

---

3 **(as) common as dirt**: lacking in manners or refinement.
  ex *I can't believe he just put his elbows on the dinner table like that. Why, he must be **as common as dirt!***
  Everyone thinks I'm common as dirt just because of the way I talk.
  *Why on earth did you invite men who are **common as dirt** to such a fancy event?*

place with the columns. I pulled you down off them columns and how you loved it, having them **colored lights**[4] going! And wasn't we happy together, wasn't it all okay till she showed here? [*Stella makes a slight movement. Her look goes suddenly inward as if some interior voice had called her name. She begins a slow, shuffling progress from the bedroom to the kitchen, leaning and resting on the back of the chair and then on the edge of a table with a blind look and listening expression. Stanley, finishing with his shirt, is unaware of her reaction.*] And wasn't we happy together? Wasn't it all okay? Till she showed here. **Hoity-toity**[5], describing me as an ape. [*He suddenly notices the change in Stella*] Hey, what is it, Stella? [*He crosses to her.*]

STELLA [*quietly*]: Take me to the hospital. [*He is with her now, supporting her with his arm, murmuring indistinguishably as they go outside.*]

---

4   The colored lights could be a symbol of Stanley and Stella's relationship and the representative of the array of emotions they have for each other ranging from love and passion to anger and frustration. Stanley is attempting to reassure Stella that despite losing all of her wealth, she is happier with him and is also trying to manipulate Stella into doubting her trust in Blanche, who is actively trying to take away her source of happiness (Stanley).

5   Hoity-toity: having or showing the insulting attitude of people who think that they are better, smarter, or more important than other people
     a bunch of **hoity-toity** snobs

희곡 04 The Glass Menagerie by Tennessee Williams

JIM: [Abruptly]: You know what I judge to be the trouble with you? Inferiority complex! You know what that is? That's what they call it when a fellow low-rates himself! Oh, I understand it because I had it, too. Uh-huh! Only my case was not so aggravated as yours seems to be. I had it until I took up public speaking, and developed my voice, and learned that I had an aptitude for science. Before that time I never thought of myself as being outstanding in any way whatsoever.

LAURA: Oh, my!

JIM: Now I've never made a regular study of it, [Sits armchair right]—**mind you**[1], but I have a friend who says I can analyze people better than doctors that make a profession of it. I don't claim that's necessarily true, but I can sure guess a person's psychology. Excuse me, Laura. [Takes out his gum] I always take it out when the flavor is gone. I'll use this scrap of paper to wrap it in. I know how it is when you get it stuck on a shoe. Yep—that's what I judge to be your principal trouble. A lack of confidence in yourself as a person. Now, I'm basing that fact on a number of your remarks and also on certain observations I've made. For instance, that **clumping**[2] you thought was so awful in high school. You say that

---

1 mind (you): used when you want to make what you have just said sound less strong
   ex *He's very untidy about the house; **mind you**, I'm not much better.*
   *I know I'm lazy - I did go swimming yesterday, **mind**.*
2 clump: to walk with loud, heavy steps
   ex *I could hear him **clumping** [=clomping] down/up the stairs.*

you even dreaded to walk into class. You see what you did? You dropped out of school, you gave up an education because of a clump, which as far as I know was practically non-existent! A little physical defect is what you have. Hardly noticeable even! Magnified thousands of times by your imagination! You know what my strong advice to you is? You've got to think of yourself as superior in some way!

LAURA: In what way would I think?

JIM: Why, man alive, Laura! Just look about you a little. What do you see? A world full of common people! All of 'em born and all of 'em going to die! Now, which of them has one-tenth of your strong points? Or mine? Or anybody else's, **for that matter**[3]? You see, everybody excels in some one thing. Some in many! Take me, for instance. My interest happens to lie in electro-dynamics. I'm taking a course in radio engineering at night school, Laura, **on top of**[4] a fairly responsible job at the warehouse. I'm taking that course and studying public speaking.

LAURA: Ohhhh.

JIM: Because I believe in the future of television! I want to be ready to go right up along with it. You see, I'm planning to **get in on the ground floor**[5].

---

3 for that matter: used to show that a statement is true in another situation
   He's never been to Spain, or to any European country **for that matter**.
   I haven't seen him for years or her either, **for that matter**. [=I also haven't seen her for years]
4 on top of something: in addition to something, especially something unpleasant
   We missed our flight, and **on top of** that we had to wait seven hours for the next one.
5 get in on the ground floor: become part of an enterprise in its early stages
   He was able to **get in on the ground floor** of the computer industry.

I've already made all the right connections and all that remains is for the industry itself to **get under way**[6] **full steam**[7]! You know, knowledge—Zzzzzp! Money—Zzzzzp! Power! **Wham**[8]! That's the cycle democracy is built on! [His attitude is convincingly dynamic. LAURA stares at him, even her shyness **eclipsed**[9] in her absolute wonder. He suddenly grins.] I guess you think I think a lot of myself!

LAURA: No-o-o-o!

---

6 get under way: to begin to happen:
   ex The Democratic convention **gets under way** tomorrow in Chicago.
7 full steam: (of a steam engine) using the greatest possible amount of steam, in order to travel as fast as possible, or work as hard as possible:
   ex **At full steam**, the ship could move from the tropics to the Arctic in a matter of weeks.
   참고 full steam: working as hard as possible
   ex The company is pressing ahead **at full steam** with development of the electric car.
       She's tireless. She is **going full steam**, it seems, 24 hours a day.
8 wham: used to imitate the sound of a loud, sudden noise or to say that something happened very quickly
   ex **Wham**! The wind slammed the door shut.
       Everything seemed fine and then **wham**! all hell broke loose.

장문 독해 지문
번역

1 일반영어 지문 번역

일반영어 01 고통의 진정한 의미 (What Suffering Does)

    지난 몇 주 동안, 많은 사람들과 대화를 할 기회가 있었는데, 대체로 말은 하지 않아도 인생의 가장 중요한 목표는 최대한 행복을 누리는 것이라고 으레 생각하는 것 같았다. 당연하다. 흔히 사람들은 자신의 미래를 계획할 때, 앞으로 누리게 될 행복한 삶이나 즐거움에 대해 이야기한다. 오늘날 미국 사회의 화두는 행복이다. 지난 해 한 분기 동안 집계한 것만 보아도, 온라인 서점 아마존에 행복을 주제로 한 책들이 1천 권이나 쏟아져 나왔다.

    하지만 다음과 같은 현상을 주목해 보자. 사람들은 과거를 떠 올릴 때, 행복에 대해서만 이야기하는 것은 아니다. 오히려 과거의 시련이 자신에게 가장 의미있는 기억으로 남아 있는 경우가 종종 있다. 사람들은 행복을 추구한다. 하지만, 결국 시련을 통해서 성숙해 진다고 느낀다.

    물론 고통 자체를 미화할 수 없다는 점은 분명히 밝혀야겠다. 경우에 따라, 실패는 실패일 뿐이다. (실패를 한다고 누구나 제2의 스티브 잡스가 될 수 있는 것은 아니다) 마찬가지로 고통은 때로는 그저 상처만 줄 뿐이고 그래서 최대한 빨리 벗어나야 한다.

    하지만, 분명히 고통을 승화시키는 사람들이 있다. 프랭클린 루즈벨트 대통령의 경우, 소아마비를 앓고 나서, 오히려 더 깊이 있고 타인의 고통에 공감할 수 있는 인물이 되었다는 점을 생각해 보자. 육체적인 고통이나 전쟁 등의 사회구조적 고통을 통해 때로는 타인의 관점에서 인생을 보게 되는 경우가 종종 있다. 다른 사람들이 겪는 고통에 대해 세심하게 이해하게 되는 것이다.

    하지만 고통의 진정한 의미는 행복 중심의 사고방식에서 추구하는 바로 그 논리 이면의 다른 모습을 볼 수 있게 해 준다는 점이다. 행복의 논리는 우리가 얻을 수 있는 혜택을 최대한 늘릴 수 있는 방법에 골몰하기를 바란다. 반면에 어려움이나 고통은 그와는 다른 방향으로 나아가게 만들어 준다. (대안: 행복의 논리대로라면, 우리는 기쁨을 최대한 늘릴 수 있는 방법에 골몰하게 된다. 반면에, 시련과 고통을 통해 우리는 그와는 다른 시각을 가지게 된다.)

    첫째, 고통을 겪으면, 스스로의 내면으로 더 깊이 침잠하게 된다. 신학자인 폴 틸리치는 그의 글에서 고통을 견디는 사람들은 삶의 일상적인 생활 밑에 자리잡고 있는 내면의 모습을 보게 되고, 스스로 믿고 있던 자신의 모습과는 다른 모습을 발견하게 된다고 말한 바 있다. 예를 들자면, 위대한 음악 작품을 작곡할 때 느끼는 고뇌나, 사랑하는 연인을 잃어버리고 느끼는 슬픔은 자신들이 스스로의 성품의 가장 밑바닥이라고 생각했던 것을 산산이 깨 부수고, 그 아래에 숨겨져 있던 모습을 드러낸다. 그리고 다시 그 밑바닥마저 깨 부수고, 그보다 더 아래에 숨겨져 있는 본질적인 모습을 드러낸다.

    그리고 나서, 고통을 통해 사람들은 자기 자신의 한계, 즉 자신이 통제할 수 있는 것과 그렇지 못한 것에 대해 더 정확하게 깨닫게 된다. 사람들은 이와 같이 더 깊은 고통에 처하게 되면, 당장 벌어지는 일에 대

자신이 어떠한 결정도 할 수 없다는 사실에 직면할 수 밖에 없다. 고통을 겪는 상황에서는 고통을 더 이상 느끼지 말자고 스스로 아무리 다짐해도 소용이 없다. 또 이미 고인이 되었거나 자신의 곁을 떠난 사람에 대한 그리움을 멈추고 싶다고 멈출 수 있는 것이 아니다. 그리고 심지어 마음의 평안이 다시 돌아 올 때 조차도, 혹은 슬픔이 가시기 시작하는 바로 그 순간에도, 상처가 아물어가는 진정한 이유가 무엇인지는 확실치 않다. 이와 같은 치유 과정 역시 개인의 힘으로는 어쩔 수 없는 무엇인가 자연적인 힘이나 절대자가 개입하는 듯한 느낌을 가지게 된다.

이러한 상황을 겪는 사람들은 종종 자신들보다 더 큰 섭리가 자신을 이끌고 있다는 느낌을 받는다. 링컨 대통령은 남북전쟁을 치러야 하는 고통을 겪어야 했다. 하지만 남북 전쟁이 끝날 무렵 다시 대통령에 당선되었다. 링컨은 이러한 경험을 통해 자기 자신뿐만 아니라 미국이라는 나라 전체를 고뇌와 구원이라는 도도한 흐름이 이끌고 있다는 사실을 느끼게 되었다. 그리고 자기 자신은 그와 같은 초월적 역할에 있어서 단순한 도구에 불과했다는 생각도 가지게 되었다.

어려움을 겪고 있는 사람들이 소명 의식을 느끼기 시작하는 때가 바로 이 때이다. 그들이 상황을 자기 뜻대로 좌우할 수 있는 것은 아니다. 하지만 그렇다고 또 아무 것도 할 수 없는 것만도 아니다. 그들은 자신들이 겪는 고통의 방향을 결정할 수는 없다. 그러나 고통에 대응하는 방식은 결정할 수 있다. 그들은 때로는 고통에 대해 존엄하게 대처해야 한다는 도덕적 책임감을 느낀다. 시련에 대해 이처럼 당당하게 대처해야 한다고 생각하는 사람들은 자신들이 행복의 차원이나 개별적인 효용성의 차원을 넘어 훨씬 깊이 있는 차원에 있다는 점을 느낀다. 그들은 "내 아이를 잃은 상실감이 아주 크다. 그러니 여기저기 파티를 부지런히 쫓아다니고 마음껏 즐기면서, 내 감정을 추스려야 하겠다"라는 식으로 말하지는 않는다.

이러한 종류의 고통에 대한 올바른 대응방식은 쾌락이 아니다. 오히려 성스러운 태도가 필요하다. 그렇다고 해서 순수하게 종교적 의미의 성스러움을 말하는 것은 아니다. 이 때의 성스러움이란 희로애락이 담겨 있는 삶에 대해 인간으로서의 존엄성을 지킨다는 측면에서 관조하는 시각을 말한다. 다시 말하여, 삶의 고통들을 도덕적 맥락에 놓고 고통을 성스러운 것으로 승화시켜 그 고통을 이겨낼 수 있도록 만드는 것이다. 사랑하는 자식을 잃은 부모들이 재단을 설립하는 경우가 그런 경우다. 또 링컨 대통령은 미국의 연방 체제를 유지하기 위해 자신을 희생했다. 강제수용소에 갇혀 있던 사람들은 심리학자 빅토르 프랑클의 도움을 얻어, 자신들이 사랑했던 사람들은 이미 고인이 되었지만, 그들의 희망과 바람대로 다시 살아가겠다는 삶의 의지를 다질 수 있었다.

고통에서 회복한다는 것은 질병에서 회복되는 것과는 다르다. 고통을 겪은 사람들이 회복할 때에는 온전히 치유되는 것이 아니다. 그들은 과거의 모습과 달라졌을 뿐이다. 그들은 개별적인 효용성이라는 논리를 과감하게 거스르고 오히려 역설적으로 행동한다. 사랑하는 사람 사이의 다짐들은 거의 대부분의 경우 항상 고통이 따를 수 있다. 하지만 이런 사람들은 그러한 고통의 가능성을 피하지 않고, 오히려 사랑을 향해 더 과감하게 뛰어든다. 심지어 최악의 상황과 가장 가슴 아픈 결과를 경험하더라도, 더 상처를 무릅쓰고 행동한다. 그들은 자신이 추구하는 예술이나, 사랑하는 사람, 그리고 자신의 신념에 깊숙이 그리고 오히려 감사하는 마음으로 혼신을 다해 자신을 던진다.

그 과정에서 겪는 고통은 두렵기는 하지만 하나의 선물(fearful gift)로 볼 수도 있다. 그리고 그것은 고통과 동등하면서도 또 다른 선물, 즉 통상적인 의미의 행복과는 차원이 전혀 다르다.

자신감의 양극화 현상 (The bluster imbalance)

여성들은 아무래도 자신감이 부족한 것 같다. 하지만 그렇다고 해서 필요 이상으로 과도한 자신감을 가지도록 유도하지는 말았으면 좋겠다.

최근 주로 여성 직장인들을 겨냥하여 쏟아져 나오는 자기 계발서들이나 기사들을 살펴보자. 예를 들어, "자신감이라는 비밀(The Confidence Code)"이나 "과감하게 요구하자(Lean In)"와 같은 책들이다. 이런 내용들을 보면, 남성과 여성이 느끼는 자신감에 큰 차이가 있다는 것을 알 수 있다.

몇 가지 걱정스러운 현상들과 그 근거들 중에서도 특히 여성들은, 아무리 성공한 경우라고 해도, 스스로에 대해 회의적인 생각을 많이 가지고 있다. 우리는 자신의 다음 행보에 대해 끊임없이 회의적인 생각을 하며, 과거에 실패한 경험을 떠올린다. 여성들은 중요한 회의가 있을 경우, 자신의 의견을 밝히려고 하지 않는다. 반면에 남성들은 여성들에 비해 아는 것이 더 적은 경우에도 스스럼없이 허풍을 떨거나 자신의 능력을 과시하면서, 조금이라도 유리한 위치를 차지하거나 상대방의 말을 끊고 자기 주장을 펼친다. 심지어 익명이 보장되는 정치 여론 조사에서도, 여성들은 설령 자신들이 잘 알고 있는 내용이라도, 자신의 의견에 대한 질문을 받으면, 잘 모른다는 의견을 제시하는 경우가 남성들에 비해 더 많다.

여성들은 자신의 의견을 밝힐 때에도, 자신들의 의견에 대해 사과를 하거나, 예를 들어, 저는 잘 모르지만 이라는 말처럼 미리 자신감이 없는 듯한 표현을 사용하는 경우가 아주 많다. 아니면 자신 있게 의견을 말하지 않고 말 끝을 올려 자신 없는 모습을 보인다. 여성들은 충분히 승진이나 봉급 인상을 요구할만한 자격이 있는 경우에도, 과감하게 요구하지 못한다. 반면에 남성들은 승진이나 봉급인상을 요구하기에 턱없이 부족한 경우에도, 거리낌없이 요구한다.

이와 같이 여성들이 자신감이 부족한 모습을 보이면, 소위 유리 천장이 더 단단해 진다. 왜냐하면 어떤 일은 자신감이 있으면 성과가 더 높게 나타나기 때문이다. 그리고 더 중요한 것은 자신감 있는 모습을 보이면 다른 사람들이 우리 여성늘에 대해 더 능력이 있는 것으로 인정해 주기 때문이다. 한 연구에서는 경영대학원에 다니는 학생들에게 예를 들어, 섀독 여왕(Queen Shaddock)이나 갈릴레오 로바노(Galileo Lovano) 등과 같이 사실 현실에서는 존재하지 않지만, 허구적인 역사적인 인물들이나 사건들을 알고 있는지 질문을 던졌다. 그 결과, 비록 허구적인 인물들이지만 그들을 마치 잘 알고 있는 것처럼 과시한 학생들이 다른 동료 학생들로부터 가장 높은 평가를 받은 것으로 나타났다.

물론 여기에는 우리가 잘 알고 있는 광범위한 성별 고정관념이 자리잡고 있고, 이러한 고정 관념은 주로 아직 경험이 많지 않은 대학생들을 대상으로 한 소규모 실험이나 외부 기관의 검증을 거치지 않은 기업 내의 설문 조사 등을 통해 근거가 있는 것처럼 제시되는 것이 사실이다. 하지만 정말 똑똑하고 능력은 있지만 끊임없이 자기 자신에 대해 회의를 가지는 여성들을 친구로 둔 한 사람의 젊은 여성으로서, 또 신문에 칼럼을 쓰고 있는 저널리스트로서, 필자가 보기에는 많은 부분이 설득력이 있다. (칼럼 지면은 특히 여성들의 목소리가 부족하다는 비판을 많이 받는다. 하지만, 이와 같이 여성 필자가 적은 것은 남성들은 신문사에서 먼저 요청을 하지 않아도 자신들이 먼저 신문사로 기고하는 경향이 더 많고 기고 요청을 받으면, 승낙하는 경우가 더 많기 때문이다.)

그러므로 선천적인 이유이든 혹은 사회에 의해 길들여졌기 때문이든, 여성들은 스스로를 낮게 평가하는 경향이 있는데, 이제 좀 더 자신감 있는 태도를 보일 필요가 있다.

하지만, 소위 자신감의 격차 문제가 왜 단순히 여성들의 문제로만 인식되어 왔는지, 또 왜 여성들에게 가장 좋은 해결책이 경쟁 상대인 남성들의 행동방식을 똑같이 따라 하는 것이어야 하는지는 필자도 분명히 이해할 수 없다.

여성들이 자신감이 부족하다는 점을 보여주는 연구들에서는 또 남성들의 경우 지나치게 자신감이 넘친다는 점을 보여준다. 앞에서 이야기한자신감이라는 비밀(The Confidence Code)이라는 책에서는 콜롬비아 경영대학원에서 실시한 한 연구의 사례를 들고 있다. 그 연구에서는 남성들은 흔히 자신의 실제 능력보다 30% 정도는 과장해서 생각하는 경우가 있다는 점을 보여준다. 마찬가지로, 지난 주 YouGov에서 발표한 설문조사 결과를 보면, 설문대상자들에게 평균적인 미국인들과 비교하여 자신의 지적 능력이 어느 정도라고 생각하는지 물어보았다. 그러자, 남성들 중에서는 자신들이 훨씬 더 지적이라고 응답한 비율이 대략 25%이었던 반면에 여성들의 경우는 15%에 불과한 것으로 나타났다. 역시 자기 자신에 대해 과대 포장하는 성향은 남성들이 더 강한 것 같다.

간단히 말하여, 남성들은 여성들에 비해 자기 과시가 훨씬 더 강하다. 그것은 사교 행사이든, 직장에서든 아니면 심지어 익명을 전제로 한 전화 설문 조사나 미국에서 내로라하는 신문의 칼럼 면에서도 마찬가지이다. 그리고 고용주들이나 동료들이 계속 과도한 자신감을 능력과 혼동하며, 자기 과시하는 사람을 높이 평가하고 직장에서 승진을 시켜주는 한, 여성들이 남성과의 경쟁에서 성공할 수 있는 유일한 방법은 단순히 좀 더 자신감을 가지는 차원을 넘어, 남자들처럼 매사에 자신을 과대 포장하는 형태로 되어야 할 것이다.

근검절약도 그렇지만, 이와 같이 과도한 자신감을 보이는 행동도 개인이 성공하기 위한 목적으로는 유용할지 모르지만, 사회 전체에는 해를 끼칠 수 있다. 필자가 보기에 이런 식으로 서로 과시하기 위한 경쟁이 과열되어서는 최소한 기업 발전에도 도움이 되지 않는다. 그리고 그래서는 건설적인 정치적 논의 자체가 나타날 수 없다. (혹시 케이블 TV의 뉴스 프로그램이나 대통령 후보 토론회를 보신 분들은 잘 알 것이다. 저는 잘 모르지만이라는 표현을 사용하면 일단 사람들이 좋아하지 않는다.) 내 생각에는 여자들에게 지금보다는 좀 더 자신감을 가지라고 이야기하는 것이 쉬우면 쉬웠지, 다 큰 남자들에게 과시하고 싶은 생각을 자제하라고 설득한다고 들을 것 같지는 않다. 그러므로 해결책은 남들보다 다 허세를 잘 부릴 수 있는 방법을 배우는 것이 아니라, 과도한 허세에 대한 우리 사회의 인식을 바꾸는 것이다. 그러므로 이제는 여성들까지도 성공을 위하여 과도한 자신감으로 무장해야 한다고 주장하기 보다는, 앞으로 유권자들이나 학생들, 직장 상사들 그리고 TV 시청자들에게 남자든 여자든 제일 목소리가 큰 사람에 대해서는 우선 의심을 하도록 강조하는 것이 좋겠다.

일반영어 03 뇌에 대한 세 가지 속설 (Three Myths About the Brain)

　19세기 초, 프랑스의 신경생리학자 피에르 플루랑스(Pierre Flourens)는 일련의 혁신적인 실험들을 실시했다. 비둘기, 닭, 개구리 등을 비롯한 다양한 동물들의 뇌 조직 중에서 점점 더 큰 부분들을 차례대로 제거하는 실험이었다. 그는 실험 이후에 동물들의 행동에 변화가 있는지 관찰했다.

　그가 발견한 사실들은 분명했으며 합리적인 일관성이 있었다. 그는 1824년에 쓴 글에서 대뇌엽(大腦葉)의 앞면이나, 뒷면, 또는 상부나 측면에서 특정한 대뇌엽 조직을 제거해도 대뇌엽의 기능에 지장을 주지 않는다고 적었다. 이 실험이 시사하는 것은 뇌엽의 작은 일부만 있어도 충분히 지적인 능력을 발휘할 수 있다는 것이다.

　그 결과, 우리가 흔히 잘못 알고 있는 한 가지 속설이 나타나게 되었다. 우리는 우리 뇌의 극히 일부분만 사용한다는 것이다. 가장 흔히 드는 이야기는 우리 뇌의 10%밖에 활용하지 못한다는 것이다. 이런 주장을 초기에 제기한 사람은 또 한 명의 19세기 과학자인 샤를 에드와르 브라운 세카르(Charles-douard Brown-Squard)였다. 그는 1876년 인간의 두뇌의 능력에 대해 글을 쓰면서, 자신의 뇌를 충분히 활용하는 사람은 거의 없으며, 뇌의 능력을 완전히 활용하는 사람은 절대 없다고 밝혔다.

　하지만 플루랑스의 생각은 틀렸다. 한 가지 이유는 인간의 정신적인 능력에 대한 그의 측정 방법이 조잡했고 그가 실험 대상으로 선택한 동물들이 인간의 뇌 기능을 연구하기에는 적합하지 않았기 때문이다. 오늘날, 신경과학계에서는, 과거 수 십 년 동안 그래왔던 것처럼, 우리가 두뇌의 잠재력을 거의 활용하지 못하고 있다는 주장을 모두 받아들이지 않고 있다.

　하지만 이러한 속설은 지금도 남아 있다. 영화 루시(Lucy)에서 여자 주인공은 자신의 뇌가 가진 잠재력을 최대한 활용하여 초인적인 능력을 발휘한다. 이 주인공이 그러한 속설이 가장 최근에 나타난 대표적 사례일 것이다.

　뇌에 관한 속설들이 등상하는 전형적인 과정을 살펴보자. 먼저 관심을 끌만한 실험 결과가 나오면, 예를 들어, '뇌엽(lobe) 중 일부만 있어도 충분하다는 식으로, 아직 추론의 단계이기는 하지만, 제법 그럴듯한 결과에 대한 해석이 등장한다. 그리고 그러한 해석은 인간은 자신의 뇌의 10%만 사용한다는 식으로 확대해석 되거나 왜곡된다 이와 같이 과도한 추론은 결국 대중 문화에서 속설로 자리잡게 되고, 처음에 그러한 속설을 낳았던 일부 사실과는 상관없이 뿌리를 내리게 된다.

　또 하나의 속설은 뇌의 좌반구와 우반구가 근본적으로 다르다는 주장이다. 흔히 좌뇌는 논리와 분석적인 면을 담당하고 있다고 생각하는 반면, 우뇌는 열정과 창의성을 담당한다고 본다. 이러한 과장된 속설의 발단은 1860년대에 있었던 한 가지 관찰 결과로 거슬러 올라간다. 뇌에 대한 당시의 관찰 결과, 좌뇌가 손상될 경우, 우뇌의 손상에 비해, 언어 능력과 운동능력에 판이하게 다른 영향을 미친다는 결과가 나왔다.

　물론, 좌뇌와 우뇌 사이에 이와 같은 차이나 그보다는 잘 드러나지 않는 차이가 있는 것은 사실이기는 하지만, 좌뇌와 우뇌의 기능상 차이에 대해 지나치게 부각된 것이 사실이다. 사실, 뇌의 양쪽 부분은 차이점보다는 서로 비슷한 점이 더 많다. 그리고 대부분의 뇌의 활동에서는 양쪽을 모두 쓰게 된다. 특히 창의성이나 고도의 논리적인 활동처럼 복합적인 경우에는 더 그렇다.

　최근 몇 년 동안에는 뇌에 관한 새로운 속설이 나타나기 시작했다. 이 속설의 주인공은 '미러 뉴런(mirror neurons)'이다. 이 속설의 내용은 짧은 꼬리 원숭이들에게서 발견할 수 있는 일군의 뇌 세포들이 인간의 정신을 이해하는 데 있어서 중요한 단서를 제공할 것이라는 생각이다.

　미러 뉴런은 짧은 꼬리 원숭이가 과일을 잡기 위하여 손을 뻗치는 것과 같이 자신이 행동을 할 때 활성화된다. 또 다른 동료 원숭이가 똑 같은 동작을 취하는 것을 관찰할 때에도 역시 활성화된다. 그래서 일부 과학자들은 미러 뉴런 세들이 있기 때문에 원숭이가 다른 원숭이들의 행동을 이해할 수 있게 되며, 그 이유는 원숭이가 자신의 뇌에서 그 행동을 똑같이 모방하기 때문이라고 주장해왔다. 또 인간의 뇌에도 미러 시스템이 있어서 (상당히 신빙성이 있는 주장이다) 우리가 행동들을 이해할 수 있도록 만들어 준다는 주장도 있었다. 뿐만 아니라, 미러 시스템은 자폐증과 같이 미러 시스템이 제대로 작동하지 않아 발생한다고 알려진 각종 장애의 원인이 되기도 하지만, 언어 구사, 모방 또는 공감 능력 등과 같은 다양한 정신적 능력의 바탕을 이룬다는 주장도 하고 있다.

미러 뉴런의 존재에 대한 주장은 이제 단순히 실험실에만 머무는 것이 아니라 우리의 일상생활에서도 쉽게 볼 수 있다. 예를 들어, 월드컵 경기를 볼 때 흥분하는 이유는 우리 뇌에 있는 미러 뉴런 때문에 마치 우리가 경기장에 있는 것처럼 착각해서 자신이 직접 공을 차거나 패스하는 것처럼 느끼기 때문이라는 이야기를 들어 보았을 것이다.

하지만 다른 속설들의 경우와 마찬가지로, 이러한 추론 역시 뒷받침할 수 있는 실증적인 데이터들은 없다. 우리는 이제 신체적인 움직임 자체가 있어야만 특히 우리의 이해가 결정되는 것은 아니라는 점을 잘 알고 있다. 왜냐하면, 우리는 스스로 할 수는 없는 일이라도 (예를 들어, 새처럼 날거나 뱀처럼 미끄러지듯이 나아가는 동작) 이해는 할 수 있기 때문이다. 그리고 한 가지 동작도 여러 가지 다양한 방법으로 해석할 수 있기 때문이다 (예를 들어, 물병을 기울이는 동작은 물을 붓고 있거나, 채우거나 아니면 비우는 동작 등 다양하게 해석될 수 있다) 추가로 좀 더 연구를 해 본 결과, 예를 들어 뇌성마비나 뇌졸중 또는 루게릭병 환자에서 근육 운동 시스템에 문제가 있다고 해서 동작들을 이해하거나 (월드컵 경기들을 즐길 수 있는) 능력이 없어지는 것은 아니라는 사실을 알게 되었다. 따라서, 미러 뉴런의 기능에 대해 최근에 정립된 이론들에서는 미러 뉴런이 행동들을 이해할 때 수행하는 역할보다는 운동 능력의 제어에서 수행하는 역할을 더 강조한다.

그러니 제발 관심을 가져주기 바란다. 지금 당장 잘못된 속설을 막으려는 조그만 노력이 훗날 신경과학계에서 터무니 없는 이론이 나타나는 것을 막을 수 있으니 말이다.

언론의 기계적 중립성으로 인한 현실의 왜곡
(The distorting reality of 'false balance' in the media)

언론 매체가 기계적 중립성을 보이는 것은 흔한 일이다. 기계적 중립성이란 어느 한 쪽에 치우치지 않는다는 인상을 주기 위하여 분명한 근거가 없거나 심지어 신뢰성에 의심이 가는 주장에 대해서도 똑 같은 비중을 두어 보도하는 태도를 말한다. 하지만 유력 언론 매체가 기계적 중립성 문제를 해결하기 위해 의미 있는 조치를 취하는 것은 흔치 않은 일이다.

이번 달 초, BBC방송 이사회는 과학적인 내용들의 보도에 있어서 BBC방송의 공정성에 대해 평가한 보고서를 발표했다. 보고서에서는 기후 변화와 같은 문제의 경우, 다양한 각각의 관점들이 똑 같은 과학적 근거를 가지고 있는 것은 아니라고 결론 내렸다. 다양한 의견들에 대해 해당 의견의 근거는 생각하지 않고 동일한 시간과 비중을 줄 경우, 공론의 전개 과정에서 기계적 균형만 맞출 위험성이 있다.

이는 영국 뿐만 아니라 미국의 모든 언론 매체들에게 소중한 교훈이다. 그리고 과학적인 사실의 보도에만 국한되는 문제도 아니다. 물론 거의 모든 사안에는 다양한 측면이 있는 것이 사실이다. 그렇다고 해서, 모두 자동적으로 동일한 가치를 가지는 것은 아니다.

하지만, 불행하게도 너무 많은 언론 매체들이 사실이 아닌 주장과 실제 사실에 대해 같은 비중을 두면서까지 균형을 맞추는 것에만 온통 관심을 쏟고 있다. 예를 들어, 언론 매체들이 기후 변화 논쟁에 대해 정확하게 보도하고 싶다면, 코미디언인 존 올리버의 사례를 따르는 것이 좋겠다.

그는 최근 기후 변화를 재미있게 다룬 한 가상 논쟁에서 기후 변화를 부인하는 쪽의 인원은 3명으로 하고 과학적인 증거를 가지고 있는 전문가들은 97명을 출연시켜 논쟁을 하는 모습을 보여주었다. 그것이 오히려 통계학적 대표성을 갖는 토론이 된다는 점을 역설하기 위한 의도였다. 하지만, 실제 언론에서는 소위 균형을 맞추기 위해 스스로 왜곡하게 되고, 그 결과 항상 우리를 실망시키지 않는 폭스 뉴스와 같은 방송에서는 기후변화의 위협은 과장되었는가?(Is the climate change threat exaggerated?)와 같은 프로그램이 만들어진다. 이러한 프로그램들에서는 주장이 팽팽하게 맞서고 있는 논란의 양측 주장에 대한 증거들을 비교해 보겠다고 약속한다. 그러니 지구온난화에 대해 과학계에서는 대부분 사실로 인정하고 있다는 점을 알고 있는 미국 국민들이 60%에 불과하다는 것도 무리가 아니다. 30% 정도는 기후 변화가 과학적인 근거가 있다는 점에 대해 잘 모르고 있다.

이러한 보도 행태를 보이는 것은 보수 우파 진영의 선정적인 방송 프로그램들만 그런 것이 아니다. 진보적인 언론 감시 단체인 미디어 매터즈(Media Matters for America)의 분석에 따르면, 2013년도에 유엔의 산하기구인 '기후변화에 관한 정부간 협의체(IPCC)'의 5차 평가보고서에 대해 보도하는 과정에서, 월스트리트 저널이나 워싱턴 포스트와 같은 주류 언론 매체들은 3%에 불과한 기후변화를 부인하는 사람들에게 과학계에서 그들이 실제 차지하는 비중의 5배 이상의 비중, 즉 15% 정도의 비중을 두고 보도했다고 밝혔다. 그 결과 환경보호 운동가이자 언론인인 빌 맥기번(Bill McKibben)이 말한 것처럼, 인류 역사상 가장 위험한 일이 될 수도 있는 기후변화가 실제 일어나고 있다는 것을 언론이 국민들에게 제대로 인식시키지 못하는 문제가 발생하고 있다. (실제, 로스앤젤레스 타임즈가 최근 기후변화에 있어서 인간의 영향을 부인하는 사람들의 반박 투고 내용에 대해서는 지면에 싣지 않겠다는 방침을 발표했는데, 이는 매우 이례적인 일이다.)

정치학자 토마스 만과 노엄 온스타인은 애초에 중립적으로 볼 수 없는 사안을 무조건 중립적으로 보려고 할 경우, 오히려 사실을 왜곡할 수 있다고 자신들의 글에서 밝혔다. 그리고 이러한 사실은 과학적인 현상에 대한 보도의 경우에만 나타나는 현상은 아니다. 언론 매체들은 정치적인 논란의 상반된 입장을 제대로 거르지 않고 전할 때에도 비슷한 양상을 보인다. 그 결과, 모든 논쟁은 서로 경중이 같은 양측 사이의 논쟁으로 그 의미가 축소된다. 2013년 공화당 의원들이 의료보험 개혁 법안 문제를 빌미로 정부 기능을 일시적으로 마비시켰을 때, 언론계에서 많은 사람들은 양측이 똑같이 문제가 있다는 식의 양비론을 보였다. 하지만 의료개혁법안은 결국 나중에 의회에서 통과되었고 대법원에서도 합헌성을 인정해 준 사안이다.

진보적인 매체인 The Nation에 칼럼을 쓰고 있는 에릭 올터만은 한 번은 글을 통해어떤 주장이 아무리 터무니없고, 비논리적이며 단순히 사실이 아니라고 하더라도, 편집자들이나 기자들 중에 객관성에만 너무 집착하는 경우들이 너무나 많다고 밝혔다. 이러한 태도는 지구온난화 문제를 비롯하여 한 사회가 직면하고 있는 가장 시급한 문제들에 대한 일반인들의 이해에 아주 큰 영향을 미치게 된다.

환경 문제에 대한 갤럽의 2014년 여론 조사 결과를 보면 미국 국민 중 42%는 지구온난화의 심각성에 대해 언론에서 대체로 과장하고 있다고 생각하는 것으로 나타났다. 우리는 기계적인 중립성이라는 생각에 현혹되어서 지구온난화가 일어나고 있다는 사실은 믿으면서도 우리에게 심각한 영향을 미치지는 않을 것으로 생각하고 있는 것이다. 그 결과, 우리가 선출한 정치인들이 기후 변화의 위협에 대한 노력을 게을리해도 제대로 책임을 묻지 않고 있다. 기후변화의 위험성은 시간이 흐를수록 점점 커지고 있지만 말이다.

결국, 사실 면에서 어느 한쪽으로 치우쳐 있는 사안에 대해 구태여 균형을 맞추려고 하는 자체가 언론인으로서의 윤리에 맞지 않는 것이다. 또 진실을 말하고 정확하게 판단한다는 자랑스러운 우리 언론의 전통에 비추어 보아도 우리가 버려야 할 점이다. 그러한 행태는 백 번 양보해서 평가해도, 언론인으로서 태만한 행동이며, 정말 냉정하게 평가한다면 언론의 역할을 내팽개치는 행동이기 때문이다.

이제는 우리 언론도 논쟁 거리들에 대해 무비판적으로 앵무새처럼 되풀이하기 보다는 BBC 방송의 과감한 사례를 따라 언론으로서 제대로 된 편집권의 판단을 행사해야 하지 않을까? 왜냐하면, 진실이라고 생각되는 측면을 더 많이 보도한다고 해서, 그것이 편파 보도라고 볼 수 없기 때문이다. 오히려 그런 보도 태도야말로 진정한 저널리즘이다.

위험한 정치적 갈등 (Dangerous Divisiveness)

미국 국민들 중에, 정치적 신념이 거의 종교적인 신앙심에 가까운 사람들이 늘고 있다. 이러한 상황에서 이념적 좌표의 양 극단에 있는 사람들은 선이냐 악이냐, 천사냐 악마냐, 자신의 가치관의 보호냐 파괴냐는 식의 종교적 양자택일의 논리로 보게 된다.

지난 주에 연구 조사 기관인 '시민과 언론을 위한 퓨 리서치 센터'에서 발표한 조사 결과를 직접 인용해 보자. 공화당과 민주당 지지자들은 지난 이십 년 동안 과거 어느 때보다 이념적인 차이에 따라 뚜렷하게 나뉘고 있다. 그리고 상대 당을 지지하는 사람에 대한 반감도 더 깊고 광범위하게 나타나고 있다.

보고서의 내용을 조금 더 인용해 보자.

모든 사안에서 항상 보수적인 견해를 유지하는 미국 국민과 항상 진보적인 견해를 유지하는 미국 국민들의 전체 비율은 지난 이십 년 동안 10%에서 21%로 두 배 이상 늘었다. 그리고 이념적 사고는 과거 어느 때 보다 지지 정당 별로 뚜렷하게 나뉘고 있다. 그 결과, 공화당과 민주당 지지자들 사이의 이념적인 공통분모가 줄어 들었다. 오늘날 공화당 지지자 중 92%는 민주당의 중도파보다 이념적으로 오른쪽에 있으며, 민주당 지지자 중 94%는 공화당의 중도파보다 이념적으로 왼쪽에 있다.

그렇다고 이념적인 양극화 문제에 있어서 양측이 모두 똑같은 것은 아니다. 보고서에서도 분명히 밝히고 있는 것처럼, 민주당 지지자 중 공화당에 대해 미국의 국가 발전을 저해하는 세력으로 보는 비율이 27%인 반면 공화당 지지자 중 민주당이 미국의 국가 발전을 저해하는 세력으로 보는 시각은 36%에 달했다. 또 정치적 성향이 같은 사람들끼리 함께 사는 것이 중요하다고 대답한 비율도 보수적 성향의 사람들 사이에서 더 높게 나타났다. 그 밖에도, 진보적인 사람이 가까운 친척 중에 공화당을 지지하는 사람과 결혼을 했을 경우, 못마땅하게 생각하는 비율보다 보수적인 사람이 가까운 친척 중에 민주당 지지자와 결혼을 한 사람이 있을 경우, 싫어하는 비율이 더 높은 나타났다.

이러한 현상이 누드러진 시기는, 어느 정도는, 특정 정파를 지지하는 성향이 강한 라디오 시사 토크쇼들과 이념적 성향이 노골적인 케이블 뉴스 방송들이 인기를 얻기 시작한 때와 일치한다. 이러한 프로그램들은 수익을 올리는 것에만 혈안이 되어 자극적인 발언으로 사람들을 선동하고, 감정을 자극하며 생각이 다른 사람들을 적대적으로 몰아간다.

그리고 이러한 언론 매체의 청취자들이나 시청자들 혹은 독자들은 그 내용들을 맹목적으로 신봉한다. 그래서 경직된 흑백 논리를 고집하며, 유연한 태도를 보이려고 하지 않는다. 또 누군가가 조금만 자신의 신념에 대해 망설이는 태도를 보여도 그 신념을 포기한 것처럼 매도하는 분위기를 만든다. 이러한 상황은 그 자체로 매우 위험하다.

오늘날 우리의 정치 풍토에서는 조금만 잘못해도 극도로 민감하게 받아들이거나 기분 나쁘게 받아들일만 한 요소들이 지뢰밭처럼 여기 저기 널려 있다. 그래서 어떤 입장을 이야기하든 나쁜 의도가 숨어있는 것으로 함부로 단정짓는다. 그리고 일부 견해는 실제로 그러한 의도가 깔려 있는 경우가 있어서, 문제가 더 복잡한 양상을 띄게 된다.

이러한 현상은 비교적 최근에는 오바마 대통령에 대한 다양한 견해들에서 극명하게 나타난다. 오바마 대통령에 대한 입장은 자신이 주로 어떤 이념을 고집하고 있는가에 따라 맹목적인 지지로 해석되기도 하고 맹목적인 증오감으로 받아들여진다. 이러다 보니 한 쪽에서는 오바마 대통령이 정당하게 이룩한 업적들도 아예 무시하는가 하면, 또 다른 한쪽에서는 잘못된 정책에 대해서도 무조건 오바마 대통령을 옹호하게 된다.

객관적인 시각에서 보자면 오바마 대통령의 국정운영은 여러 가지 측면에서 반대 세력에 발목을 잡혀 온 것이 사실이다. 몇 가지 예를 들어 보자. 오바마 대통령이 취임하고 나서, 극우 보수 세력인 티 파티 세력이 부상하기 시작했다. 그리고 당시 상원 공화당 원내 대표였던 미치 맥코넬 의원은 보수 세력의 가장 시급한 문제가 오바마 대통령의 재선을 막는 것이라는 주장을 하여, 우리의 귀를 의심하게 만들었다. 물론,

자신들의 바람대로 되지는 않았다. 그 밖에도 유권자들의 권리를 막으려는 터무니없는 시도도 있었다. 그리고 코크 형제와 같이 막대한 재산을 가진 보수 기업인들이 정치권에 진출하는 일도 있었다. 또 가장 최근의 인구조사 이후에 자신들의 선거에 유리하게 노골적으로 선거구를 획정하는 작태가 있었다. 그 뿐만 아니라 공화당이 장악한 의회에서 유례를 찾아볼 수 없을 정도로 국정 운영의 발목을 잡아왔다.

하지만 정부의 규모와 역할에 대해서는 실질적이고 합리적인 논쟁이 있어야 한다. 그 밖에도, 경제를 성장시키고 확장하는 방안, 경제적 약자들을 단기적으로나 장기적으로 지원할 수 있는 방안, 또 국제사회에서 마지막으로 남아 있는 강대국으로서 미군의 역할, 그리고 다수 시민들이 원하는 민주적인 욕구를 존중하면서도, 특히 개인이 사회적 소수자일 경우, 개인의 권리를 보호하거나 그 권리에 대한 인식을 높일 수 있는 방안 등에 대해서도 합리적인 논쟁이 있어야 한다.

우리는 이러한 문제들이 발생할 때마다 한 가지씩 해결해야 한다.

일부 윤리적인 문제들의 경우, 절대 모호한 태도를 가져서는 안 되는 경우도 있다. 예를 들어서, 인간은 자신의 출생이나 성장, 또는 자신이 스스로 생각하는 정체성을 이유로, 일반적인 경우와 다른 대우를 받아서는 안 된다. 또 여성들은 출산과 관련된 모든 선택권을 누릴 수 있어야 한다. 그리고 미국 사회를 충격에 빠뜨리고 있는 총기 난사사고에 대해서는 어떤 식으로든 조치를 취해야 한다

하지만 예를 들어, 관타나모 지역 수용소 시설을 존속시키는 문제, 무인기의 사용, 정부의 감청 등과 같은 기타 문제들의 경우에는 누가 정권을 잡고 있던지 상관없이 철저하고 당파를 초월하여 철저히 검증이 필요한 부분이 있다. 한 가지 이유는 이들 정책들이 공화당 정권과 민주당 정권에 모두 해당 되는 부분이 있기 때문이다.

우리는 자신이 적극적으로 지지하는 대상이 과연 옳은지 끊임없이 자문해 보아야 한다. 그 이유는 단순히 적대적인 세력으로부터 방어하기 위한 것뿐만 아니라 우호적인 세력들을 유지하기 위해서도 필요하기 때문이다. 또 우리가 지지하는 세력과 적대적인 세력이 반드시 모든 문제에 있어서 서로 다르거나 대립하고 있지 않다는 점을 이해하기 위해서도 필요하다. 특정한 견해를 지나치게 쉽게 믿고, 또 무비판적으로 맹신하게 되면, 양심과 원칙을 저버리는 행동을 하기 쉽고, 심지어 그러한 결과를 조장할 수 있다.

일반영어 06 교육은 사업이 아니다 (Teaching Is Not a Business)

　오늘날 교육 개혁을 주장하는 사람들은 학교에 심각한 문제가 있고, 그 해결책은 기업들에게서 배울 수 있다고 생각한다. 일각에서는 경쟁을 활용해야 한다고 주장한다. 또 다른 사람들은 주로 온라인 학습과 같은 방법을 통해 기존의 판도를 바꾸는 혁신적 방법을 주장하기도 한다. 양 측 모두 교육 문제의 해결책은, 보이지 않는 시장의 손이든 혹은 시장을 변화시키는 첨단기술의 위력이든 상관없이, 단순히 교사와 학생의 개인적인 차원을 벗어나야 한다는 생각을 공통적으로 가지고 있다.

　하지만 두 가지 방법 모두 호들갑을 떠는 것만큼 성과가 있는 것은 아니다. 거기에는 그럴만한 이유가 있다. 본질적으로 복잡 미묘한 인간 관계를 정면으로 다루지 않고 우회하는 방법으로는 교육 문제를 개선하는 것이 불가능하기 때문이다. 청소년들이 성공적인 학교 생활을 하기 위해서는, 스스로가 자신의 미래를 결정할 수 있다는 사실, 즉 추구할만한 목표를 가지고 있다는 점을 믿어야 한다. 청소년들에게는 자신들을 믿고 이끌어 줄 사람이 필요하다. 바로 이 부분이 선생님들의 역할이 중요한 의미를 가지는 지점이다. 가장 효과적인 방법만 활용하면 선생님들과 학생들 사이의 결속력을 더 높일 수 있다.

　오늘날 시장의 주요 논리가 교육 정책의 논의를 지배하고 있다. 비중이 큰 읽기 과목과 수학 과목의 성적이 마치 학생의 학업 성과를 측정하는 유일한 기준처럼 취급되고 있다. 마치 기업에서 실적이 유일한 기준인 것과 마찬가지이다. 이와 같은 중요 과목의 성적이 좋지 않으면 해당 과목을 가르치는 선생님은 해고 당하고 학생들의 성적이 좋은 선생님은 성과급을 받는다. 마치 기업들이 실적이 좋은 직원에게는 보너스를 주고 실적이 저조한 직원들은 해고하는 방식과 똑같다. 기업들이 자신들의 영업 할당 실적을 채우지 못하는 지점은 폐쇄하고 유망한 다른 지역에 새로운 점포를 내는 것과 마찬가지로, 학생들의 성적이 저조한 학교들은 폐교 조치하고, 새로 채용한 선생님들과 교직원들을 갖춘 소위 구조조정 시범 학교들(turnaround model schools)이 그 자리를 차지한다.

　이러한 방식은 연구 단계에서는 타당하다고 생각 할 수도 있다. 하지만 실제로는 아주 실패한 정책이다. 교사들에게 정작 필요한 재교육은 실시하지 않고, 오히려 해고하면 결국 교사들의 사기가 떨어지게 된다. 또 경우에 따라, 그 때문에 교직을 원하는 대학생들이 교직을 포기할 가능성이 있다. 베이비 붐 세대에 속한 나이 많은 교사들이 정년퇴직을 하면서 교사들의 수가 부족해질 것이라는 우려가 점차 현실로 나타나면서, 앞으로 교원 부족 대란이 나타날 가능성이 높다. 교사들 사이에는 협력이 필요하다. 그런데, 교사들에게 성과급을 지급하면 과도한 경쟁을 부추길 수 있다. 또 학교를 폐쇄할 경우, 성적이 저조한 것에 대해 모든 선생님들을 모두 책임이 있는 것으로 취급하는 셈이며, 학생들이 겪는 어려움에 눈을 감는 것이나 다름없다. 학교 개혁을 강조하는 사람들은 어떠한 핑계도 용납할 수 없다는 태도를 보이고 있는데, 어려운 가정 형편을 어떻게 핑계거리라고 할 수 있는가?

　교육 관계자들도 기업들에서 배울 점이 없는 것은 아니다. 하지만 경쟁만능주의나 '파괴적 혁신'과 같이 반짝 유행하는 개념들에 현혹되어서는 안된다. 정작 효과가 있는 방법들은 오랜 시간 동안 이미 실효성이 입증된 전략들이다.

　생산과 서비스 시스템을 끊임없이 그리고 항상 개선해야 한다. 이 말은 경영의 대가 에드워즈 데밍(W. Edwards Deming)이 50년 동안 역설해 온 경영 원칙이다. 제2차 세계 대전 이후 일본의 기업들은 그가 창안한 계획, 실행, 평가, 개선의 4단계 품질 관리 방식을 그대로 활용했으며, 포춘지 선정 500대 기업에 속하는 많은 기업들 역시 이 방식에 관심을 기울여 성과를 보았다. 한편 하버드 경영대학원 역사학과 교수이자 풀리처 상을 수상한 바 있는 알프레드 챈들러 교수는 기업들이 성공하는 비결은 조직 역량을 구축하고, 효과적인 시스템을 가동시키는 한편, 조직 내의 학습 분위기를 장려하는 것이라고 밝혔다. 챈들러 교수는 그러한 기업 문화를 구축하기 위해서는 시간이 걸리며, 경영진이 일시적으로 유행하는 경영 개념에 현혹될 경우, 그러한 기업 문화가 순식간에 무너질 수도 있다고 강조했다.

내가 알고 있는 성공적인 교육 정책들은 모두 교사와 학생 사이의 개인적인 유대감 강화를 목표로 한다. 그 방법은 학교 내에서 학생들을 도와줄 수 있는 확고한 지원 시스템을 구축하는 것이다. 유아 교육을 담당하는 학교들 중 우수한 학교들은 교사와 학생 사이에 아주 긴밀한 관계를 구축하여, 아이들이 스스로 모든 것을 결정하고, 어른들은 항상 가까이에서 관심을 가지고 지켜보는 방법을 취한다.

학교 개선 방안(Organizing Schools for Improvement) 이라는 이름으로 시카고 공립 학교들을 대상으로 대규모 연구를 한 결과, 대상 학교들 중 100개 학교들은 상당히 큰 성과를 보았지만, 나머지 100개의 학교들은 별 성과가 없었던 것으로 나타났다. 학생, 교사, 부모 그리고 학교 운영자들 사이의 사회적 신뢰가 있느냐 없느냐의 문제가 가장 관건이 된 것으로 보인다.

한편, YouthBuild 운동은 지난 25년 동안, 수 십 만 명의 고등학교 중퇴자들을 대상으로 내실있는 직업 실무 경험과 교실 내의 개별 지도를 제공했다. 사실 이 학생들은 학교들이 포기한 상황이었는데, 이들 중 71%는 고등학교 졸업에 준하는 학력(GED)을 인정받았다. 이는 전국의 고등학교 졸업율과 비슷한 수준이다. YouthBuild의 학생들은 선생님들이 포기하지 않도록 적극 지원해주었기 때문에 교육을 받아야겠다는 의지를 가질 수 있었다고 밝혔다.

교육에서는 이와 같이 교사와 학생 사이의 개인적인 관계가 아주 중요하다. 이러한 이야기는 뉴욕 시민 개방 대학의 중퇴 방지 교육 과정에 참여하고 있으며, 현재 커뮤니티 칼리지에 다니는 대학생들로부터도 들을 수 있었다. 이 과정을 통해 고등학교 졸업율을 두 배나 높일 수 있었다.

이러한 정책과, 비슷한 철학을 바탕으로 한 많은 다른 정책들 역시 성과가 매우 높다는 것이 이미 입증되었다. 그런 상황에서도 공립학교들은 첨단 기술이 앞으로 교육의 미래라고 보고 수 십 억 달러의 막대한 예산을 투입하고 있다. 하지만 요란스러웠던 주장들과는 달리, 그 결과는 실망스러웠다. 빌 & 멜린다 게이츠 재단의 교육담당 총괄사업부장이자 교육기술 기업의 투자자이기도 한 톰 반더 아크는 "성과를 입증할만한 데이터가 별로 없다. 가시적인 실적 문제의 경우에는, 실제 성과가 없으니 전혀 근거가 없다고 봐도 무방하다"고 밝혔다.

우선 선생님들이 훌륭하면, 얼마든지 첨단 기술을 효과적인 용도로 활용할 수 있다. 하지만, 이러한 흐름은 소위 미래학자들이 아니라 선생님들이 주도할 수 있도록 해 주어야 한다. 가르치고 배우는 과정은 인간적인 호흡이 중요한 분야라서 단순히 컴퓨터나 시장이 똑같이 모방할 수 없다. 기업 모델이 각급 학교의 개혁에서 큰 성과를 보이지 못한 것도 무리가 아니다. 결국 학교 교육에서는 어떠한 방법도 선생님과 학생간의 인간적인 관계를 대신할 수는 없다.

경제성장의 발목을 잡는 불평등 (Inequality Is a Drag)

　지난 30여 년 동안, 미국 정치권에서 내로라하는 사람들은 거의 누구나 부자 증세와 저소득층에 대한 경제적 지원 확대가 경제 성장을 저해할 것이라는 관점에 동의해왔다.
　진보 진영에서는 대체로 이러한 문제에 대해 감수할만한 가치가 있는 희생이라고 보았다. 그들의 주장은 경제적으로 곤란한 일부 국민들을 도울 수 있다면, GDP감소라는 형태로 어느 정도 희생이 있어도, 충분히 감수할만 하다는 것이었다. 한편, 보수 정치인들은 낙수 효과론(trickle-down economics)을 주장해 왔다. 그들의 주장은 경제성장에 가장 효과적인 정책은 부자 감세와 저소득층에 대한 복지 혜택 축소를 통해 경제 성장률을 높이는 것이며, 그렇게 되면 자연히 모든 경제 주체에게 이득이 돌아간다는 것이었다.
　하지만 새로운 견해의 타당성을 뒷받침하는 증거들이 속속 나타나고 있다. 새로운 견해란 이 논쟁의 전제 자체가 잘못되었고, 공정성과 효율성은 어느 한 쪽을 포기해야 하는 문제가 아니라는 것이다. 왜 그럴까? 시장 경제는 어느 정도 불평등한 요소가 있어야 효과적으로 작동하는 것이 사실이다. 하지만 오늘날 미국의 경제적 불평등은 워낙 심각하여, 미국 경제에 커다란 해를 끼치고 있다. 그리고 이는 결국 부자증세와 저소득층 복지 확대를 통한 소득의 재분배가 경제 성장률을 낮추기보다 오히려 높일 수 있다는 점을 시사한다.
　이러한 견해에 대해, 단순히 희망사항에 불과하다고 무시해 버리고 싶은 생각이 들 수도 있다. 즉, 부자들에 대한 세금을 깎아주면 경제성장을 촉진하고, 그 결과 정부의 세수를 늘릴 수 있을 것이라는 보수 우파 진영의 환상과 마찬가지로 진보진영이 가지고 있는 신기루에 불과하다는 것이다. 하지만 실제로 다름 아닌 IMF와 같은 국제금융기관에서 발표한 자료들을 보면, 불평등이 높아지면 성장의 발목을 잡는 반면, 부의 재분배는 경제 성장에 도움을 준다는 점을 분명히 보여주는 증거들이 있다.
　이번 주 초, 국제 신용평가사인 스탠다드 앤 푸어스 (S&P)의 발표로, 불평등과 경제 성장에 대한 새로운 견해 한층 힘이 실리게 되었다. S&P에서 불평등이 심화되면, 경제 성장의 발목을 잡는다는 사실을 뒷받침하는 연구 결과를 발표한 것이다. 사실 이번에 발표한 내용은 S&P가 자체적으로 연구한 결과는 아니고, 다른 연구 결과를 요약한 것이고, 그들의 분석 결과를 전적으로 받아 들일 수는 없다. (우리는 S&P가 미국의 국채에 대한 신용 등급 강등 결정과 같은 터무니없는 결정을 내린 적이 있다는 점을 기억할 필요가 있다) 하지만 S&P가 불평등에 대한 새로운 견해에 대해 공식적으로 인정했다는 사실은 이 견해가 이제는 대세로 자리잡고 있다는 점을 잘 보여준다. 지금 현재로서는 이미 소득 수준이 높은 사람들에게 더 유리한 환경을 조성하고 저소득층의 삶을 더욱 어렵게 만드는 정책이 경제 성장에 도움이 된다고 믿을 만한 근거는 없다. 반면에, 그 반대가 사실일 것이라고 생각할만한 근거는 충분하다.
　특히, 불평등, 재분배 및 성장에 대한 세계 각국의 증거들을 체계적으로 분석해 보면 (IMF 연구원들이 사용한 것이 바로 그 방법이다) 경제적 불평등 수준이 낮은 국가들의 경우, 경제 성장의 속도가 떨어지기보다 오히려 빨라진다는 것을 알 수 있다. 더 나아가 선진국에서 일반적인 수준으로 소득의 재분배가 이루어질 경우 (미국의 경우는 선진국들의 평균 수준보다 훨씬 떨어진다) "경제 성장이 더욱 높게 그리고 지속적으로 이루어질 가능성과 매우 밀접한 관계"가 있다. 즉, 부유층을 더 부유하게 만들어준다고 해서 국가 전체의 부가 늘어난다는 논리는 증거가 없는 반면, 저소득층의 가난을 줄여주었을 때 얻을 수 있는 경제 전체의 이득은 크다는 것을 보여주는 분명한 증거들은 있다.
　하지만, 그것이 가능한 이유가 무엇일까? 부자들에게 세금을 높이고 가난한 사람들에게 도움을 주면 돈을 벌겠다는 동기가 줄어들지 않을까? 그렇기는 하다. 하지만 금전적인 동기만 경제 성장에서 중요한 것은 아니다. 기회도 마찬가지로 매우 중요하다. 소득의 불평등이 극심해지면, 많은 사람들이 자신들의 잠재력을 활용할 수 있는 기회를 박탈당하게 된다.
　이 점을 생각해 보자. 과연 저소득층 자녀들 중 똑똑한 아이들이, 부유한 가정의 자녀들과 비교하여,

양질의 교육을 받고 자신의 적성에 맞는 진로를 선택하는 등 자신의 능력을 발휘할 수 있는 기회를 똑같이 누리고 있는가? 물론 그렇지 않다. 더군다나 이 문제는 단순히 불공정성 차원의 문제에 그치는 것이 아니라, 사회 전체적으로도 손실이 큰 문제이다. 불평등이 극심하면 인적자원들을 낭비할 수 밖에 없기 때문이다.

그리고 정부가 불평등을 줄이는 정책들을 펼치면 인적 자원의 낭비를 줄여서, 경제 성장을 촉진시킬 수 있다.

예를 들어, 현재 저소득층의 근로 의지를 떨어뜨리는 제도라고 보수층으로부터 끊임없이 공격을 받고 있는 '식료품 지원 쿠폰(food stamp)'에 대해 이미 잘 알려진 사실들을 생각해 보자. 과거의 증거들을 보면, 식료품 지원 쿠폰을 받는 사람들의 경우, 일을 하려는 의지가 다소 떨어지는 것은 사실이다. 아이를 혼자 키우는 싱글맘들의 경우에는 특히 더 그렇다. 하지만 한편으로는 어렸을 때 식료품 지원 쿠폰 혜택을 받은 가정에서 자란 사람들이 나중에 성장해서 그렇지 못한 사람들에게 비해 건강 면에서나 생산성 면에서 더 나았다는 사실도 보여준다. 이는 결국 그들이 미국의 전체 경제에 더 큰 기여를 한다는 것을 의미한다. 식료품 지원 쿠폰 제도의 목적은 물론 개인의 경제적인 어려움을 돕기 위한 것이다. 하지만 이 제도가 궁극적으로는 미국의 경제 성장에도 도움이 되었을 것이라고 추론하는 것이 타당하다.

필자는 오바마 대통령의 의료개혁도 결국 같은 결과를 낳을 것이라고 생각한다. 국가가 지원하는 의료보험 혜택을 받게 되면, 일부 사람들 사이에서는 근로 시간을 줄이려는 시도도 나타날 것이다. 하지만 궁극적으로는 꼭 필요한 의료보험을 받을 수 있기 때문에, 미국 근로자들의 생산성이 전체적으로 높아지게 될 것이다. 의료보험 혜택을 잃을까 두려워하지 않고 얼마든지 직장을 바꿀 수 있기 때문에 자신들의 능력을 더 잘 활용할 수 있다는 점은 두말할 나위도 없다. 전체적으로 볼 때, 의료 보험 개혁은 사회적 안정성 뿐만 아니라 경제적 성장에도 도움이 될 것이다.

불평등에 대한 이러한 새로운 관점이 궁극적으로 정치 담론까지 바꿀 수 있을까? 분명히 그렇게 될 것이다. 그 동안의 결과들을 보면, 부자들에게 유리하고 가난한 사람들에게 냉정한 제도는 경제성장을 이룰 수 있는 제도가 아니다. 반면에 우리 경제의 공정성을 더 높일 경우, 경제 성장도 달성할 수 있다. 이제는 부자들을 위한 '낙수효과론'을 버리고 저소득층을 위한 '분수효과론'을 강조할 때이다.

과잉보호는 이제 그만 (Relax, your kids will be fine)

　1693년 철학자 존 로크는 아이들에게 "건강을 해칠 수도 있는 과일"은 너무 많이 먹여서는 안 된다고 경고한 바 있다. 그런데 3백 여 년이 지난 오늘날에도 이처럼 자녀들의 양육에 있어서 잘못 알고 있는 사실들이 너무나 많다. 자녀들을 끊임없이 지켜보지 않으면 마치 죽기라도 할 것처럼 불안감을 가지고 있는 부모들이 많다. 미국에서는 법도 마찬가지로 과도한 경우들이 있다. 이번 달에 사우스 캐롤라이나에서는 데브라 하렐이라는 여성이 9살짜리 딸이 공원에서 혼자 놀도록 방치했다는 혐의로 감옥에 수감되는 사건이 발생했다. 당시 아이는 휴대폰을 가지고 있었고, 아무 일도 없었는데도, 잠깐이기는 하지만 사회복지 시설의 보호를 받았다.

　이와 같이 아이 엄마에 대한 과도한 처벌은 선진국들에서 자녀 양육에 대한 불안감이 얼마나 심각한지 잘 보여준다. 대부분의 객관적인 기준에서 보면, 오늘날의 부모들은 과거의 부모들보다 훨씬 더 아이의 양육에 신경을 쓰고 있다. 1965년 세탁기와 즉석 조리 식품들이 등장하면서, 미국의 부부들은 평균적으로 일주일에 8시간 정도 여유 시간이 생기게 되었다. 하지만 시간들이 오히려 그 시간보다 조금 더 넘는 시간들을 자녀 양육에 썼다. 오늘날의 아버지들은 과거 세대보다 훨씬 더 자녀 양육에 직접 참여하는 경향이 강하다. 그리고 직장 생활을 하는 엄마들 역시 1960년대의 전업 주부들보다도 더 많은 시간을 자녀들의 양육에 투자하고 있다. 이는 부모와 자녀 모두에게 도움이 된다. 자녀들에게는 원래 부모의 사랑과 관심이 필요한 법이다. 또 부모들도 설거지를 하는 것보다는 책을 읽어주거나 정원에서 아이들과 공놀이를 하는 것이 더 보람 있는 일이기 때문이다.

　이러한 상황에서는 소득 계층의 문제와 직결되는 두 가지가 있다. 한 가지는 하위 소득계층과 관련이 있다. 가난한 가정의 부모들이 과거의 가난한 부모들에 비해 자녀들과 보내는 시간이 더 많은 것은 사실이지만, 그래도 오늘날 부유한 가정의 부모들에 비해 자녀들과 같이 보내는 시간보다는 더 적고 아이들에게 만족할 만큼 뒷바라지를 질 하지 못하고 있다. 이러한 상황은 특히 발육에 아주 중요한 유아 시절에 두드러지게 나타난다. 이 문제에 있어서, 미국은 아직 미흡하다. 미국 정부는 학령기의 아동들에게는 많은 재원을 투입하고 있지만 출산 후 2,3년간의 유아 교육에 대한 투자는 다른 선진국들에 비해 훨씬 적은 편이다. 우리 이코노미스트가 과거에도 지적한 것처럼, 만약 미국이 어린 자녀가 있는 가난한 가정들에 대한 지원을 늘린다면, 장기적으로 큰 성과를 볼 수 있을 것이다.

　두 번째 문제는 사실 첫 번째 문제보다 입증이 쉽지는 않다. 그런데 이 문제는 경제적 단계의 또 다른 지점, 즉 부유한 계층에서 나타난다. 그리고 다른 일에는 매우 합리적이면서도 자녀 문제만은 그렇지 않은 이코노미스트의 독자들에게도 해당된다. 다시 말하여, 교육 수준이 높고, 부유한 부모들 중에서 자녀 양육에 대한 관심이 지나친 경우이다. 한 가지 이유는 안전 문제이다. 부모들은 자녀들에게 끊임없이 관심을 기울이지 않으면, 아이들이 목뼈라도 부러지거나 땅에 떨어진 컵케이크라도 집어 먹지 않을까 노심초사한다. 또 하나의 문제는 과도한 교육열이다. 부모들은 자녀들을 중국어 과외나 바이올린 교습, 펜싱 교습 등에 일주일에 여섯 번은 보내지 않으면 좋은 대학에 들어가지 못한다고 불안해 한다. 미국의 부촌 팔로 알토나 영국의 부촌인 첼시의 도로를 보면 아이들을 태우고 각종 과외 장소로 이동하는 미니 밴들을 쉽게 볼 수 있다.

　자녀들의 안전에 대한 두려움은 전혀 근거가 없다. 우리가 보통 범죄 드라마를 보면서 받는 인상과는 달리, 선진국의 아동들은 정말 의외라고 할 정도로 안전한 편이다. 물론 차 길을 건널 때 양쪽을 잘 살펴보기만 한다면 말이다. 1950년대는 보수적인 정치인들이 정말 좋았다고 이야기하는 소위 '황금기'였다. 심지어 그런 1950년대에도 아이들이 다섯 살이 되기 전에 사망할 확률이 지금보다 다섯 배는 높았다. 하지만 그 당시에는 자녀들이 마음껏 돌아다니는 것에 대해 크게 걱정하지 않았다. 그 당시에, 대부분의 미국 아이들은 걷거나 자전거를 타고 학교에 등교했다. 하지만 요즘에는 겨우 10% 정도에 불과하다. 부모들의 불안감 때문이다. 아이들은 원래 어느 정도는 나무 위에 올라가거나 기차를 타는 것처럼 위험해 보이는 일도 경험해 봐야. 스스로 어려움을 극복하는 법을 배우는 법이다. 그러다가 혹시라도 넘어져 무릎이 다치거나, 혼자 기차를 탔다가 가끔 이상한 사람을 만나는 일이 있더라도 말이다. 자유는 아이들에게 신나는 일이다. 게다가 아이들의 자율성을 키워줄 수도 있다.

또 하나 부모들이 흔히 가지고 있는 불안감은 자신의 자녀가 명문 대학에 들어가지 못할 지도 모른다는 불안감이다. 이러한 두려움은 나름대로 일리가 있기는 하다. 오늘날에는 공부를 잘하는 것이 과거 어느 때보다 중요해졌다. 하지만, 양육 방식은 일단 어느 수준을 넘어서고 나면, 많은 부모들이 생각하는 것만큼 아이들의 실력에 크게 영향을 미치지 않는다. 예를 들어, 미국의 미네소타와 스웨덴에서 한 연구 결과들을 보면, 일란성 쌍둥이들을 같은 가정에서 키우거나 서로 다른 가정 환경에서 떨어져서 키웠다고 해도 지적인 수준에서는 거의 같은 결과가 나타났다. 콜로라도에서 이루어진 한 연구에서는 지적으로 우수한 부모들에게 입양되어 자란 아이들이라고 해서 일반적인 지적 수준의 부모들에게 입양된 아이들에 비해 특별히 더 지적인 것은 아니라는 결과가 나왔다. 고용 시장에서도 양육방식보다는 선천적인 능력이 더 중요한 것으로 나타났다. 미국에 입양된 한국 아동들을 대상으로 한 대규모 연구 결과, 소득 수준이 가장 높은 가정에 입양된 아이들이라고 해서, 나중에 성인이 되었을 때 소득 수준이 가장 낮은 가정에 입양된 아이들보다 특별히 연봉 수준이 더 높지는 않은 것으로 나타났다.

그렇다고 해서, 부모들의 양육이 영향을 미치지 않는다는 말은 아니다. 자녀들을 입양하는 부모들은 대개 사전에 철저하게 검증된다. 그러므로 입양을 하는 부모들은 성품이 온화하고 능력이 있고 또 경제적으로 중산층이라는 성향을 가지고 있다. 하지만 쌍둥이들과 입양아들을 대상으로 한 연구들을 보면 가정이 화목하고 적절한 교육에 대한 자극만 주어진다면, 어느 아이든지 자신의 잠재력을 충분히 보여주는 것으로 나타났다. 이 말은 달리 표현하면, 경제적으로 여유 있는 부모들은 이제 한 시름 놓아도 된다는 말이다. 자녀들에 대한 관심을 줄이고, 자녀들이 가끔은 햇볕을 쬐면서 마음껏 뛰어 놀도록 하는 것이 좋다는 말이다. 부모도 남는 시간을 자신의 취미 활동에 쏟거나 아니면 잠이라도 더 자면 더 행복해 질 것이다. 그리고 부모의 스트레스가 줄어들면, 자녀들 역시 감사하게 생각할 것이다. 비록 여러분들이 과일과 채소는 어떻게 해서든 더 먹이려고 하겠지만 말이다.

아직도 "보스톤에서 대학을 다녔다"고 말하는 하버드 대학 출신들
(Harvard Alums Still Say They Went to College in Boston)

최근까지만 해도 나는 한 가지 순진한 생각을 가지고 있었다. 그것은 바로 출신 대학교에 대해 질문을 받았을 때, 설마 지금도 하버드 대학 졸업생들은 "보스톤에서 대학을 다녔다"고 대답을 하거나 예일 대학 출신들은 "뉴헤이븐에서 대학을 다녔다"거나 프린스턴 대학 출신들은 "뉴저지에서 대학을 다녔다"거나 스탠포드 대학 출신들은 "베이 지역에서 대학을 다녔다"는 식으로 이야기하지는 않을 것이라는 점이었다. 나는 으레 이런 식의 대화 방법이 이제는 민망하고 진부한 표현이 되어서 아무도 쓰지 않을 줄 알았던 것이다. 그런 표현은 소설 "위대한 개츠비"의 등장인물인 닉 캐러웨이처럼 소설 속의 주인공들이나 사용하는 표현으로 생각해 왔다. "위대한 개츠비"에서는 캐러웨이가 "1915년에 뉴 헤이븐에서 대학을 다녔다"고 말하는 대사가 나온다.

그래서 '슬레이트'에서 함께 일하고 있는 동료들의 의견을 물어보았다. 그 중 많은 사람들은 '유에스 뉴스 앤드 월드 리포트'에서 선정하는 일류대학들 출신이다. 나는 동료들 중에서 많은 사람들로부터 이와 같이 돌려서 말하는 대답을 들은 적이 있다는 이야기를 들었다. 그리고 더 충격적인 것은 그 중 몇몇은 자신들도 조금씩 다르기는 해도 그런 식으로 돌려서 이야기를 한 적이 있다는 것이었다.

아직도 이러한 표현을 사용하는 사람들이 있다는 사실을 알았으니, 예일, 프린스턴, 또는 하버드의 학생들과 졸업생들이나 그 밖의 누구든지 자신이 졸업한 명문 대학에 대해 해당 지역의 이름을 들어 돌려 이야기하고 싶은 분들이 있다면 이제는 제발 그런 표현은 그만 썼으면 좋겠다. 이제 정말 그러지 말자. 물론 여러분이 배려심이 있고 똑똑한 분이라는 것은 잘 안다. 하지만 이렇게 말하는 습관을 가지고 있으면 왠지 자기 우월감에 빠져 잘난척하는 재수없는 사람이라는 인상을 줄 수 있기 때문이다.

물론 대학 학창 시절과 그 지역에 대해 이야기하다가 대학 이름이 자연스럽게 나올 때도 있다. 예를 들어, "보스톤에서 대학을 다녔다. 그래서 레드 삭스팀을 응원하게 되었다"는 말은 할 수 있다. 이런 경우는 괜찮다. 이처럼, 당장에 이야기하고 있는 주제와는 상관이 없는 경우에는 여러분이 다닌 바로 그 유명한 명문 대학에 대해 구태여 이야기할 필요가 없기 때문이다. 하지만 "어느 대학을 나오셨나요?"와 같이 직접 대학 이름을 물었는데, 구태여 애매하게 돌려서 말할 필요는 없다.

일류 대학 출신들이 이러한 습관에 대해 나름대로 제시하는 가장 큰 이유는 자신들이 하버드나 예일 또는 프린스턴 대학에 다녔다고 하면, 어떤 사람들은 어색한 표정을 짓거나, 그 말을 한 사람을 불편하게 만들거나 심지어 적대적인 감정을 드러내는 사람들도 있다는 것이다. 사실, 하버드 출신들 중에는 자신이 하버드를 나왔다고 이야기하는 것에 "하버드 나왔다고 폭탄 선언을 했다(dropping the H-bomb)"고 말하는 경우도 자주 있다. 아마 영어의 수많은 표현 중에서 이 말처럼 참 듣기 민망할 정도로 잘난척하는 것 같은 느낌을 주는 표현도 없을 것이다. 하버드 출신이라는 점을 밝혔을 때 대화에서 가지는 감당하기 힘든 위력의 문제는 하버드 교지인 "하버드 크림슨"에서도 단골 메뉴로 계속해서 다루는 주제이다. 예를 들어서, 2002년에 MSNBC 방송의 아이린 카르몬 기자가 방송한 내용을 한 번 살펴보자. 당시 보도에는 흥미로운 부제목이 붙어 있었는데, "여자들을 유혹할 때 일류대학이 도움이 될까? 오히려 독이 될까?"였다 (사실 일류대학 출신이라는 것이 여성과 남성의 역학관계에서는 복잡미묘하게 작용하는 면이 있다) 마찬가지로, 프린스턴 대학 출신들은 "프린스턴 출신이라는 폭탄선언(P-bomb)"이라는 비슷한 표현을 쓴다. 이 표현이 암시하는 점은 프린스턴이라는 명칭에서 특히 "프린스"까지 세 글자가 나오는 순간, 가벼운 대화도 어색해져 버리고, 이제 막 시작되려는 인간 관계도 아예 무산시켜 버린다는 것이다.

물론 분명히 숫자는 많지 않겠지만 사람들 중에는 하버드, 예일, 프린스턴 대학 출신이라는 이야기를 들으면 불편한 반응을 보이는 사람들도 있을 것이다. 그런 사람들은 자기 자신에 대한 자신감이 없는 사람들이고, 매년 소위 일류대학 졸업자들 중에는 참 한심한 사람들도 많다는 점을 미처 생각하지 못하는 사람들이다. 하지만 명문대를 졸업한 사람이 상대방이 보일 반응까지 염려하면서, 자신의 학력에 대해 미리 애매하게 말할 필요는 없다. 하버드 출신이라는 이야기를 듣고 열등감을 보이는 사람들은 스스로 자신감이 없다는 점을 보여줄 뿐이다.

한편 만약 여러분이 하버드 출신이라는 것을 가급적이면 말하려고 하지 않는다면, 그 경우에는 당신 스스로 그 점을 의식하고 있다는 것을 보여준다. 그런 행동은 어떤 의미에서는 여러분 자신이 하버드 대학에 대한 과장된 사회적 통념을 그대로 인정한다는 의미이고 아이비 리그 대학이 우월하다는 생각을 그대로 따르는 셈이다. "하버드"라는 이름이 가지는 효과를 걱정한다는 사실 자체가 그 이름을 지나치게 의식한다는 점을 보여준다. 하버드도 단순히 한 대학교에 불과하고, 또 하버드에 입학하는 것은 하버드에 들어가지 못한 (혹은 아예 입학 신청을 하지 않은) 사람들과 비교해 볼 때, 실력보다는 신입생들의 사회경제적 배경이나 운이 더 크게 작용한 결과라는 점을 인정하면 "보스톤에 있는 대학"이라는 식으로 돌려서 말하는 표현이 정말 유치하다는 생각을 하게 될 것이다.

아니면 이렇게 생각해 보자. "보스톤에 있는 대학을 다녔다"라고 말하거나 "뉴 헤이븐에 있는 대학을 다녔다"라고 말하는 것은 일류 대학 출신들 사이에서만 서로 통하는 암호 같은 것이라고 말이다. 사람들 중에는 그러한 암호를 알아차리는 사람들이 있을 것이다. 그들은 아마 여러분처럼 일류 명문 대학을 다니고 엘리트 의식이 있는 사람들과 함께 많은 시간을 보낸 사람들일 것이다. 하지만 여러분과 대화를 나누는 상대가 그러한 암묵적인 힌트를 아는 사람이라면, 불쾌한 느낌을 가지게 될 것이다. 여러분의 출신 대학에 대해 솔직하게 이야기해도, 담담하게 받아들이지 못할 것이라는 인상을 준 것으로 생각할 것이기 때문이다. 그리고 만약 상대방이 그러한 힌트를 알아차리지 못한다면, 그 사람은 애매하게 이야기한 것에 대해 의아하게 생각할 것이다. 그리고 나서 나중에서야 여러분이 예일 대학교를 졸업했다는 것을 알게 된다면, 그 사람도 불쾌하게 생각할 것이다. 자기가 그러한 사실조차 담담하게 받아들이지 못할 정도로 자신감이 없다는 인상을 준 것으로 생각할 것이기 때문이다. 어느 쪽이든, 상대방은 여러분에 대해 거만하다는 인상을 가지게 될 것이다.

다양한 발전 모델 (The Structures of Growth)

우리는 대부분 어떤 일이든 발전하기 위하여 노력한다. 그리고 앞으로 얻게 될 성과들은 직선형, 즉 꾸준히 비례해서 나타날 것이라고 생각하는 경향이 있다. 다시 말하여, 어떤 분야든 실력을 갖추기 위하려 노력하면 할수록 꾸준히 좋아질 것이라는 관점이다.

하지만 캐나다의 작가 스콧 영이 최근 자신의 블로그에 올린 글에서도 지적한 것처럼, 대부분의 분야에서 나타나는 발전은 직선적인 형태를 보이지 않는다. 언어를 배울 때에나 달리기를 할 때와 마찬가지로, 때로는 처음에는 급격히 상승하다 후반부에는 완만하게 상승하는 로그함수적 곡선의 형태로 발전하기도 한다. 즉 처음에 시작할 때에는 성과가 빨리 나타나지만, 점차 실력이 늘다 보면, 더 개선하는 것은 점점 힘들어진다.

스콧 영은 블로그에서 로그함수적 발전에 해당하는 활동을 하려면 마음 가짐이 달라야 한다고 밝혔다. 초기에 발전 속도가 빠른 단계에서는 모든 것이 순조롭게 이루어진다. 하지만, 이 때에 꾸준히 노력하는 습관을 유지하도록 애써야 한다. 그렇지 않으면 다시 퇴보하게 된다. 그리고 나서 발전 속도가 느린 정체기가 찾아 오면 그 동안의 습관들을 깨야 한다. 단순히 잘하는 차원을 넘어서 아주 탁월한 경지에 이르기 위해서는, 그 동안 굳어 있고, 자신의 발전을 가로막는 습관들을 깨야 한다.

예를 들어, 타이거 우즈가 골프 대회에 처음 출전했을 때를 생각해 보자. 우즈는 너무나 싱겁게 우승을 했지만, 강도 높은 연습을 계속 유지해야 했다. 하지만 일단 정체기에 도달하게 되면, 최고의 경지에 도달하기 위하여 자신의 스윙을 완전히 바꾸어야 했다.

다른 분야의 경우, 발전 속도가 지수함수적으로, 즉 처음에는 완만하다가 점점 빨라지는 경우가 있다. 이러한 활동들의 경우, 기본기를 다지는 것에만 몇 주나 혹은 심지어 몇 년의 시간이 걸리는데, 그래도 별 성과를 느끼기 힘든 경우가 있다. 하지만, 약 1만 시간의 오랜 노력을 들이고 나면, 어느 날 갑자기 그 일이 편하게 느껴지고 실력도 기하급수적으로 늘게 된다.

학문적인 지식을 습득하는 과정은 이와 같은 영역에 속한다. 대학원에서 여러 해에 걸쳐 기본적인 내용을 철저하게 익혀야 그 분야의 구조들을 완전히 체득하게 되고 또 그 개념들을 창의적으로 활용할 수 있게 된다. 아이스 하키는 이러한 활동에 해당된다. (사실 스케이트를 능숙하게 타는 것만 해도 몇 년 동안의 시간이 걸린다)

이와 같이 후반부에 가속도가 붙는 활동들의 경우, 초기 단계에서 포기하는 경우가 많다. 그러므로 처음에 원하는 성과를 얻지 못해도 미련스러울 정도의 노력이 필요하다. 하지만 나중에 발전 속도에 가속도가 붙는 단계에 이르면, 유연한 태도를 가져야 그 동안 공들여서 배운 능력이 창의적으로 꽃을 피우게 된다. 화가 고흐의 경우에도 몇 년 동안 꾸준히 그림의 기초를 배웠다. 하지만 그림에 대한 기본기를 닦은 다음에는 자신의 상상력을 마음껏 발휘하여 창작 활동을 했다.

그 밖에 또 다른 발전 모델도 있다. 일부 분야의 경우, 계단식으로 실력이 늘어난다. 실력이 늘다가 정체기가 찾아 오기도 하지만 그 뒤에 계단을 올라가는 것처럼 한 단계 도약이 나타나고 다시 또 정체기와 도약이 반복된다. 다른 분야의 경우에는, 마치 해변가에 파도가 계속 치면서, 파도와 함께 침전물이 조금씩 쌓이는 형태로 나타난다. 처음 일부 자료들을 공부하면, 마치 파도가 지나간 후처럼 지식의 침전물들이 남는다. 그 후 같은 내용을 반복해서 볼 때마다, 더 많은 파도에 의해 침전물이 쌓이는 것처럼 지식들이 쌓이게 된다.

하지만 다른 분야들은 V자형으로 나타난다. 이 경우에는, 일단 밑 바닥까지 내려가고 나서야 비로소 발전할 수 있다. 다른 나라로 이민 가는 경우가 이런 경우에 해당한다. 이민을 가면, 일단 아주 단순한 것부터 시작하여 그 사회에 대해 배워야 비로소 그 사회에서 성공할 수 있다. 도덕적인 성장도 이와 비슷한 양상을 보인다. 인생의 실패들을 극복하기 위해서는 일단 밑바닥까지 내려가서 자신의 실패를 곰곰이 따져 봐야 한다. 우선은 치욕의 쓴 맛을 봐야 다시 발전하기 위한 노력을 하겠다는 열망을 가지게 된다.

이와 같이 다양한 발전 모델들에 대해 생각해 보면 진정으로 성공적인 사람들은 자신들의 사고 방식을 완전히 정반대로 뒤집어 볼 수 있는 능력이 있다는 점을 다시 깨닫게 된다. 많은 분야에서 처음에는 원칙을 고수하고 절제하는 것이 처음에는 효과가 있다. 하지만 점차 실력이 늘게 되면, 유연하고 즐겁게 하는 것이 더 효과적이다. 정치에 입문한 경우, 선거를 치르고 당선된 후에는 '선거 유세'분위기에서 벗어나서 '직무 수행'의 분위기로 빨리 전환해야 한다. '선거유세' 단계에서는 즉각적인 만족감을 느낄 수 있는 반면, '직무수행' 단계에서는 발전 속도가 처음에는 완만하다. 그래서 이 단계에서는 경험과 인내심, 그리고 오랜 시간 갈고 닦은 경륜이 필요하다.

이렇게 생각해 보면, 어떤 능력을 갖추는 과정은 그 자체가 인성을 기르는 활동이라는 것을 알 수 있다. 무엇인가를 배우려면 단지 할 일만 안다고 되는 것이 아니라, 자연스럽게 나타나는 자신의 욕구를 극복할 수 있도록 스스로를 단련시켜야 하기 때문이다. 로그함수적인 발전의 경우, 초기에 빠르게 발전하는 단계에서는 스스로의 성취감에 도취하여 안주하려는 욕구와 싸워야 한다. 그 후의 단계에서, 많은 사람들이 여러분을 칭찬할 때에는 자기 스스로 도취되지 않도록 경계해야 한다.

미국 사회는 즉각적으로 성과가 나타나는 활동들을 높이 평가하는 경향이 뚜렷하다. 그런 활동들의 예로는 스포츠와 연예계에서 유명 스타가 되는 경우들이 있다. 반면에 정치인이나 특정 분야의 장인이 되는 것처럼 오랜 시간이 걸리는 일들은 제대로 평가해 주지 않는다. 어린이들의 구기 종목 선택에서도 비슷한 경향이 나타난다. 그래서 야구와 같이 기본기가 탄탄해야 하는 스포츠보다 축구처럼 당장 성과가 나타나는 쪽으로 선호도가 바뀌고 있다.

마지막으로, 이와 같이 발전 모델에 초점을 맞추어 생각하다 보면, 자기 자신으로부터 눈을 돌릴 수가 있다. 중요한 점은 여러분이 날 때부터 어떤 특성들을 가졌는가가 아니다. 아래와 같이 스스로 자문해 보아야 할 질문들을 생각해 보자. "내가 일하고 있는 분야는 어떤 발전 모델이 적용되는가? 나는 발전 곡선에서 어느 지점에 있는가? 나는 해당 분야의 모델로부터 어떤 영향을 받고 있는가?"

이러한 질문들에 대한 핵심적인 대답은 거울을 들여다 볼 때 나오는 것이 아니다. 그 해답들은 뒤로 물러나서 거리감을 두고 전체를 조망해 볼 때 나타난다. 그러한 태도가 어느 경우이든 더 바람직하고 건강한 시각이다.

일반영어 11 다이어트의 유혹과 거짓말 (Diet Lures and Diet Lies)

우리 집도 여느 집과 마찬가지이다. 다른 사람들에게 차마 보여줄 수 없는 물건들로 가득 차 있다. 민망한 내용의 책들에다 촌스러운 옷까지. 게다가 향초는 얼마나 많은지, 우리 집에 와 본 사람은 내가 아주 고약한 냄새가 날만한 모종의 일을 꾸미는 것으로 생각할지도 모른다.

하지만 뭐니뭐니해도 가장 민망한 것은 주방 찬장 안 타바스코 소스 병 옆에 있다. 흰 색 바탕에 초록색으로 된 약병이다. 마케팅 전문 용어로 소위 "보충제"라고 하는 약이다. 먹기만 하면 다른 노력 없이도 날씬한 몸매를 유지할 수 있다고 하는 바로 그 약이다.

물론 나도 그 말을 믿을 정도로 순진하지는 않다. 다들 마찬가지일 것이다.

약병에는 가르시아 캄보지아(Garcinia Cambogia)라고 적혀있다. 캡슐 형태의 알약에는 열대 과일인 가르시아 캄보지아에서 추출한 분말 가루가 포함되어 있다. 약병에는 마치 신비한 효능이 있는 것처럼 주장하는 내용이 적혀 있다. 지방이 체내에 흡수되는 것을 막는다는 것이다. 아니면 최소한 그런 기능을 할 가능성이 있다는 것이다. 또 식욕을 억제한다고 한다. 아니, 극히 소수이긴 하지만 그런 효과를 봤다고 하는 사람들도 있다. 또 스트레스로 인해 폭식하는 것을 조절할 수 있다고 주장하기도 한다. 하지만 입증된 이론은 아니다.

나는 아마 18개월 전에 인터넷에서 그러한 내용을 처음 본 것 같다. 그리고 그 내용에는 TV에 자주 출연하는 오즈 박사의 추천서 비슷한 내용이 함께 적혀 있었다. 그래서 나도 생각해 봤다. '혹시 또 모르잖아. 어차피 손해 볼 것 없지.' 그리고 나서 몇 분 후 나도 모르게 신용카드 번호를 키보드로 입력하고 "주문" 버튼을 눌러 버렸다. 이런 식으로, 매 년 말도 안 되는 내용에 속아 넘어 가는 수 많은 사람들의 대열에 나도 동참하게 된 것이다. 사실, 이번이 처음은 아니다.

오늘날 패스트 푸드, 각종 스낵 푸드, 그리고 탄산 음료의 문제점을 파헤치는 내용이 엄청나게 많다. 관련 책들이 쏟아져 나오는가 하면, 문제점을 지적하는 다큐멘터리 프로그램도 많다. 바람직한 일이다. 좋은 방향이다.

하지만 한 가지 주의할 점이 있다. 대대적인 광고공세를 펼치며 우리의 비만에 일조하고 있는 패스트푸드에 대해 경각심이 높아지는 것은 좋다. 하지만 그 문제에 신경 쓰느라, 역시 대대적인 광고 공세를 펼치는 각종 비만 치료제나 다이어트 제품 그리고 다이어트 프로그램들에 대해서 꾸준히 문제점을 지적하는 것을 소홀히 해서는 안 된다는 사실이다. 이들 제품은 온갖 효능을 과장하고 또 소비자들은 많은 돈을 쏟아 붓고 있지만, 실제로는 비만 해결에 전혀 도움이 되지 않는다. 이러한 다이어트 제품들의 문제점도 소홀히 하지 말아야 한다.

그런데 이러한 다이어트 제품들은 조만간 사라질 조짐이 보이지 않는다. 더 심각한 문제는 이러한 제품들이 성행하는 이유는 오늘날 우리의 다이어트 문화 때문이기도 하고 또 그로 인해 계속 유지되기도 한다는 점이다. 오늘날 우리 사회에는 칼로리 섭취량에 맞추어 소모량을 늘려야 비만을 피할 수 있다는 기본적인 원칙은 소홀히 하고, 다이어트에 대한 미시적인 이론들이나 비만의 원인을 복잡한 원인에서 찾으려는 지엽적인 과학적 주장들로 넘쳐나고 있다.

물론 이러한 원칙은 지나치게 단순화한다는 문제점은 있다. 또 항상 이러한 원칙에는 여러 가지 예외적인 사항들이 있다는 점에 대해서도 매번 새롭게 느끼게 된다. 그리고 칼로리는 같다고 해도 음식에 따라 공복감의 느낌이 다르고 그래서 계속 먹고 싶은 욕구를 더 느끼는 경우가 있다는 점도 알게 된다.

하지만, 체중 감량 문제에 가장 인정받고 있는 의사들의 이야기를 들어보면, 대개는 칼로리에 대한 기본적인 원칙이 과거와 마찬가지로 지금도 가장 효과적이라고 한다. 그리고 아주 공들여서 식단을 짜고 각종 다이어트 방법을 동원하는 것이 유행하고 있지만, 그러다 보면 오히려 기본적인 다이어트의 원칙을 소홀히 하게 되는데, 그래서 심각한 문제라고 한다. 왜냐하면, 기본적인 본성과 근본적인 생물학적 사실을 어떤 식으로든 이용하거나 속이거나 혹은 초월할 수 있다는 생각을 가지도록 조장할 수 있기 때문이다.

콜럼비아 대학교 부속 병원의 비만 문제 전문가인 루돌프 라이벨 박사는 필자와의 대화에서 "다이어트의 경우에는 열역학의 일반법칙들이 적용되는 셈"이라고 말했다. 그는 이어서 "만약 칼로리는 똑 같다는 전제 하에, 햄버거를 먹는 경우에 비해 오로지 수박으로만 식단을 짜서 먹는다고 가정하면, 수박 다이어트가 더 효과가 있을까? 그런 식의 주장은 겉으로만 보면 일리가 있어서 보이지만 실제로는 그렇지 않다. 다이어트의 문제는 근거 없는 상상력의 관점이 아니라 화학과 물리학의 과학적 관점에서 보아야 한다"고 말했다.

하지만 우리는 온갖 상상력을 발휘하고 있다. 우리는 수많은 가능성들 중에서 우리 입맛에 맞는 이론만 용케 골라내어, 다른 방법보다 특히 효과가 있는 것처럼 부각시킨다. 다이어트를 하기 위하여, 글루틴 성분이 들어있는 밀가루 음식을 아예 먹지 않는 사람이 있는가 하면, 탄수화물이 많은 전분을 전혀 섭취하지 않는 사람들도 있다. 또 돈이 많아 넉넉하게 살면서도 고대 원시인들의 식단을 모방한 다이어트를 하는 사람들도 있다. 모두 티모시 페리스라는 소위 "웰빙 전문가"의 주장을 충실히 따르는 사람들이다. 이들은 심지어 자신들의 대변 무게까지 측정할 정도라고 한다.

그 동안 교육 수준이 높아지고 다이어트에 대한 이해가 늘어나기는 했지만, 그렇다고 이러한 유행들이 사라지지는 않고 있다. 앞으로도 수시로 유행하는 다이어트를 내 놓으면 또 거기에 현혹되는 사람들이 있을 것이고, 또 거금을 쏟아 붓게 될 것이다.

이번에는 흉부외과 전문의로 유명한 닥터 오즈의 경우를 살펴보자. 그는 병원에 있는 시간보다 TV에 출연하는 시간이 더 많은 사람이다. TV에서 오즈 박사가 다른 어느 주제보다 많이 다루는 내용이 바로 다이어트인데, (자기 말에 의하면) 아주 새로운 방법으로 살을 뺄 수 있다는 것이다. 그는 "마술"이나 "기적" 또는 "혁명적"이라는 표현들을 스스럼없이 사용하면서, 여성의 임신기간에만 분비되는 HCG호르몬 주사, 그린 커피빈 보충제, 라즈베리 키톤 보충제 등을 소개하거나 마치 효과가 아주 높은 것처럼 추천했다. 그는 한 방송에서는 시청자들에게 "지금 제가 소개하는 방법은 지방이 스스로 연소하여 몸에서 배출시킬 수 있는 방법"이라고 말하기도 했다.

라이벨 교수는 이러한 주장들은 모두 과학적으로 논리가 맞지 않는다고 주장한다. "그것은 마치 미 항공우주국(NASA)에 가서 별자리 표를 보면서 유로파라는 목성의 네 번째 위성에 갈 수 있는 방법을 찾아보는 것이나 다름없다. 그 정도로 터무니없다"라고 말했다.

오즈 박사의 웹사이트에는 "체중감량 정보(Weight Loss Directory)"라는 메뉴가 있는데 그 밑에는 "복부비만 해결 단기 완성(Rapid Belly Melt)"이나 "신진대사 촉진법(Mega Metabolism Boosters)" 등의 세부 항목들을 볼 수 있다. 게다가 카시니아 캄보지아의 효능에 대해 지겨울 정도로 칭찬하고 있다.

그러면 누구나 솔깃하지 않을 수 없다. 그러다 보면 그 말을 그대로 믿는 사람도 있다. 나도 그랬다. 대학 다닐 때 소위 "탄수화물 차단제"라는 약을 먹고도 아무 효과가 없었고 수 십 년 동안 유행한다는 다이어트는 다 해 보고 나서 결국 다이어트에 가장 효과적인 방법은 결국 단 한 가지, 즉 음식 섭취량을 줄이고 규칙적인 운동을 하는 것 뿐이라는 결론을 내리고도 말이다.

카시니아 캄보지아 약병은 아직도 내 주방 찬장 안에 있다. 아직 반쯤 남아 있기 때문이다. 그 동안 매일 두 알씩 일주일 동안 먹어도 아무 효과가 없었다는 점을 알고서야 정신을 차렸다. 만약 앞으로도 계속 과장광고에 현혹되지 않는다면, 그 약병을 버릴 수 있지 않을까.

일반영어 12 훌륭한 품성 (The Mental Virtues)

　우리는 누구나 군인에게 필요한 자질은 잘 알고 있다. 영화에서 볼 수 있는 전쟁 영웅들은 용감하고 충성스러우며 극한 상황에서도 침착한 모습을 잃지 않는다. 하지만 하루 종일 컴퓨터 앞에 앉아서 일하는 직장인들의 경우는 어떨까? 혼자서 업무를 보거나 컴퓨터를 가지고 일하는, 오늘날 정보화 시대의 직장인들도 생활 속에서 자신의 인격을 드러내고 또 인격을 키울 수 있을까?
　물론 가능하다. 혼자서 사무실에 일하는 경우에도 누구나 생각은 한다. 수많은 정보의 홍수 속에서 제대로 판단하는 것은 총탄이 빗발처럼 쏟아지는 전장에서 싸우는 것과는 전혀 다른 차원의 인격적 도전인 것이 사실이다. 하지만 그러한 상황에서도 자신의 인격이 고스란히 드러날 수 밖에 없다.
　베일러 대학의 로버트 로버츠와 위튼 대학의 제이 우드는 2007년에 공저로 출판한 "지적인 덕목(Intellectual Virtues)"이라는 제목의 책에서 일부 지적인 덕목들을 추려서 보여주었다. 각각의 덕목에 대해 여러분도 스스로 자신이 얼마나 갖추고 있는지 평가 해 보기 바란다.
　첫째, 탐구욕이다. 선천적이든 후천적이든, 다른 사람들보다 유독 호기심이 많은 사람들이 있다.
　둘째, 용기이다. 지적인 용기가 분명하게 드러나는 경우는 사람들이 싫어하는 것을 알면서도 자신의 소신을 가지는 용기이다. 하지만 이보다 잘 드러나지는 않지만, 성급한 결론을 내릴 때 얼마나 위험할 수 있는지에 대해 아는 것도 용기이다. 경솔한 사람은 몇 가지 단편적인 정보들을 취합해서 논리적인 비약을 통해 아주 터무니없는 음모론을 주장하기도 한다. 반면에, 완벽주의자는 자신의 생각이 틀릴까 두려워서, 정말 확신을 하는 경우 이외에는 자기 생각을 선뜻 표현하려고 하지 않는다. 로버츠와 우드의 주장에 따르면, 지적인 용기는 어떤 경우에 과감해야 하는지 아니면 어떤 경우에 신중해야 하는지 알고 있고, 또 스스로 결정하는 것이다. 철학자 토마스 쿤은 과학자들이 종종 자신들이 가지고 있는 기존의 패러다임과 맞지 않는 사실들은 일단 무시하는 경향이 있다는 점을 지적한다. 하지만 지적으로 용기 있는 사람은 웬만해서는 직시하기 힘든 문제를 있는 그대로 보려고 노력한다.
　셋째, 소신이다. 남들이 조금이라도 반대한다고 해서 자신의 신념을 포기해서는 안된다. 반면에, 자신의 생각이 틀렸다는 객관적인 증거들이 분명히 있음에도 불구하고 자신의 생각을 무조건 고수해서도 안된다. 이와 같이 무소신과 고집스러움 사이의 중용을 지키는 것이 바로 소신있는 신념이다. 소신있는 사람은 확고한 근거를 가지고 타당한 세계관을 가지고 있으면서도, 새로운 정보에 대해 흔쾌하게 수용한다. 이러한 사람은 자신의 신념이 가지고 있는 강점과 증거의 강점을 서로 잘 접목시킬 수 있는 사람이다. 소신은 정신적으로 유연해야 나타낼 수 있는 자질이다.
　넷째, 겸손이다. 자신이 지위를 얻고 싶은 욕구가 있다고 해서 정확성을 희생시키지 않으려는 태도를 말한다. 겸손한 사람은 자신의 허영심과 우쭐한 생각을 억누르려고 애쓴다. 글을 써도 자기 자신이 똑똑한 것처럼 보이려는 사람들과는 다르게 쓴다. 그러한 사람은 절대 자신을 대단하다고 생각하지 않는다. 연구를 하는 사람 중에서도 겸손한 사람은 자신의 연구 주제에 대해 마치 다 터득한 것처럼 오만한 태도를 보이지 않는다. 겸손한 사람은 인생의 어떠한 단계에서든 다른 사람으로부터 배우는 것에 대해 마음을 열고 있는 사람이다.
　다섯째, 자신의 중심을 잡아야 한다. 선생님이 한 이야기라고 해서 또 작가가 쓴 글이라고 해서 무조건 받아들여서는 안 된다. 반면에 자신의 일에 일가견이 있는 사람이 방향을 제시해주는 것을 무조건 거부하는 것도 문제가 있다. 자기 중심은 권위에 승복해야 할 때와 그렇지 않을 때, 자신이 존경하는 사람을 따라야 할 때와 그렇지 않을 때, 그리고 전통을 고수해야 할 때와 그렇지 않을 때를 판단할 때 생긴다.
　마지막으로, 아량이다. 아량은 자신이 아는 것을 남에게도 기꺼이 알려주고, 좋은 결과가 있을 때에는 다른 사람에게 그 공을 넘겨 주려는 태도에서 시작된다. 하지만, 다른 사람들이 원하는 대로 그들의 이야기를 들어주고, 다른 사람의 장점을 찾으려고 노력하며, 다른 사람들이 실수를 하더라도 의기양양하게 그

잘못을 비판하지 않으려는 노력도 역시 아량에 해당한다.

사람은 누구나 이러한 덕목 중 일부 덕목에서는 남들보다 나은 반면에 일부 덕목에서는 다른 사람들보다 부족한 면이 있을 것이다. 하지만 나는 최근 의사 결정에 대한 주류 언론의 자료들이 우리의 정신에 대해 마치 우리 몸과 분리된 기관 취급을 하고 마치 컴퓨터처럼 프로그래밍을 할 수 있는 것으로 생각을 하는 것을 보고 깜짝 놀랐다.

사실, 인간의 정신은 인간의 본성에서 매우 중요한 부분이다. 그리고 제대로 사고한다는 것은 인간의 허영심, 게으름, 확실성에 대한 욕망, 고통스러운 진실을 회피하고 싶은 욕구 등 인간의 원래 본성을 거스르려는 노력이다. 올바른 생각을 한다는 것은 단순히 올바른 생각을 할 수 있는 방법을 받아들인다는 의미만은 아니다. 오히려 도덕적인 행동이며 올바른 품성이 필요한 행동이다. 다시 말하여, 우리가 추구하는 고귀한 이상을 위하여 그보다 낮은 단계의 본성에 저항하는 행동이다.

사상가인 몽테뉴는 한 때 이런 글을 남겼다. "우리는 다른 사람의 지식을 가지고 자신의 지식을 늘릴 수 있다. 하지만 다른 사람의 지혜를 들었다고 우리가 지혜를 가지게 되는 것은 아니다." 그 이유는 지혜는 단순히 지식을 모아 놓은 것이 아니기 때문이다. 지혜란 자신의 한계에 대처하는 방법을 안다는 도덕적 차원의 의미를 말한다. 워렌 버핏은 자신의 특기인 투자 분야에서 비슷한 이야기를 한 적이 있다. "투자는 지능지수가 160이라고 해서 지능지수가 130인 사람에게 이기는 게임이 아니다. 일단 보통 사람의 지능만 갖추고 있으면, 다른 사람들을 곤경으로 몰아가는 충동에 대해 자제력을 가지는 것이 가장 필요하다."

오늘날 우리의 일상 생활에서도 자신의 인격을 시험할 수 있는 기회들이 아주 많다. 그러므로 사무실에서 혼자 앉아 일하면서도 얼마든지 자신의 인격을 발휘할 수 있다. 단지 영화의 소재로 맞지 않을 뿐이다.

일반영어 13 위기로 치닫고 있는 미국의 정치 (Is American democracy headed to extinction?)

정부가 제 기능을 발휘하지 못할 때, 그 이면에는 민주주의 자체가 쇠락하고 있는 것일까?

고대 아테네의 경우 민주주의가 쇠락하여 와해되기까지 고작 250 년 밖에 걸리지 않았다. 아테네에는 민중들이 직접 스스로를 통치하는 인류 역사상 전혀 새로운 정부의 형태가 만들어졌다. 그러한 정치구조는 매우 효과적이라는 것이 입증되었다. 아테네인들은 물질적 부와 국력을 키울 수 있었으며, 페르시아의 침공을 물리칠 수 있었다. 그리고 자신들이 알고 있던 주변의 세계에서는 최강의 국가로 자리매김했으며, 건축, 철학 및 예술 분야에서 오늘날까지도 눈부신 업적을 남겼다. 하지만 각종 특권과 부정부패가 만연하고 국정 운영의 문제점이 뿌리를 내리게 되면서, 아테네의 찬란한 불꽃도 꺼져 버렸다.

그로부터 2천 여 년이 지난 뒤, 민주주의는 미국 헌법에서 다시 그 모습을 찾아 볼 수 있게 되었다. 이번에는 직접 민주주의가 아닌 대의민주주의의 형태였다. 아테네에 이어 이번에도 민중들의 합의를 통한 정부 형태가 합리적이라는 점이 입증되었다. 미국은 경제, 문화 및 군사적인 측면에서 전세계에서 가장 부강한 나라가 되었다. 유럽에서는 민주주의 체제가 권위주의적인 왕정체제와 극우 파시스트나 공산당의 독재체제를 극복하고 대세를 이루었다. 최근 수 십 여 년간, 민주주의가 확산되면서 그 동안 남아 있던 일부 권위주의 체제는 이제 소수로 전락하게 되었다.

미국에서 시작된 두 번째 민주주의의 실험이 시작 된지도 이제 250년이 다가오고 있다. 미국식 민주주의는 아테네의 첫 번째 민주주의만큼 성공적이었다. 하지만 아테네의 역사를 통해 얻을 수 있는 교훈은 지금 성공하고 있다고 해서 영원히 성공하는 것은 아니라는 점이다. 민주주의는 거저 얻어지는 것이 아니다. 민주주의는 국민들의 의지를 모아 만들어 가야 하는 정부 형태이다. 그리고 지속적인 노력이 없으면 쇠퇴할 수 밖에 없다. 오늘날 미국과 영국의 경우, 리더십을 통해 민주주의를 잘 키워야 함에도 불구하고 민주주의는 와해되고 있다. 만약 민주주의의 모범 국가라고 할 수 있는 이들 나라에서조차 민주주의 불꽃이 꺼져 버린다면, 다른 나라에서도 민주주의가 지속될 것이라는 기대감을 가지기 힘들 것이다.

단순히 정부가 민주적이라는 것만으로는 부족하다. 정부는 민주주의를 실질적으로 실천해야 한다. 그렇지 않으면, 민주주의는 쇠락을 면할 수 없다. 영국 정부의 경우, 무능이 점점 심해지고 있다. 영국의 헌법학자인 앤소니 킹(Anthony King)은 영국의 정부에 대해 "정치적 안정"이 30년도 채 안 되는 짧은 기간에 "정치적 혼란"으로 퇴보했다고 밝혔다. 10년간에 걸친 신노동당(New Labor)의 통치 기간 동안에 그러한 논리가 시험대에 올랐고, 결국은 그의 주장이 사실이라는 점이 확인되었다. 1997년 영국에서는 총선 승리를 통해 신노동당 정부가 새롭게 들어섰다. 토니 블레어 정부는 대처 총리 시절의 경제적 불평등의 대세를 바꾸어 달라는 민심의 바탕 위에 정치적 의지를 가지고 있었다. 당시 정부는 민주 정부에서 기대할 수 있는 모든 의회권력을 확보했을 뿐만 아니라, 10년 동안 꾸준히 이어진 경제 성장의 혜택을 톡톡히 보고 있었다. 하지만 막강한 권력을 확보했음에도 불구하고 미흡한 협치구조 때문에 결국은 실패하고 말았다. 이와 같이 허약한 협치구조는 애초에 의도했던 어떠한 성과도 보이지 못했고, 영국의 경제적 불평등은 그 전의 정권보다 오히려 더 악화되었다.

그 다음에 들어선 중도 우파 연립 내각 역시 마찬가지로 무능하다는 점을 입증했다. 새로 들어선 정부는 전세계 경제 위기의 타격을 입은 영국 경제를 살려야 한다는 임무를 가지고 있었다. 하지만 독점적인 금융 서비스를 유지하고, 서민들을 희생하는 대신 부자들에게 유리한 긴축 정책을 펼치는 등, 경제 위기의 원인들에 대해 무능력하게 대응하는 모습을 보였다. 이번에도 다시 한 번 영국 정부는 비록 악의적인 의도가 있던 것은 아니었지만 무능한 모습을 보였다. 이들 두 정부들은 경제적 부의 편중 현상을 제대로 해결하지 못했고, 그 결과 이제 정치적으로 통제할 수 없는 지경까지 이르렀다.

한편, 미국의 민주주의는 겉으로 보기보다 훨씬 더 심각한 문제를 가지고 있다. 미국 정부의 3부, 즉 입법부, 행정부, 사법부는 견제와 균형의 원리를 통해 작동하도록 되어 있다. 하지만 견제가 오히려 정치의 발목을 잡게 되었다. 그리고 미국은 자신에게 필요한 협치구조를 확보하지 못하고 있다. 바로 이 지점에서 불평등과 정부의 무능이 적나라하게 드러나고 있다. 현재 미국의 정치 권력은 헌법 질서에 따른 정치권보다는 오히려 각종 선거후원단체, 연구집단, 미디어 및 로비 단체들과 같은 이해집단들에게 넘어간 상태이다.

오늘날과 같이 막대한 비용이 드는 정치 상황에서, 선거에 출마하는 후보들은 일상적으로 계속되는 선거 운동 자금을 확보하기 위해 후원자들에 의존할 수 밖에 없다. 원래 시장의 영역에 있어야 하는 돈이, 금전적인 것과는 전혀 상관이 없어야 하는 정치로 흘러 들어가도록 방치해 두면, 결국 돈줄을 쥐고 있는 사람들이 어떤 후보가 승리하게 될 것인지 결국 자신들이 후원하려는 후보가 될 것이다 —그리고 그들이 당선되고 나서 내릴 의사결정에 영향을 미칠 수 있는 힘을 가지게 된다. 돈 많은 지지자들은 자신들이 정치에 영향력을 행사하는 데에 있어서 두 번의 기회를 가질 수 있다. 한 가지는 유권자로서의 기회이고 또 한 가지는 후원자로서의 기회이다. 그렇지 못한 일반인들은 유권자로서의 기회 밖에 없다. 하지만, 가진 자들의 정치적 영향력이 커지면서, 유권자의 역할은 결국 그 가치가 떨어지게 만든다. 흔히 선거에 출마한 후보들이 돈을 쫓는다고 생각하는데, 그것은 오해이다. 오히려 돈이 후보들을 쫓는다고 보는 것이 맞다.

아테네에서는 부자들이 더 많은 재산을 가지게 되고, 공정한 규칙에 맞추어 경쟁하는 것을 거부하고 확립된 정부 체제를 약화시키면서 민주주의가 와해되기 시작했다. 현재 미국과 영국이 바로 그 지점에 도달하고 있다.

지금으로부터 거의 한 세기 전, 지금 우리가 겪고 있는 위기와는 차원이 다른 자본주의 민주주의의 위기를 겪고 있던 시절, 미국 대법원의 루이스 브란데이스(Louis Brandeis) 판사는 다음과 같은 경고를 남겼다. "우리는 민주주의냐 아니면 일부 극소수에게 부가 편중되는 사회냐 사이에서 선택할 수 있다. 하지만 그 두 가지 모두 가질 수는 없다." 미국의 민주주의가 그 당시 어려움을 극복할 수 있었던 것은 두 가지 이유가 있었다. 첫째, 민주주의를 파괴하는 것은 단순히 불평등 자체만이 아니라, 그 후에 불평등과 위법한 행동들이 결합되어 나타난 결과라는 점이다. 더군다나, 당시에는 민주주의가 위기로부터 교훈을 배울 수 있었다. 루즈벨트 대통령의 뉴딜(New Deal) 정책은 경제적인 '약육강식'의 무자비한 투쟁을 완화시키는 역할을 했다. 기본적으로는 1933년에 통과시킨 은행법이 주요 수단이었다. 그 결과, 일반 서민들도 새롭게 사회보장제도의 혜택을 누릴 수 있었다.

아테네의 사례에서 얻을 수 있는 교훈은 성공을 하면 현실에 안주하기 쉽다는 사실이다. 대부분의 사람들은, 특히 특권을 가지고 있는 사람들은 타인에 대한 관심을 버리게 되고 민주주의를 소홀히 하게 된다. 전세계 금융 위기가 시작되고 나서 6년이 흐른 지금, 모범적인 민주주의 국가들에서 나타나는 징후들을 보아도, 특권을 누리고 있는 사람들이 타인들을 배려하지 않고, 정치권 역시 과거의 교훈으로부터 배우지 못하고 있다는 점을 알 수 있다. 글로벌 금융 위기는 미국과 영국에서 전혀 통제를 받지 않던 금융 산업에서부터 시작되었음에도 불구하고 금융 산업을 규제해야 한다는 목소리가 제대로 제기되지 못했다. 경제적 불평들은 계속해서 정치적 불평등으로 이어졌으며, 민주 정부는 이제 해결할 수 있는 힘과 능력을 모두 상실하고 있다. 브란데이스 판사의 경고는 결국 틀린 것이 아니었다. 오히려 그는 시대를 앞선 사람이었던 것이다.

일반영어 14. 낯선 이에게 말 걸기 (Hello, Stranger)

지하철이나 버스를 타 본 사람들은 아마 나름대로의 불문율을 잘 알고 있을 것이다. 예를 들어, 다른 승객과 가능하면 눈길을 마주 치지 않고, 공간의 여유만 있으면 최대한 서로 떨어져 있어야 한다. 하물며 전혀 낯선 이에게 말을 거는 것은 절대 금물이다. 하지만 그러한 불문율이 사실은 틀렸다면 어떨까?

행동과학을 연구하는 니콜라스 에플리(Nicholas Epley)와 줄리안 슈로더(Juliana Schroeder)는 한 가지 실험을 했다. 두 사람은 시카고 주변의 한 기차역에서 평소 기차로 출퇴근하는 승객들의 도움을 얻어 그러한 불문율을 깨는 실험을 해 보았다. 우선 승객들에게 스타벅스의 5달러짜리 상품 교환권을 주고, 기차를 타고 가면서 실험에 참가하겠다는 동의를 받았다. 승객들을 두 집단으로 나누어, 한 집단에게는 그날 아침 출근하면서 옆 자리에 앉은 사람에게 말을 걸어보라고 일러 두었다. 또 다른 집단의 경우에는 출근시에 평소의 습관대로 아무에게도 말을 걸지 않고 혼자 가만 있으라고 이야기해 두었다. 그 결과, 기차에서 내릴 때쯤, 옆 좌석의 낯선 사람과 대화를 나누었던 통근 승객들은 그렇지 않은 사람들에 비해 출근 시간이 더 유쾌했던 것으로 나타났다.

만약 옆 좌석에 앉은 낯선 사람에게 말을 거는 것에 대해 불편한 느낌이 있다면, 여러분만 그런 것이 아니다. 에플리 박사와 슈로더 연구원은 같은 기차 역에서 첫 번째 실험군에 속한 사람들과는 다른 사람들에게 낯선 사람과 대화를 나눈다면 어떤 느낌이 들 것인지 예상을 해 보라고 부탁했다. 그러자, 그들은 그냥 자기 혼자 조용히 가는 것이 더 편할 것으로 생각한다고 대답했다.

그렇다면 승객들의 최초의 예상과 실제 경험 후의 결과 사이에는 왜 이렇게 큰 차이가 있는 것일까? 대부분의 사람들은 대화를 시작하는 것이 우선 힘들 것이라고 생각했다. 사람들은 자신들이 말을 붙여도 대화를 하고 싶어하는 사람들은 전체 승객 중 절반도 안될 것으로 보았다. 하지만 실제로는 대화를 시도한 사람들 중 단 한 사람도 상대방으로부터 차가운 반응을 느끼지 않았다고 밝혔다. 그리고 대화 내용도 시종일관 유쾌했다고 전했다.

과학전문잡지인 사이언스(Science)에 실린 2004년도의 한 연구 결과에 따르면, 우리가 매일 겪는 다른 일상적인 일들과 비교해 볼 때, 출,퇴근에 대해 고역이라고 생각하는 느낌이 더 강한 것으로 나타났다. 다른 사람과의 접촉을 피하면서 우리는 집단적인 착각에 빠져 있는지도 모른다. 하지만 그러한 착각이 틀린 것 같다. 예를 들어, 버스나 기차에서 중년 여성과 유행의 최첨단을 걷는 젊은이가 나란히 앉아 있다고 가정해 보자. 중년 여성은 캔디 크러시 사가(Candy Crush Saga)라는 스마트 폰 게임에 빠져 있고, 옆 좌석의 청년은 아이튠즈에서 음악을 듣는 것에만 열중한다면, 서로 공감을 나눌 수 있는 좋은 기회를 놓치게 된다.

개개인들도 마찬가지지만 각국 정부들 역시 매일 매일의 출퇴근을 좀 더 쾌적하게 만들기 위하여 많은 돈을 투자하고 있다. 소음을 막을 수 있는 헤드폰부터 좀 더 쾌적한 좌석 공간에 이르기 까지 다양한 분야에 많은 노력을 기울이고 있다. 하지만 연구 결과, 사회적 자본 즉 우리와 함께 대중 교통을 이용하는 낯선 이들과 서로 대화를 나누는 노력에 투자하는 것이 성과가 더 높다면 어떨까?

낯선 사람들의 경우 좋은 점은, 정작 사랑하는 사람들에게는 오히려 무뚝뚝한 경우라도 낯선 이들을 만날 때에는 밝은 표정을 짓는 경향이 있다는 점이다. 동료 연구진 중의 한 사람인 리즈는 대학원생인데, 자신의 남자 친구 벤자민이 자신과 있을 때에는 걸핏하면 신경질을 부린다는 것을 알게 되었다. 하지만 어쩔 수 없이, 낯선 사람이나 아는 정도의 사람과 대화를 해야 하는 상황에서는, 그런 벤자민도 유쾌한 모습을 보였다. 그리고 그러한 유쾌한 반응이 불쾌했던 기분을 해소시키는 경우들이 종종 나타났다.

행동과학을 연구하는 연구자로서 좋은 점 한 가지는 배우자나 연인에게서 마음에 안 드는 점이 있을 경우, 그것을 연구 과제로 삼아 수 십 쌍의 다른 커플들을 모아서 근본적인 원인을 알아 볼 수 있는 실험을 할 수 있다는 점이다. 리즈는 실험을 통해 자신의 가설을 검증해 보고, 대부분의 사람들이 "벤자민 효과"를 보이고 있다는 점을 알았다. 물론 이 효과는 남자 친구의 이름을 따서 자신이 붙인 이름이다. 즉, 대부분의 사람들이 자신의 배우자나 연인보다는 오히려 낯선 사람과 함께 있을 때 더 유쾌한 모습을 보이고, 그 결과 자신들이 처음 생각했던 것보다 더 유쾌한 기분을 느낀다는 점이다.

하지만 많은 사람들은 으레 우리의 행복이 우리 주변의 가까운 사람들과의 관계에 따라 결정되는 것이지, 일상생활에서 마주치는 사소한 인간 관계에 의해 영향을 받지는 않을 것이라고 생각하는 것 같다. 이러한 생각이 타당한지 확인하기 위하여 필자들이 가르치고 있는 대학의 학생인 길리언 샌드스트롬은 사람들에게 자신들이 매일 만나게 되는 다양한 사람들과의 접촉에 대해 그 회수를 모두 집계하여 확인해 주도록 부탁했다.

그녀는 피실험자들에게 생활을 하면서 주머니에 빨간색과 검정색으로 된 2개의 숫자 집계용 클리커를 가지고 다니도록 했다. 피실험자들은 자신들과 가까운 관계에 있는 사람들 (즉, 긴밀한 관계인 경우)과 만날 때에는 빨간색 클리커를 눌렀다. 그리고 잘 모르는 사람들 (즉, 비교적 낯선 관계인 경우)을 만날 때에는 검정색 클리커를 눌렀다. 결과를 보니 내성적인 사람이든 외향적인 사람이든 모두 사회적 상호작용이 더 많은 날일수록 행복도가 높게 나타났다.

더 놀라운 점은, 친밀도가 낮은 관계의 사람들과의 접촉 역시 적어도 친밀도가 높은 사람들과의 상호작용만큼 행복에 미치는 영향이 높다는 점이었다. 이러한 사실은 어쩌다 마주치는 낯선 사람이 우리의 행복에 상당한 영향을 미칠 수 있다는 것을 보여준다.

최근 한 실험에서, 우리는 길 가던 사람들을 세워서 5달러짜리 스타벅스 상품교환권을 주고 손님들로 붐비는 스타벅스 매장에 들어가도록 부탁했다. 우리는 일군의 피실험자들에게는 계산할 때 직원에게 미소를 짓고 간단한 대화를 하되,진심으로 마음을 열고 대화하도록 부탁했다. 또 다른 일군의 피실험자들에게는 가능하면 효율성의 측면에서 행동하도록 부탁했다. 말하자면, 들어가서 아무 말 없이 계산만 하고, 볼 일이 끝났으면 그냥 가라는 것이었다. 그 결과, 스타벅스 매장에서 직원과 이야기를 나누며 조금 더 여유있는 시간을 가졌던 피실험자들은 떠날 때에 더 유쾌한 기분을 느낄 수 있었다. 결국, 우리는 효율성이라는 것에 대해 과대평가하고 있다는 생각이 든다.

심지어 잠시 스쳐 지나가는 것처럼 쳐다보는 것도 영향을 미친다. 많은 사람들이 아마 독일어로 wie Luft behandeln라고 하는 심리학적 표현, 즉 누군가가 시선을 피해 허공을 쳐다보는 듯한 느낌을 겪은 경험이 있을 것이다. 낯선 사람과 눈을 마주치는 것을 피하려는 불문율은 그다지 나쁜 해를 끼칠 것 같지는 않다. 하지만 그렇지 않을지도 모른다. 예를 들어 보자. 중서부 지역의 한 대학에서 한 가지 실험을 했다. 그 연구에서는, 대학생 나이 또래의 한 여성을 시켜, 대학 교정에서 학생들을 지나치며 실험을 했다.

그 여성은 세 가지 동작을 취했는데, 지나치는 사람과 눈을 마주치거나, 마주치면서 미소를 짓거나, 아니면 상대방의 귀 쪽의 허공을 쳐다보는 시선을 보이며, 의도적으로 눈길을 피하는 식이었다.

이 여성 실험자 뒤에는 또 다른 연구원이 따라 다니며, 그녀와 마주친 사람들에게 설문 조사를 해 보았다. 그 결과, 그녀가 허공을 응시하여 마치 투명 인간 대하는 듯한 취급을 받은 사람들은 다른 사람들로부터 소외되고 있다는 느낌이 더 강했다고 심정을 털어 놓았다.

길 거리에서 낯선 사람의 존재를 인정하는 듯한 태도만으로도 그 사람의 소위 실존적 고민을 덜어 줄 수 있다는 것이다. 그리고 우리가 다른 사람들로부터 존재를 인정받는 것도 우리에게 똑 같은 효과를 가져다 준다. (한 가지 주의할 점이 있기는 하다. 다른 일부 연구들에서는, 누군가 낯선 사람이 의도적으로 자신을 쳐다보면 그 사람을 피하려는 경향을 보인다는 결과들도 있었다.)

또, 타인들과 친밀감을 느낄 때 얻을 수 있는 장점은 양쪽 모두에게 도움이 되는 것으로 나타났다. 에플리 박사와 슈로더 연구원은 병원 등의 대기실에서 한 사람이 낯선 사람에게 이야기를 먼저 걸면, 두 사람 모두 기분이 좋아졌다는 반응을 보인다는 사실을 발견했다. 낯선 사람에게 먼저 다가가는 행동은 그 사람들의 프라이버시를 침해해서 기분 나쁘게 만들 수도 있다고 생각하는데, 전혀 그렇지 않다. 오히려 상대방의 기분도 좋게 만들 수 있다.

그러니 고독을 즐기는 것이 더 낫다는 속단은 이제 버리고 먼저 다른 사람에게 다가가는 것이 좋겠다. 그러면, 최소한 우리가 길을 걸을 때, 반대 방향에서 다가오는 낯선 사람을 마치 투명 인간 보듯이 무시하는 태도만은 피할 수 있을 것이다. 우리가 낯선 사람에게 말을 걸면, 나만의 시간은 좀 잃어버릴 수도 있겠지만, 아마 그보다 훨씬 많은 것을 얻을 수 있지 않을까?

자기 성찰인가, 아니면 자아 도취인가? (Introspective or Narcissistic?)

일기 쓰는 것을 좋아하는 사람들이 있는가 하면 반대하는 사람들도 있다.

일기를 쓰는 사람들은 대개 일기에 대해 자기 자신을 이해하고 개인적으로 성장하는 과정의 한 부분으로 본다. 그들은 자신이 깨달은 점이나 겪은 일들이 기억 속에서 사라지는 것을 원하지 않는다. 그들은 글을 통해서 생각을 정리하고, 자신의 경험을 되새겨보고 자신의 감정을 잘 이해하기 위하여 글로 표현해야만 한다.

일기 쓰기에 반대하는 사람들은 일기를 쓸 경우, 자기 집착과 자아 도취를 조장할 수도 있다는 점을 걱정한다. 영국의 소설가이자 신학자인 C.S. 루이스는 수시로 일기를 썼는데, 일기를 쓰면서 오히려 슬픔이 더 커졌고 자신의 신경쇠약증이 더 악화되었다고 우려했다. 조지 마샬 장군도 2차 세계 대전 당시에 일기를 쓰지 않았다. 왜냐하면 "일기를 쓰다 보면 스스로를 속이거나 결정을 내릴 때 망설일 가능성이 있다"고 보았기 때문이다.

문제는 자기 자신에게 집착하지 않으면서도 자아 성찰을 할 수 있는 방법이 무엇인가 하는 점이다.

심리학자들을 비롯한 많은 사람들이 이러한 의문에 대해 연구했다. 이들 연구의 결론은 성찰의 가장 핵심적인 부분에는 한 가지 역설이 있다는 것이다. 우리 자신의 모습은 가까이에서 자세하게 들여다 볼 때보다, 거리를 두고 떨어져서 볼 때 더 정확하게 볼 수 있다. 가능하면 자신의 모습에서 멀리 떨어져서 자신을 볼수록, 자신에 대해 더 정확하게 이해할 수 있다는 것이다.

문제는 우리 인간의 정신은 매우 깊고, 복잡하며 변화무쌍하다는 점이다. 철학자 칸트는 이 점에 대해 다음과 같은 유명한 발언을 한 바 있다. "우리 인간은 아무리 철저하게 성찰을 한다고 해도, 비밀에 가려져 있는 행동의 동기들을 완전히 이해할 수는 없다." 그와 동시에 우리가 스스로 생각하는 자신의 가치와 정체성은 자신에 대해 스스로 판단을 내릴 때 마다 크게 달라진다.

이와 같이 자기 행동에 대한 불가해한 측면과, 자신의 정체성과 판단의 연관성이 함께 나타나면, 자기 기만이나 합리화 그리고 감정에 치우친 판단이 나타날 수 밖에 없다.

사람들은 지나치게 가까이에서 자신의 모습을 지켜 볼 때, 대개의 경우 자신에 지나치게 골몰하거나 아니면 과도하게 단순화할 가능성이 있다. 자신에 골몰하는 행동은 우리가 간혹 한 밤 중에 잠이 깨어 고민에 휩싸이는 경우와 비슷하다. 갑자기 밤 중에 잠이 깨면, 주변의 세상은 온통 어둠에 휩싸여 있는데, 우리의 정신은 끊임없이 꼬리에 꼬리를 물고 자기만의 생각에 빠지게 된다. 그렇게 되면 끊임없이 생각만 반복하고 행동은 하지 않는다. 자기만의 생각에 골몰하여 우울증에 사로잡혀 있으면, 결국 우울증만 더 심해져 진다.

또 지나친 단순화에 빠진 사람들은 스스로를 진정으로 이해하지 못한다. 그래서 자신의 욕망을 설명하기 위하여 인위적인 이유들을 꾸며 낸다. 예를 들어, 사람들은 평소 자신이 원하는 배우자의 이상형을 이야기하지만 정작 그와 같은 막연한 기준과는 전혀 딴 판인 사람과 결혼한다. 부동산 업자들 역시, 많은 사람들이 정작 집을 살 때에는 처음에 자신들이 원했던 집과는 전혀 거리가 먼 집을 사게 된다는 사실을 잘 알 것이다.

우리는 자기 자신을 구축하고 있는 요소들을 하나씩 분석하는 방식보다는 일정한 거리를 두고 그 과정에서 나타나는 자신의 모습을 전체적으로 파악할 때 더 정확하게 자신을 파악할 수 있다. 그러기 위해서는 몇 가지 방법이 있다.

첫째, 자기 자신과 시간상 거리를 두는 방법이다. "위기 상황 심리 치료 프로그램(Critical Incident Stress Debriefing)"이라고 하는 프로그램에서는 트라우마의 희생자들에게 사건이 일어난 직후에 자신의 감정을 글로 표현하도록 하고 있다. (이유는 피해자들이 감정을 마음 속에 쌓아두어서는 안되기 때문이라는 것이다) 하지만 그렇게 한 사람들은 외상후 스트레스 장애를 더 많이 겪었으며, 그 후 몇 주 동안 오히려 우울증이 더 심해졌다. 거리감을 두지 않고 바로 분석을 한 결과 오히려 트라우마 치유를 힘들게 만들고, 고통이 가시지 못하게 만들어 버렸다. 하지만 시간이 어느 정도 흐른 후에 트라우마에 대해 글로 표현을 한 사람들은 사건들에 대해 더 넓은 시야를 가지고 볼 수 있었다. 그러한 방법이 그들의 삶에 큰 도움이 되었다.

둘째, 표현 방식을 통해 자신과의 거리를 둘 수 있다. 대개의 경우, 남들에게는 조언을 잘 하는 사람도 스스로에게 조언을 할 때에는 서툰 모습을 보인다. 그러므로 스스로에 대해 성찰해 볼 때 자신을 다른 사람이라고 객관화해 보는 것이 바람직하다. 자신을 제 3자라고 생각해 보는 것이다. 오즐렘 아이듀크(Ozlem Ayduk)와 에탄 크로스(Ethan Kross)라는 연구자가 한 연구에 따르면 자기 자신에 대해 거리감을 두고 객관적으로 보려고 노력하는 사람은 자기 자신의 주관에 사로잡힌 사람보다 자기 성찰을 더 효과적으로 한다고 한다.

마지막으로 스토리 텔링 기법을 활용하는 방법이다. 버지니아 대학의 티모시 윌슨 교수는 자신의 책 "우리 자신의 이방인(Strangers to Ourselves)"이라는 책에서 우리는 자신에 대해 고고학자의 관점으로 보아서는 안 된다고 밝혔다. 고고학자는 각각의 감정을 세밀하게 분석하고 무의식의 세계에까지 깊이 파고 들어가려고 하기 때문이라는 것이 그 이유이다. 그보다는 문학평론가의 관점을 가져야 한다는 것이다. 그래서 좀 더 긴 호흡으로 삶 전체를 조망해 보는 관점을 가져야 한다. 이와 같은 관점을 가지면 단지 이성적으로 분석을 하는 방법보다 우리 스스로 겪는 경험들을 더 유연하게 이해할 수 있다.

윌슨은 책에서 이렇게 밝히고 있다. "요지는 (우리가 느끼는 감정에 대한) 정보들을 과도하게 의도적으로 그리고 의식적인 방법을 통해 분석하려고 시도하거나, 장점과 단점들을 분명하게 따지려고 하지 말아야 한다는 것이다. 우리는 우리 스스로, 자신의 감정들을 다 설명할 수는 없어도, 상황에 따라 변화하는 우리의 무의식이 우리의 진정한 감정들을 찾아내도록 내버려 두고, 또 그러한 감정들을 믿어야 한다."

화가인 척 클로스(Chuck Close)의 자화상들 중 한 작품을 생각해 보자. 그림 전체가 얼굴 하나로만 가득 채워져 있는 그림이다. 모공 하나까지 다 볼 수 있을 정도이다. 어떤 사람들은 그와 같은 방식으로 자신을 성찰하려고 한다. 하지만 다른 사람들은 좀 더 폭 넓은 관점에서, 즉 용서, 구원, 좌절, 승화를 다루는 더 긴 호흡의 맥락에서 자신의 모습을 본다. 성숙이란 가까이에서 분석하던 단계에서 전체적으로 조망해 볼 수 있는 단계까지 변화하는 것이다. 그렇게 되면 자신이 스스로 강점이나 약점이라고 생각하는 것에 대해 초점을 맞추기 보다는 우리가 살아가며 느끼는 '공감'에 더 역점을 두게 된다. 그러한 공감이 다른 사람들이나 자기 자신 그리고 생존을 이해할 때 반드시 필수적인 수단이기 때문이다.

결혼식 전에 치러야 할 한 가지 싸움 (The one fight to have before your wedding)

전세계의 약혼한 여성들이여, 단결하라! 그대들이 잃을 것은 남편의 이름 밖에는 없으니.

나는 며칠 후에 결혼한다. 그리고 결혼 준비를 하다 보면 항상 그렇다고 귀에 따갑게 들었던 것처럼, 살얼음판을 걷는 듯한 그 과정에서 아주 사소한 문제들을 둘러싸고 피곤한 싸움이 계속 일어났다. 하지만 나의 경우 내가 제일 마음에 안 들었던 점은 호칭 문제였다.

구체적으로 말하면, 여성들의 이름이 문제였다. 아니, 결혼과 함께 여성의 이름을 빼 버리는 전통 때문이었다고 말하는 것이 더 정확할 것이다.

사건의 발단은 이렇다. 결혼 준비에서 청첩장이나 봉투, 그리고 좌석 배치 명표와 같은 문제는 친정 엄마가 책임지기로 했다. 무엇보다 이 문제는 엄마가 나보다 훨씬 더 호불호가 강하기 때문이었다. 나는 사실 청첩장의 재질이 고고학 발굴 현장에서 몰래 도굴한 고대 이집트의 파피루스 종이든, 아니면 재활용한 화장실 휴지든 아니면 아예 디지털 초청장은 없고 종이 청첩장만 있든 전혀 상관이 없었다. 아니면 인터넷 청첩장 전문 업체인 Evite.com만 사용해도 전혀 문제 없는 사람이다.

하지만 까칠한 예비 신부로서 절대 양보할 수 없는 문제가 한 가지 있다. 그 문제는 페미니스트를 자처하는 나의 약혼자도 적극 찬성하고 있는 부분이다. 그것은 바로 여성들의 이름들을 어떻게 표기할 것인가의 문제이다. 구체적으로 말하면, 여성들의 이름을 그대로 다 표기할 것인가의 문제였다.

나는 항상 결혼한 여성들을 공식적으로 지칭해야 할 때 남편의 이름에 따라 부르는 것이 싫었다. 여러분도 짐작이 갈 것이다. 우리 사회에서는 로버츠 스미스와 제인 스미스(Mr. Robert Smith and Mrs./Ms. Jane Smith) 와 같은 형태의 표현보다는 로버츠 스미스씨 부부(Mr. and Mrs. Robert Smith)라는 표현을 사용한다. 나는 결혼하고 나서 여성들이 남편들의 성을 그대로 따르는 것은 어느 정도 이해한다. 가족간의 화합을 위해서 그럴 수도 있고 또 유아원에서 어린 자녀를 데려 올 때 혼선을 피하기 위한 목적일 수도 있고 그 밖의 여러 가지 이유가 있을 것이다. 나는 개인적으로 내 이름을 모두 그대로 유지하기로 결정했지만 말이다. 하지만, 결혼한 여성의 이름까지도 빼앗는 것이 과연 타당할까? 결혼한 여성들도 자신만의 정체성을 가지고 있다. 결혼한 여성들은 단순히 배우자의 부속물이 아니라는 이야기이다.

그래서, 내 결혼식을 준비해야 할 때가 왔을 때, 나는 어떠한 경우이든 결혼한 부부들을 지칭할 때에는 반드시 여성의 성과 이름을 그대로 다 표기하겠다고 선언했다. 친정 엄마는 처음에는 반대했다. 그래도 전통인데 함부로 무시할 수는 없지 않느냐는 것이었다. 하지만 결국에는 내 의견을 존중해주기로 동의해 주셨다.

하지만 그 문제는 친정 엄마나 내가 생각했던 것보다 훨씬 더 어려운 문제였다.

엄마가 청첩장 인쇄업자에게 초청 문구의 앞 부분에 "[엄마의 이름] 여사와 [아빠의 이름] 씨는 여러 하객 분들을 모시고 ···"라고 써 달라고 부탁했다. 그러자 여성이었던 인쇄업자는 경악을 금치 못했다. 그 동안 수없이 청첩장을 인쇄를 해 봤지만 한 번도 그렇게 관례에 어긋나는 일은 해 본 일이 없다고 불만이 많았다. 엄마는 깜짝 놀라서 나에게 전화를 했다. 마치 내가 원하는 문구가 질서정연한 이 우주의 질서를 무너뜨리기라도 할 것처럼 확신하는 것 같았다.

나는 엄마에게 그 인쇄업자는 그만두게 하고 우리가 선택하는 문구가 무엇이든 간에 군말하지 않고 들어줄 수 있는 사람을 찾아 보라고 부탁했다. 결국 엄마는 내 말대로 해 주셨다.

그 다음에는 청첩장에 상대방의 이름을 인쇄할 차례가 되었다. 엄마는 큰 맘 먹고 전문적인 서체 전문가를 고용했다. 엄마는 서체 전문가에게 엑셀 파일을 보냈다. 그 파일에는 우리가 초청한 사람들의 이름이 담겨 있었다. 그녀에게 우리가 쓴 대로 그대로 써서 인쇄하라고 지시했다. 만약 그렇지 않으면, 신부가 보통 성격이 아니라 가만있지 않을 것이라고 단단히 일러두었다. 서체 전문가도 순순히 그러겠다고 했다.

하지만 결혼한 내 지인들이 받은 청첩장 봉투에는 어떻게 적혀 있었을까? 아니나 다를까 "로버츠 스미스

부부(Mr. and Mrs. Robert Smith)"라는 식으로 적혀 있었다. 심지어 최소한 한 사람의 경우에는, 여성 인권 의식이 높아 결혼 전의 이름을 그대로 유지하는 사람인데도, 그렇게 적혀 있었다.

나는 처음에 우리가 업자들을 잘못 선정해서 그런 것으로 알았다. 아마 서체 전문가가 자기도 모르게 선의의 실수를 했을 수 있지 않을까. 그래서 나는 인터넷에서 검색을 해 보았다.

그런데, 인터넷에도 이와 같은 반 여성주의적인 전통을 유지해야 한다는 의견이 거의 대다수였다.

인터넷에서 호칭에 대한 지침을 살펴보니 무명의 소위 전문가에서부터 크레인앤코(Crane & Co.)와 홀마크(Hallmark)처럼 유명한 문구 업체에 이르기까지 공통적으로 결혼한 여성의 경우에는 이름을 빼는 것이 낫다고 권하고 있었다. (이와 관련하여 전통적인 예의범절 전문 기관인 에밀리 포스트 연구소에서 권하는 내용을 보면 다소 모호한 면이 있다.) 그런가 하면, 예법에 어긋나지 않으면서도, 이렇게 터무니없는 전통을 피할 수 있는 방법에 대해 고민하는 예비 신부들이 쓴 웹사이트나 게시판의 글들도 그에 못지 않게 많았다.

물론, 부부를 지칭할 때, 이와 같이 남편의 이름만 쓰는 전통은 청첩장에만 국한된 문제는 아니다. 이러한 문제는 동창회, 교회의 단체, 자선 기관에 우편물을 보내거나 심지어 광고성 우편물을 보낼 때에도 또 같다. 심지어 사회적으로 저명하고 성공한 여성들의 사교 클럽 중에도 회원을 지칭할 때 남편의 이름을 따서 부르는 경우를 봤다.

하지만 여성의 정체성을 남편에게 완전히 맡기는 듯한 이와 같은 케케묵은 전통을 앞으로도 계속 유지해야 한다는 부담감이 특히 짜증나게 느껴지는 경우는 바로 결혼을 준비하는 과정에서 나타난다. 이 때는 각각의 인격체로 성장한 두 사람의 성인이 법적으로나 정신적으로 서로 하나가 된다는 것에 대한 의미를 진지하게 모색하게 되는 과정인데도 말이다.

그래서 나는 전세계의 모든 예비 신부들에게 호소한다. 결혼 준비를 하다 보면 훨씬 더 의미가 없으면서 돈만 더 들어가는 일들이 수없이

많지만, 여러분들이 결혼 준비를 하면서 가족들이나 친구들 그리고 업자들에게 결코 양보할 수 없는 한 가지가 있다면, 바로 이 문제라는 인식으로 싸워주기 바란다. 그리고 결혼한 여러분들의 여성 동지들에 대해 결혼 전 그녀의 원래 이름으로 불러주도록 하자. 그리고 결혼한 다음에는 그녀들도 여러분에 대해 똑같이 불러달라고 요청하라.

2 문학 지문 번역

1 소설

소설 01 An American Tragedy by Theodore Dreiser (미국의 비극)

　이번의 색다른 모험에서 클라이드가 받은 영향은 이런 세상에 처음 발을 들여놓은 세상 물정 모르는 풋내기가 받을 만한 그런 영향이었다. 그만큼 간절한 호기심과 욕망에 이끌려 발을 들여놓고 굴복하기는 했지만, 오랫동안 귀가 따갑게 들어 온 도덕적인 교훈과 자신의 소심한 결벽성 때문에 돌이켜 보니 모든 일이 벌을 받을 만한 타락한 짓이었다고 말할 수밖에 없었다. 그의 부모가 이런 짓을 천박하고 수치스러운 행동으로 가르친 것은 어쩌면 옳은 일이었는지 몰랐다. 하지만, 클라이드는 전날 밤 새로운 경험을 하고 난 이후, 그 모든 경험과 그 경험이 벌어진 새로운 세상에 대해, 역겹기도 하고 한편으로는 도덕적으로 문제가 있지만 또 한편으로는 매력을 느낄 수 밖에 없었다. 더군다나 그보다 더 흥미로운 또 다른 경험을 통해 그 기억이 조금이나마 희미해질 때까지는 어쩔 수 없이 그 때의 경험에 관심을 느끼게 되었고 더 나아가 쾌감을 가지고 되새겨 보게 되었다.

　더구나 클라이드는 이제 돈을 어느 정도 버는 이상, 자기가 가고 싶은 곳에 가고, 하고 싶은 일도 마음대로 할 수 있다고 스스로 생각하고 있었다. 마음이 내키지 않으면 그런 곳에 다시 갈 필요가 없었다. 어쩌면 그런 곳처럼 심하게 천박하지 않거나, 혹은 좀 더 세련된 다른 장소에 갈 수도 있었다. 두 번 다시는 그런 식으로 떼를 지어서 가고 싶지는 않았다. 시벌링이나 도일이 교제하는 부류의 여자를 어디선가 찾아낼 수 있다면 그런 여자와 사귀고 싶었다. 그래서 지난 밤에 있었던 일에 대해 마음이 심란하기는 했지만, 클라이드는 처음 환락을 경험한 그 장소는 아니더라도 새로운 쾌락에 벌써 마음을 빼앗겼다. 할 수만 있다면 도일처럼 자유분방하고 거리낌 없는 여자를 사귀고 그녀를 위해 돈을 쓰고 싶었다. 그런 생각이 들자 이런 식으로 욕망을 충족시킬 기회가 몹시 기다려졌.

　그러나 이 무렵 그 일보다도 더 흥미 있고 그의 목적에 훨씬 잘 맞는 일이 생겼다. 헤글런드와 래터러가 클라이드에게 적잖이 관심을 보이면서 접근하여 자신들의 일이나 향락 계획에 끼워 주려고 한다는 점이었다. 이런 일이 가능했던 것은 두 사람에 대해 클라이드가 은근히 품고 있는 우월감에도 불구하고, 아니 오히려 그런 우월감을 그들이 느끼고 있었기 때문이었다. 첫 번째 색다른 경험이 있은 지 얼마 안 되어 래터러는 클라이드를 자기 집에 초대했다. 클라이드는 그의 집안이 자신의 집안과는 아주 다르다는 것을 곧 눈치챌 수 있었다. 그리피스 집안에서는 모든 것이 엄숙하고 근엄하며 교리나 신앙의 무게가 느껴질 만큼 조용한 분위기가 감돌았다. 하지만, 래터러의 집안은 이와는 정반대라고 할 수 있었다. 래터러와 함께 사는 어머니와 여동생은 특별한 신앙이 있는 것은 아니지만, 어느 정도의 도덕심은 갖추고 있었다. 하지만,

두 사람의 인생관은 도덕군자에게는 자칫 방종하다고까지 보일 정도로 느슨했다. 엄격한 도덕이니 까다로운 예법이니 하는 것은 아예 처음부터 마음에 두고 있는 것 같지 않았다. 래터러도, 그보다 두 살 아래인 루이즈도 하고 싶은 대로 자유롭게 행동하면서도 별로 개의치 않았다. 그러나 그의 여동생 루이즈는 약삭빠르고 개성이 강해서 아무에게나 쉽게 자신을 맡기는 타입은 아니었다.

이 모든 상황에서 흥미로운 점은 클라이드가 어느 정도 세련된 기질이 있어서 대부분의 이런 일을 의심의 눈길로 바라보면서도, 여전히 그런 원초적인 삶의 모습과 그것이 가져다주는 자유로움에는 어느 정도 매력을 느끼고 있었다는 사실이다. 적어도 이런 사람들과 교류하면서 그는 전에는 가 보지 못한 곳을 갈 수 있고, 해 보지 못한 일을 할 수 있으며, 과거에는 생각조차 못한 사람이 될 수도 있었다. 특히 같은 또래의 여자들이 그에게 매력이나 호감을 느끼는지 초조하고 불안해 하다가, 이제는 기분이 좋아지고 자신감이 생겼고, 좀 의구심이 들기는 하지만 이 문제에서 해방된 것 같은 느낌마저 들었다. 바로 그 전까지만 해도, 또 최근 헤글런드를 비롯한 일행에 이끌려 태어나 처음으로 환락의 장소를 방문하기도 했지만 클라이드는 여자들에 관한 한 여전히 그들을 다루는 기술이나 사로잡는 매력이 자신에겐 없다고 믿었다. 여자들이 그저 옆에 있거나 가까이 다가오기만 해도 마음이 움츠러들거나 몸이 뻣뻣하게 굳거나 안절부절 못하고 가슴이 두근거렸다. 또 다른 젊은이들이 지닌 것 같은 대화나 진지한 농담을 나누는 타고난 능력마저도 제대로 발휘할 수 없었다. 그러나 그는 이제 래터러의 집에 몇 번 드나들면서 이런 수줍음과 불안한 마음을 극복할 수 있는지 시험해 볼 기회가 얼마든지 있다는 사실을 깨닫게 되었다.

래터러의 집은 래터러나 그의 여동생의 친구들이 자주 모이는 장소였기 때문이다. 그런데 그들이 살아가는 방식은 하나같이 서로 거의 비슷비슷했다. 그곳에서는 춤을 추거나 카드놀이를 하거나 별로 수치심을 느끼지도 않고 거의 공개적으로 애정 행각을 벌이곤 했다. 지금까지 클라이드는 래터러 부인처럼 부모가 자식의 행실과 도덕에 이렇게 방관적이고 무관심한 태도를 보일 수 있다는 것을 상상조차 할 수 없었다. 어떤 어머니라도 래터러 부인 집에서 벌어지고 있는 자유분방한 애정 행각을 묵인하리라고는 도저히 상상할 수 없었을 것이다.

그리고 얼마 지나지 않아, 클라이드는 래터러의 호의적인 초대를 받고 몇 번 그의 집을 방문했기 때문에 자연스럽게 그들과 어울리게 되었다. 어떤 관점에서 보자면, 클라이드는 그들이 생각이나 말에 있어서 교양이 없는 것을 보고 경멸하고 있었다. 그러나 다른 관점에서 보자면, 각자 나름대로 자유를 즐기고, 마음이 내키는 대로 서로 어울린다는 점 때문에 그는 그들에게 마음이 끌렸다. 그가 그들에게 끌린 또 다른 이유는 태어나서 처음으로 용기만 낼 수 있다면 자기 또래의 여자와 사귈 수 있었기 때문이다. 클라이드는 곧 래터러나 그의 여동생 그리고 그들의 친구들의 호의적인 도움 덕분에, 이런 욕망을 채우려고 했다. 사실 그 일은 그가 래터러 집을 처음 방문했을 때 이미 시작되었다.

래터러의 여동생 루이즈는 잡화점에서 근무하고 있었는데, 늦게 퇴근하는 경우가 많았다. 그날 밤도 일곱 시쯤이 되어서야 집에 돌아왔고, 그 때문에 집안 식구들의 저녁 식사는 당연히 늦어질 수밖에 없었다. 그러는 동안 루이즈의 친구 둘이 그녀와 무엇인가 상의할 일이 있어 그녀의 집에 찾아왔다. 그들은 루이즈의 귀가가 늦어지는 데다가 래터러와 클라이드가 집에 있는 것을 보고 집에서 그냥 기다리기로 했다. 두 아가씨는 클라이드와 그가 입고 있는 새 옷에 꽤 관심이 끌렸다. 클라이드는 이성에 굶주려 있으면서도 동시에 여자들 앞에서 낯을 가렸다. 그런 클라이드가 긴장 때문에 거리를 두자, 루이즈의 친구들은 마치 클라이드가 도도해서 우월감 때문에 그런 것으로 착각하게 되었다. 그 결과, 두 사람은 이러한 클라이드의 모습에 호감을 느끼고 자신들의 매력을 뽐내려고 마음 먹었다. 클라이드의 마음을 사로 잡으려는 생각을 가지게 된 것이다. 한편 클라이드에게는 그들의 투박스러운 행동과 뻔뻔한 태도가 오히려 무척 매력적으로 보였다. 그러다 보니 그는 곧 호튼스 브릭스라는 한 아가씨의 매력에 끌렸다. 그녀는 루이즈와 마찬가지로 큰 가게에서 점원 노릇을 하는 교양없는 여자에 지나지 않았지만, 얼굴이 예쁘장하고 가무잡잡했으며 자신만만했다. 물론 그는 처음부터 그녀가 교양 없고 천박한 여자라는 것을 깨닫고 있었다. 한마디로 그가 꿈에 그리던 이상적인 여성과는 거리가 먼 여자였다.

"아니, 루이즈는 아직도 집에 오지 않았어요?" 호튼스는 래터러가 먼저 문을 열어 주자 앞쪽 창가 근처에서 창밖을 내다보고 있던 클라이드를 쳐다보면서 말했다. "이거 어떡하지. 좀 기다리야 할 것 같네요. 실례가 안된다면요." 그녀가 뽐내듯이 마지막 말을 내뱉는 것으로 보아, 남들의 시선 따위는 신경쓰지 않는다는 것을 알 수 있었다. 그러더니 그녀는 식당의 불 없는 받침쇠를 장식한 황토색 벽난로 위의 거울 앞에 서서 화장을 고치면서 거울에 비친 자기 모습에 감탄하기 시작했다. 그러자 함께 온 그레터 밀러라는 아가씨가 그 말을 받아 덧붙였다. "그래 네 말이 맞아. 루이즈가 올 때까지 설마 우리를 내쫓지는 않겠죠. 우린 식사하러 온 게 아니니까요. 지금쯤이면 벌써 식사를 끝낸 줄로 생각했거든요."

"그럴 리가 있겠니? 너희들을 쫓아낼 사람이 누가 있니?" 래터러가 냉소적인 말투로 대답했다. "너희들은 갈 생각도 없는데도 누군가 여기서 쫓아낼 것처럼 말하는구나. 어서 거기들 앉아서 레코드판이라도 듣고 있어. 아니면 하고 싶은 일을 하거나. 이제 곧 저녁 식사 준비가 끝날 거고, 루이즈도 돌아올 거야." 래터러는 아가씨들에게 클라이드를 소개하고 나서, 읽고 있던 신문을 읽으러 식당으로 들어갔다. 클라이드는 이 두 아가씨의 얼굴과 태도를 보고 나니 갑자기 망망대해 한복판에서 갑판도 없는 조그마한 쪽배로 표류하고 있는 듯한 느낌이 들었다.

"아, 제발 식사하라는 말은 하지 마세요!" 그레터 밀러가 말했다. 그녀는 아까부터 클라이드가 사귈 만한 남자인지 아닌지 판단하려는 듯 조용히 그를 살피고 나서 상대해도 괜찮을 것 같다고 결심하고 있었다. "오늘 밤은 아이스크림이랑 케이크랑 파이랑 샌드위치를 먹어야 하거든요. 루이즈에게 너무 많이 먹지 말라고 일러 두려고 했죠. 톰 오빠도 알겠지만, 오늘 밤 키티 킨 집에서 생일 축하 파티가 있어요. 큼직한 케이크를 비롯해서 여러 가지 맛있는 음식이 나오기로 돼 있거든요. 오빠도 나중에 오지 않을래요?" 그녀는 클라이드도 어쩌면 따라와 함께 어울릴지 모른다고 생각하면서 말을 맺었다.

"그 생각은 미처 못 했는걸. 저녁 먹고 나서 클라이드와 같이 연극 보러 갈 계획이거든." 래터러가 부드러운 목소리로 대답했다.

"아니, 무슨 바보 같은 소리예요." 호튼스 브릭스가 두 사람의 관심을 그레터로부터 자기 쪽으로 돌리려고 끼어들었다. 그녀는 여전히 거울 앞에 서 있었지만 몸을 휙 돌려 특히 클라이드에게 매혹적인 미소를 던졌다. 그녀는 지금 그레터가 그를 낚으려 할지도 모른다고 생각했다. "모처럼 춤을 출 기회인데. 그런 기회를 놓치면 그건 바보죠."

"그래 맞아. 너희 셋 머릿속엔 온통 춤추는 생각밖에 없으니. 너희 둘하고 루이즈 말이야." 래터러가 되받았다. "잠시도 쉬려고 하지 않으니 참 신기해. 어쨌든 난 하루 종일 서 있었더니 이젠 잠시 앉아 있고 싶어."

"아, 나한테 앉아 있으란 말은 절대 하지 말아요. 이번 주 약속이 벌써 꽉 차 있어요. 아, 맙소사!" 그레터 밀러가 도도한 웃음을 짓고 왼발로 휙 미끄러지며 춤을 추는 흉내를 내보이며 말했다. 그녀는 일부러 눈썹과 이마를 치켜세우고 연극 배우처럼 가슴 앞에 두 손을 꼭 움켜쥐었다. "너무 끔찍해요. 이번 겨울에 있을 댄스파티 생각을 하니, 호튼스, 안 그래? 목요일 밤, 금요일 밤, 그리고 토요일과 일요일 밤에 말이야." 그레터는 손가락을 꼽으면서 호들갑을 떨었다. "아, 이거야 정말! 어휴 끔찍해." 이렇게 말하면서 그녀는 클라이드를 향해 호소와 동정을 구하는 듯한 미소를 지어 보였다. "톰 오빠, 며칠 전 밤에 우리가 어디 갔었는지 한번 알아맞혀 보세요. 루이즈하고 랠프 소프랑, 호튼스하고 버트 게틀러랑, 그리고 나하고 윌리 배식이랑 이렇게 세 쌍이 웹스터 애비뉴에 있는 페그레인에 갔었어요. 아, 사람들이 어쩜 그렇게 많았는지 오빠도 한번 봤어야 해요. 샘 셰이퍼랑 틸리 번스도 왔더라고요. 그곳에서 우린 새벽 네 시까지 춤을 췄죠. 무릎이 나가는 게 아닌가 싶었어요. 그렇게 피곤해 보기는 정말 오랜만이었어요."

"아, 정말 굉장했죠!" 호튼스가 이제 자기 차례가 왔다는 듯, 연극이라도 하는 것처럼 두 팔을 번쩍 쳐들면서 끼어들었다. "이튿날 아침 회사에 나가지 못하는 줄 알았어요. 가게에서 손님들이 돌아다니는 게 겨우 보일 정도였어요. 그리고 엄마는 얼마나 길길이 뛰시던지! 아이고! 아직도 엄마는 화가 풀리지 않았지 뭐예요. 토요일이나 일요일이라면 그래도 참을 수 있지만, 다음 날 아침 일곱 시에 일어나 회사에 나가야 할 때 늦게까지 놀아선 안 된다는 거죠. 맙소사, 얼마나 잔소리 해대는지!"

"어머니가 그러시는 것도 무리가 아니다." 래터러 부인이 그때 마침 감자와 빵 접시를 들고 들어오며 한마디 했다. 그렇게 매일 돌아 다니면, 너희 둘 다 병이 날 거야. 루이즈도 마찬가지고, 루이즈한테도 늘

잔소리해 대고 있지. 잠을 더 늘리지 않으면 가게에 계속 붙어 있을 수 없거나, 그 애가 견뎌 낼 수 없을 거라고 말이다. 하지만 톰과 마찬가지로 어디 내 말을 들어 먹어야 말이지.콧방귀도 뀌지 않으니 원."

"아니, 글쎄, 나같이 직장에 나가는 놈이 늘 일찍 집에 돌아오리라고 기대할 순 없죠, 어머니." 레터러가 말했다. 그러자 호튼스가 그 말을 받았다. "어머, 전 하룻밤이라도 집 안에 틀어박혀 있으면 답답해 죽을 것 같아요. 종일 일만 하니 좀 즐겨야죠."

정말 집안 분위기가 자유 분방하구나! 정말 자유롭고 무관심한 분위기이구나! 클라이드는 이렇게 마음속으로 생각했다. 그리고 이 두 젊은 아가씨의 쾌활하고 선정적인 몸가짐은 또 어떠한가! 이 아가씨들의 부모는 이런 것에 전혀 신경을 쓰지 않는 모양이었다. 육감적인 작은 입술에 반짝반짝 빛나는 두 눈을 가지고 있는 호튼스와 사귈 수 있다면 얼마나 좋을까.

"저는 한 주에 이틀만 일찍 자도 충분해요." 그레터 밀러가 능글맞게 말했다. "우리 아버지는 저를 보고 제 정신이 아니라고 생각하지만, 전 그 이상 자면 도리어 몸에 해가 돼요." 그러고 나서는 재미있다는 듯이 깔깔 웃어 댔다. 클라이드는 어법에도 맞지 않는 교양 없는 말투에도 불구하고 오히려 강렬한 인상을 받았다. 그들에게서 젊음과 쾌활함 그리고 자유와 삶에 대한 사랑을 느낄 수 있었기 때문이다.

소설 02 The Age of Innocence by Edith Wharton (순수의 시대)

그 날 저녁 잭슨 씨가 자리를 뜨고 부인들 역시 사라사 무명 커튼을 친 침실로 물러간 후, 뉴랜드 아처는 생각에 잠겨 자기 서재로 올라갔다. 평소처럼 불을 담당하는 하인이 난롯불을 꺼지지 않게 해 두고 램프 심지를 다듬어 놓았다. 서재에는 책들이 서가마다 열을 지어 꽂혀 있고, 벽난로 선반 위에 청동과 강철로 만든 "검객들"의 조각상들이 놓여 있었는데, 유명한 그림들의 사진들로 장식되어 있는 그 방이 그날 따라 유난히 푸근하고 반갑게 느껴졌다.

그는 난로 옆의 안락의자에 털썩 앉아 약혼녀 메이 웰랜드의 커다란 사진에 눈길을 던졌다. 그 사진은 그들이 연애를 막 시작했을 때 그녀가 준 것이었다. 그 전에 있던 다른 사진들은 치우고 이제는 탁자 위에 그녀의 사진만 남아 있는 것이다. 그는 자신이 영혼의 보호자가 되어야 할 처녀의 솔직한 이마, 진지한 눈과 쾌활하고 순진한 입을 바라보며 새삼 경외감을 느꼈다. 그가 속해 있을 뿐만 아니라 믿고 있는 사회 체제의 무서운 산물이며, 아무것도 모른 채 모든 기대를 품고 있는 바로 그 처녀는 메이 웰랜드의 낯익은 모습 속에서 낯선 사람처럼 그를 돌아보았다. 다시 한번 결혼은 그가 배워 온 대로 안전한 정박지가 아니라, 해도에도 없는 망망대해를 헤쳐 나가는 항해라는 사실을 절감했다.

올렌스카 백작 부인의 사례에 부딪치게 되자, 오래 굳어진 신념들이 흔들리며 그의 마음속에 위험스럽게도 표류하는 것 같았다. "여성들도 자유를 누릴 수 있어야 합니다. 우리 남자들만큼 자유를 누려야 한다는 말입니다."라는 그의 발언은 문제의 본질을 잘 보여주고 있었다. 그 문제는 그가 속해 있던 상류사회에서는 아예 존재하지도 않는 것처럼 암묵적으로 동의하고 있던 문제였다. "정숙한" 여성이라면 아무리 부당한 대우를 받는다고 하더라도 절대 아처가 주장한 것과 같은 종류의 자유를 요구하지도 않을 것이고, 따라서 아처 자신과 같은 너그러운 남자들은 —열띤 논쟁이 진행될 때—마치 언제든지 그 자유를 여성들에게 허용해 줄 준비가 되어 있는 것처럼 더욱 더 호기롭게 주장할 수 있었던 것이다. 이러한 말뿐인 관대함은 사실 모든 것을 묶어 놓고 사람들을 낡은 양식에 속박하는 엄격한 관습을 기만적으로 위장한 데 불과했다. 하지만, 이제 아처는 자신의 아내가 하면 종교와 사회적 관습에 따라 자신도 덩달아 격렬하게 비난을 할 만한 행동이라고 해도, 아내의 사촌인 올렌스카 백작부인이 하면 옹호할 각오가 되어 있었다. 물론 이 같은 곤란한 상황은 어디까지나 가정일 뿐이었다. 자신이, 올렌스카 백작 부인의 남편, 즉 그 폴란드 귀족 망나니가 아닌 이상, 만약 자기가 그라면 아내에게 어디까지 권리를 허용해줄까 따져 보는 것도 우스꽝스러운 일이었다. 그러나 뉴랜드 아처는 바보가 아니었으므로, 그와 메이라면 훨씬 덜 추잡하고 모호한 이유로도 서로의 유대 관계가 허물어질 수 있다는 사실을 알고 있었다. '점잖은' 남성으로서 그녀에게 자신의 과거를 숨겨야 하고, 그녀는 혼기에 든 처녀로서 숨길 과거가 없어야 한다는 이유 때문에, 그들은 진짜 서로에 대해 아는 것이 없지 않은가? 상대방에 대한 사소한 일들이 드러나기 시작하면서 서로에게 싫증이 나고 오해가 생기거나 짜증을 내게 된다면? 그는 친구들 중 행복한 결혼 생활을 한다는 친구들을 떠올려 보았으나, 메이 웰랜드와 영원히 열정적이고 애정 넘치는 부부 관계를 유지할 수 있으리라는 답을 희미하게나마 제시해 주는 사례는 하나도 찾지 못했다. 그는 이러한 관계가 되려면 먼저 경험, 다양한 재능, 자유로운 판단력이 전제되어야 하나, 메이는 이러한 요소들을 가지지 않도록 세심하게 교육받았다는 사실을 깨달았다. 자신의 결혼도 물질적, 사회적 이해로 맺어진 지루한 관계가 한쪽의 무지와 다른 쪽의 위선으로 유지되는 대다수의 결혼과 별반 다르지 않을 거라는 오싹한 예감이 스치고 지나갔다.

소설 03   Call of the Wild by Jack London (야성의 부름)

벅 덕분에 오 분 만에 천육백 달러라는 거금을 벌게 되자, 손턴은 그동안 진 빚을 다 갚고 동료들과 함께 늘 가고 싶었던 동부로 갈 수 있게 되었다. 전설 속의 '잊혀진 광산'이 있는 그곳은 그 지역의 역사만큼 오래된 역사를 간직한 곳이었다. 많은 사람들이 그곳을 찾아 떠났으나 발견한 사람은 거의 없었고 갔다가 돌아오지 못한 사람도 꽤 있었다. '잊혀진 광산'은 비극으로 물들고 미스터리에 휩싸여 있었다. 그 곳을 가장 먼저 발견한 사람에 대해 아는 사람은 아무도 없었다. 가장 오래된 전설은 채 알려지기도 전에 끊어지고 말았던 것이다. 거기에는 옛날부터 다 쓰러져 가는 오두막이 한 채 있었다고 한다. 죽어 가는 사람들의 증언에 의하면 그런 오두막이 실제로 있고 그것이 잃어버린 광산으로 가는 길의 표지이며 그곳에서 발견되는 금은 지금까지 북부에서 발견된 어떤 금보다 질이 우수하다는 것이었다.

그러나 그 오두막을 손에 넣은 사람은 아무도 없었고 이미 죽은 사람들은 말이 없었다. 손턴과 피트와 한스, 벅과 여섯 마리의 개들은 지금까지 인간과 개들이 개척하는 데 실패한 미지의 길을 따라 동부로 향했다. 그들은 유콘 강을 따라 위로 100킬로미터를 달리다가 왼쪽으로 돌아 스튜어트 강으로 들어섰다. 그러고는 마요와 매케스톤을 지나 스튜어트 강이 개울이 된 곳까지 가서 대륙의 등뼈에 해당하는 높은 봉우리들 사이를 누비고 지나갔다.

손턴은 인간과 자연에 대한 기대가 거의 없었다. 그는 야생의 삶을 두려워하지 않았다. 그는 소금 한웅큼 정도와 권총만 있으면 과감하게 야생에 뛰어들었고, 원하는 곳이라면 어디든지, 자기가 원하는 동안 여행했다. 서둘지 않고 인디언처럼 그날 여행하면서 사냥한 것으로 저녁을 즐겼다. 만일 아무것도 잡지 못하면 조만간 사냥감을 만날 거라고 굳게 믿으면서 여행을 계속했다. 그랬기 때에 동부로 향하는 여행에서 필요한 것은 직접 잡은 고기뿐이었고 썰매의 짐은 탄약과 도구 들뿐이었고, 여정은 끝없는 미래 위에 그려졌다.

벅에게도 사냥하고 물고기를 잡으며 끝없이 낯선 고장을 헤매는 것만큼 큰 기쁨은 없었다. 몇 주일은 날마다 계속 여행했다가 또 몇 주일은 이곳저곳에서 야영하면서 개들은 뛰어놀고 사람들은 얼어붙은 부식토와 자갈 사이 구멍에 불을 지펴 그 열기를 이용해 사금 채취 접시로 물속에서 사금을 골라냈다. 일행 모두 때로는 굶기도 하고, 때로는 실컷 먹을 수도 있었는데, 그것은 오로지 사냥감이 얼마나 많은지 그리고 얼마나 사냥하기에 운이 좋았는지 여부에 따라 달라졌다. 곧 여름이 다가왔고, 개들과 사람들 모두 등에 짐을 잔뜩 진 채로 산속 푸른 호수를 건넜으며, 숲에서 나무를 베어 만든 폭이 아주 좁은 배를 타고 이름 없는 강들의 물줄기를 따라, 상류로 올라가기도 하고 하류로 내려가기도 했다.

몇 달 동안 그들은 구획도 없는 광활한 지역을 꾸불꾸불 뒤로 갔다가 앞으로 갔다가 하면서 아무도 없는 곳, 만일 전설 속의 '잊혀진 오두막'이 사실이라면 사람들이 갔을 땅을 헤맸다. 그들은 여름날 때아닌 눈보라 속에서 분수령을 넘었고 수목 한계선과 만년설 사이의 헐벗은 산에서 백야를 경험하며 추위에 떨다가 모기와 파리 떼가 윙윙거리며 달려드는 여름에는 계곡으로 내려갔다. 그리고 빙하의 그늘 속에서 남부에서나 자랑하는 푹 익은 딸기와 고운 꽃을 땄다. 그해 가을에 그들은 음산한 호수 지역으로 뚫고 들어갔다. 그 지역은 슬프고 고요했다. 옛날엔 야생 조류들이 있었지만 지금은 어떤 생명도, 뭔가가 살아 있다는 흔적도 없는 곳이었다. 그저 싸늘한 바람만 불었고 쉴 만한 거처에는 물이 얼어 있었고 외로운 해변에는 우울한 잔물결이 일었다.

그 다음 해 겨울에 그들은 지금은 흔적조차 지워졌지만 전에는 사람들이 다녔던 길들을 찾아 헤맸다. 한번은 숲 속에 표지로 나무껍질을 벗겨 놓은 것을 발견하고 길을 찾았다고 생각했다. '잊혀진 오두막'이 아주 가까워진 것 같았다. 그러나 길이 어디에서 시작하고 어디에서 끝나는지 알 수 없었고, 누가, 왜 그 길을 만들었는지도 모호한 신비에 싸여 있었다. 또 한번은 세월의 때가 묻은 다 부서져 가는 사냥꾼용 오두막을 발견했는데 손턴이 먼지가 수북한 낡은 담요 밑에서 부싯돌로 불붙이는 화승총을 찾았다. 개척 초기 북서부의 허드슨베이 회사에서 만든 총이었는데 인기가 한창 좋았을 때는 수달 가죽을 판판하게 펴서 총의

키만큼 쌓아야 맞바꿀 수 있는 정도였다. 그리고 그게 전부였다. 그 옛날, 오두막을 짓고 모피 사이에 총을 남겨 둔 사내에 관해서 아무런 단서도 찾을 수 없었다.

다시 봄이 찾아왔다. 그들은 우여곡절 끝에 '잊혀진 오두막'이 아니라 넓은 계곡에서 얕은 사금 개울을 발견했다. 사금 채취 접시를 물속에서 흔들면 바닥에 노란 버터처럼 금이 고였다. 그들은 그곳에 짐을 풀었다. 그들은 매일같이 일하면서 깨끗한 사금과 금덩이로 몇천 달러를 벌었다. 금은 사슴 가죽 자루에 25킬로그램씩 나누어 담아 가문비나무로 만든 오두막 옆에 장작 쌓듯이 쌓아 놓았다. 그들은 열심히 일했고 사금 자루가 쌓여 가면서 하루하루가 꿈처럼 빠르게 지나갔다.

개들은 손턴이 잡은 사냥감을 실어 나르는 일 외에 할 일이 없었다. 그래서 벅은 불 옆에서 긴 시간을 생각에 잠겨 보냈다. 특별히 할 일이 거의 없어서 다리가 짧고 털이 많은 남자의 모습이 그를 더 자주 사로잡았다. 벅은 불 옆에서 눈을 깜박거리며 자신이 기억하는 다른 세상에서 그와 함께 이곳저곳을 헤맸다.

그 세상에서 가장 두드러진 감정은 공포인 것 같았다. 머리를 무릎 사이에 묻고 두 손을 위로 들어 올려 마주 잡은 채 불가에서 잠든 털 난 사내를 벅은 지켜보았다. 사내는 불안하게 잠이 들었다가 여러 번 깜짝깜짝 놀라 벌떡 일어났고 두려워하며 어둠 속을 응시하다가 불 위에 장작개비를 던져 넣었다. 둘은 해변을 같이 걸었는데 털 난 사내는 연방 조개를 주워 가며 먹었다. 어딘가에 도사리고 있는 위험을 찾아낼 듯이 두 눈을 두리번거렸고, 다리는 위험이 닥치면 바람같이 달아날 태세였다. 벅은 사내의 뒤를 졸졸 따라다니며 숲 속을 소리 없이 걸었다. 둘은 똑같이 사방을 예민하게 경계하면서 귀를 쫑긋하며 계속 움직였고 코를 벌렁거렸다. 사내도 벅만큼이나 예민하게 듣고 냄새를 맡았다. 털 난 사내는 나무 위로 뛰어올라 땅에서만큼 빠르게 움직일 수 있었다. 두 팔로 나뭇가지에서 나뭇가지 사이로 그네 타듯 옮겨 다녔는데 두 팔로 나뭇가지를 잡았다가 놓았다가 했고 어떤 때는 3 미터나 되는 거리를 한 번도 떨어지거나 나뭇가지를 놓치는 법 없이 옮겨 다녔다. 그에게는 나뭇가지 사이도 땅 위의 집처럼 편안해 보였다. 사내는 나무 위에 잠자리를 만들었는데 벅에게는 사내가 꼭 잡고 잠든 나무 아래에서 밤을 새운 기억들이 있었다.

털난 사내에 관한 기억과 마찬가지로 숲 속 깊은 곳에서 여전히 들리는 야성의 부름도 강렬했다. 그 소리를 들은 벅은 커다란 불안과 이상한 욕망으로 가득 찼다. 그 소리는 벅에게 뭐라고 표현하기 힘든 쾌감과 기쁨을 줬다. 정확히 알 수 없었지만 그 소리를 듣고 있으면 야생에 대한 동경과 충동을 느꼈다. 때로 그는 그 소리를 찾아 숲 속으로 들어가기도 했다. 마치 잡을 수 있는 물건이라도 되는 듯 벅은 기분이 내키면 부드럽게 저항하듯이 짖으면서 그 소리를 찾아 헤맸다. 벅은 서늘한 나무 이끼 속이나 긴 풀이 자라는 검은 흙 속에 코를 처박아 보기도 하고 진한 흙냄새에 기뻐하며 킁킁거리기도 했다. 어떤 때는 곰팡이가 잔뜩 핀 나뭇등걸 뒤에 몇 시간씩 숨죽인 채 웅크리고 앉아 눈과 귀를 활짝 열고 주변에서 움직이고 소리나는 모든 것을 지켜보았다. 그는 그렇게 숨어 있다가 알 수 없는 그 야성의 부름을 잔뜩 놀라게 해 주고 싶었다. 그러나 그는 자신이 왜 그런 짓들을 하는지 알지 못했다. 그저 그렇게 할 수 밖에 없었고 어떤 설명도 할 수 없었다.

저항할 수 없는 충동이 벅을 사로잡았다. 그는 캠프 안에 누워 한낮의 열기 속에서 나른하게 졸다가도 갑자기 머리를 번쩍 들고 귀를 쫑긋 세우고 뭔가를 주의 깊게 듣다가 벌떡 일어나 밖으로 달려 나갔다. 그러고는 몇 시간씩 숲 속 오솔길이나 검은 잡초들이 덤불을 이룬 공터를 달렸다. 그는 물기 없는 수로를 따라 내려가는 게 좋았고 기어가서 새들이 나무 속에서 어떻게 사는지 몰래 훔쳐보는 것을 즐겼다. 벅은 한 번 나가면 하루 종일 풀숲에서 엎드려 있곤 했다. 그 곳에서는 공작들이 날개를 퍼덕거리며 멋을 내며 뽐내듯이 오가는 모습을 지켜볼 수 있었다. 하지만 특히 벅이 좋아했던 것은 여름날 한 밤 중에 흐릿한 여명이 비추는 가운데 숲 속을 달리는 것이었다. 그럴 때마다, 벅은 나지막하면서도 나른한 숲의 속삭이는 소리를 들었고, 마치 사람이 책을 읽는 것처럼 숲 속의 각종 징후들과 그 소리들을 읽어 내려고 했을 뿐만 아니라, 잠들어 있거나 깨어 있을 때 항상 벅 자신을 부르는 듯한 묘한 야성의 부름 소리를 찾으려고 애썼다.

소설 04 Anne of Green Gables by Lucy Maud Montgomery (빨강 머리 앤)

다음 주 금요일이 되어서야 마릴라는 꽃으로 장식한 모자에 대한 이야기를 듣게 되었다. 마릴라는 린드 부인의 집에서 돌아오자마자 해명을 듣기 위해 앤을 불렀다.

"앤, 린드 부인 말로는 네가 지난 일요일에 장미와 미나리아재비를 얹은 우스꽝스런 모자를 쓰고 교회에 갔다더구나. 도대체 그렇게 제멋대로 굴어 어쩔 셈이니? 정말 볼만했겠구나!"

앤이 입을 열었다.

"네, 저도 분홍색과 노란색은 저한테 어울리지 않는다는 건 알아요."

"어울리지 않는다고! 색깔이 어떻든지 간에 모자에다 꽃을 다는 건 말도 안되는 짓이야. 정말 대책없는 아이로구나!"

"옷에는 꽃을 꽂으면서 모자에 꽃을 달면 왜 말이 안된다고 하는지 모르겠어요. 옷에 꽃을 단 여자 아이들이 얼마나 많았는데요. 뭐가 다른거죠?"

하지만 마릴라는 이런 애매하고 추상적인 앤의 이야기에 말려들지 않고 확실하고 구체적인 생각을 고수했다.

"그렇게 되묻지 마라, 앤 아주 멍청한 짓이야. 잔꾀로 날 어떻게 해볼 생각은 버려. 네가 그런 꼴로 들어오는 걸 보고 린드 부인은 하늘이 무너지는 줄 알았다더라. 꽃을 떼라고 말해주려 해도 너무 멀리 떨어져 있어 그럴 수가 없었다면서. 사람들이 그 일로 쑨소리를 많이 했다고 하더구나. 보나 마나 널 그 꼴로 보낸 날 분별없는 사람이라고 쑥덕거렸겠지."

앤이 눈물을 글썽이며 말했다.

"아, 정말 죄송해요. 아주머니께서 언짢아 하실 줄은 몰랐어요. 장미와 미나리아재비가 너무 향기롭고 예뻐서 모자에 얹으면 멋질 거라고만 생각했어요. 다른 아이들은 주로 모자에 조화를 꽂으니까요. 저 때문에 아주머니가 힘들어지시면 어쩌죠? 어쩌면 절 고아원으로 다시 돌려보내시는 게 나을지도 몰라요. 너무 끔찍한 일이라 도저히 못 견딜 것 같긴 하지만요. 전 아마 결핵에 걸리고 말겠죠. 지금도 이렇게 비쩍 말랐는걸요. 하지만 아주머니께 고통을 드리는 것보단 그 편이 나을 거예요."

마릴라는 자기 때문에 앤이 울고 있다고 생각하니 마음이 좋지 않았다.

"무슨 말도 안 되는 소리냐. 널 고아원으로 돌려보낼 생각은 조금도 없다. 난 네가 다른 아이들처럼 행동하고 남들한테 웃음거리가 되지 않기를 바랄 뿐이야. 이제 그만 울어라. 너한테 알려 줄 소식이 있다. 오늘 오후에 다이애나 배리가 집에 돌아왔다는구나. 배리 부인에게 스커트 본을 빌리러 갈 참인데, 너도 내키면 같이 가서 다이애나를 만나 보렴."

앤이 볼에 눈물이 채 마르지 않은 얼굴로 두 손을 잡으며 벌떡 일어섰다. 가장자리를 감치고 있던 행주가 바닥으로 떨어졌다.

"아, 아주머니, 두려워요. 드디어 때가 왔다 생각하니 겁이나요. 다이애나가 절 좋아하지 않으면 어쩌죠! 아마 제 평생 가장 비극적이고 절망적인 일이 될 거예요."

"이제 야단 법석 떨지 말고. 그리고 제발 거창한 표현들은 말하지 않으면 좋겠구나. 어린아이가 그런 표현을 쓰면 이상하게 들리니까. 다이애나는 널 좋아할 거야. 네가 신경 써야 하는 사람은 그 아이 엄마란다. 배리 부인이 널 마음에 들어 하지 않으면 다이애나가 아무리 널 좋아해도 소용없으니까. 린드 부인에게 대든 얘기며, 미나리아재비를 두른 모자를 쓰고 교회에 간 얘기를 듣는다면 배리 부인이 어떻게 생각할지 모르겠구나. 예의 바르고 착하게 굴어야 한다. 엉뚱한 소리를 해서 깜짝 놀라게 하지도 말고. 세상에, 얘가 정말로 떨고 있네!"

앤은 부들부들 떨고 있었다. 얼굴은 하얗게 질려 잔뜩 굳은 채였다.

앤이 급히 모자를 가지러 가며 말했다. "아, 마릴라 아주머니, 아주머니도 마음의 친구가 되길 바라는 아이를 만나러 가는데, 그 애 어머니가 아주머닐 싫어할지도 모른다는 생각을 하면 저처럼 떨 수 밖에 없을 거에요."

앤과 마릴라는 시내를 건너고 비탈진 전나무 숲을 지나, 지름길을 따라 언덕 과수원 집으로 갔다. 마릴라가 문을 두드리자 배리 부인이 부엌문을 열고 나왔다. 큰 키에 검은 눈동자, 검은 머리, 단호해 보이는 입매가 인상적인 모습이었다. 배리 부인은 자식들에게 엄하기로 소문이 나 있었다.

"안녕하세요, 마릴라. 어서 들어오세요. 이 아이가 입양했다는 아이로군요?"

배리 부인이 친절하게 말했다.

"네, 이 아이는 앤 셜리라고 해요." 마릴라가 소개했다.

"제 이름은 끝에 'e'가 붙어요."

앤은 떨리고 흥분되긴 했지만 중요한 점에 오해가 생겨서는 안 된다는 굳은 결심으로 가쁘게 덧붙였다.

배리 부인은 못 들은 건지, 이해를 못 한 건지 그저 악수만 청하며 상냥하게 말했다.

"잘 지내니?"

앤이 진지하게 대답했다. "정신적으로는 무척 뒤죽박죽이지만 몸은 건강해요. 고맙습니다, 아주머니." 그러고는 주위에 다 들릴 만한 소리로 마릴라에게 속삭였다. "저 별로 이상한 말 안 했죠, 아주머니?"

소파에 앉아 책을 읽고 있던 다이애나가 손님이 들어오자 책을 내려놓았다. 다이애나는 엄마처럼 눈과 머리가 검고, 뺨이 발그레했으며, 아버지를 닮아 표정이 밝고, 예쁜 아이였다.

배리 부인이 말했다. "얘가 다이애나란다. 다이애나, 앤을 데리고 정원에 나가 꽃을 보여 주렴. 눈 나빠지게 책만 보는 것보단 훨씬 나을 거야." 아이들이 나가자, 배리 부인이 마릴라에게 말했다.

"다이애나는 책을 너무 많이 읽어요. 애 아버지까지 부추기니 제가 말릴 방도가 있어야지요. 책 읽는 게 일이랍니다. 친구가 생겨 정말 다행이에요. 아무래도 밖에서 보내는 시간이 더 많아지겠죠?"

정원에서는 앤과 다이애나가 서쪽 편에 자라는 오래된 전나무들 사이로 부드러운 저녁 노을빛이 가득 비쳐드는 가운데, 아름다운 참나리 덤불 너머로 수줍게 서로를 바라보며 서 있었다.

배리 씨네 정원에는 여러 가지 꽃들이 가득했다. 지금처럼 운명과 관계된 중요한 때만 아니라면, 언제든 앤의 마음을 즐겁게 해 줄 것 같았다. 정원 주위엔 커다란 늙은 버드나무와 키 큰 전나무가 빙 둘러 자랐고, 나무 아래엔 그늘을 좋아하는 꽃들이 앞다투어 피었다. 조개껍질로 깔끔하게 가장자리를 두른 반듯한 흙길이 빨간 리본처럼 정원을 직각으로 나누었고, 길 사이로 난 꽃밭에는 오래된 품종의 꽃들이 만발해 있었다. 장밋빛 금낭화와 화려한 진홍빛 작약, 향기로운 흰 수선화, 가시가 많고 아름다운 스코틀랜드 장미, 분홍과 파랑과 흰색의 매발톱꽃, 연보랏빛 비누풀꽃, 개사철쑥과 흰줄갈풀과 박하 덤불, 보랏빛 난초인 아담과 이브, 수선화, 아기자기하고 줄기가 깃털같이 하얗고 향긋한 클로버 무리, 하얀 사향꽃 위로 불타는 창을 던지는 듯한 주홍빛 센트란투스가 한데 어우러졌다. 햇살이 아쉬운 듯 남아 정원을 비추었고, 벌들이 윙윙 날아다니고, 바람이 기분 좋게 살랑대며 여기저기를 기웃거렸다.

마침내 앤이 두 손을 꼭 잡으며 들릴 듯 말 듯한 목소리로 말했다.

"저, 다이애나, 너 혹시....……, 혹시 나를 조금이라도 좋아할 수 있을 것 같니? 내 마음의 친구가 될 만큼?"

다이애나가 웃었다. 다이애나는 말하기 전에 늘 웃기부터 했다. 다이애나가 솔직하게 대답했다.

"그래, 그럴 것 같아. 난 네가 초록 지붕 집에 살게 돼서 얼마나 기쁜지 몰라. 같이 놀 친구가 있으면 무척 즐거울 거야. 이 근처엔 함께 놀 다른 여자 아이가 없거든. 여동생은 아직 어리고 말이야."

앤이 간절하게 말했다. "영원히 내 친구가 되겠다고 맹세해 주겠니?"

다이애나가 깜짝 놀란 얼굴로 나무라듯 말했다.

"어머, 그건 아주 나쁜 행동인데."

"아, 아냐, 오해하지마. 내가 말한 swear는 욕한다는 말이 아니고 맹세하자는 말이야."

다이애나가 의심쩍은 듯 말했다. "난 한 가지밖에 모르겠는걸."

"분명 한 가지가 더 있어. 이건 전혀 나쁜 게 아니야. 그냥 엄숙하게 약속을 하는 거라고."

다이애나가 안심하며 말했다.

"그래, 그렇다면 좋아. 어떻게 하는 건데?"

앤이 엄숙하게 말했다. "일단 손을 잡아야 해. 원래는 흐르는 물 위에서 해야 하지만, 이 길에 물이 흐르고 있다고 상상하자. 내가 먼저 맹세할게. 해와 달이 사라지지 않는 한, 내 마음의 친구 다이애나 배리를 절대 배신하지 않겠다는 것을 엄숙히 맹세합니다. 자, 이제 네가 내 이름을 넣어 말해 봐."

다이애나가 웃으며 맹세를 했고, 맹세를 마치자 또 웃었다. 그리고는 말했다.

"넌 참 이상한 아이야, 앤. 네가 별나다는 소린 들었어. 하지만 난 네가 정말 마음에 들것 같아."

마릴라와 앤이 집으로 돌아가려 하자 다이애나가 통나무 다리가 있는 곳까지 배웅해 주었다. 아이들은 팔짱을 끼고 함께 걸었다. 시내에 이르자 두 아이는 내일 오후에 다시 만나자는 약속을 몇 번이나 한 후 헤어졌다.

초록 지붕 집 정원으로 들어서며 마릴라가 물었다. "그래, 다이애나랑은 마음이 잘 통하든?"

"네, 그럼요." 앤은 기쁨에 취한 나머지 마릴라가 비꼬고 있다는 것도 눈치채지 못한 채 한숨을 쉬며 말했다.

"아, 마릴라 아주머니, 지금 이 순간 프린스 에드워드 섬에서 저보다 행복한 아이는 없을 거예요. 오늘 밤에는 정말 열심히 기도를 드릴 거예요. 다이애나와 전 내일 윌리엄 벨 아저씨의 자작나무 숲에서 우리만의 아지트를 만들기로 했어요. 장작 창고에 있는 깨진 그릇들을 가져가도 될까요? 다이애나의 생일은 2월이고, 전 3월이에요. 정말 기가 막힌 우연이죠? 다이애나가 책을 빌려 준댔어요. 아주 놀랍고 흥미진진한 책이래요. 숲 뒤에 야생 나리가 있는 곳도 보여 준다고 했어요. 다이애나의 눈은 참 감정이 풍부한 것 같지 않아요? 제 눈도 그러면 좋을 텐데. 저한테 〈개암나무 골짜기의 넬리〉 노래를 가르쳐 줄 거래요. 방에 걸어 놓을 그림도 주고요. 연청색 실크 드레스를 입은 멋진 여인이 그려진 그림인데, 아주 아름답대요. 재봉틀 가게에서 선물로 얻은 거래요. 저도 다이애나한테 뭔가 줄 수 있으면 얼마나 좋을까요? 제가 키는 다이애나보다 2 센티미터 정도 크지만, 몸집은 다이애나가 더 통통해요. 다이애나는 마른 게 우아해 보인다며 자기도 살이 빠졌으면 좋겠다고 말했지만, 아무래도 절 위로하려고 한 말 같아요. 다음엔 조개껍질을 주우러 바닷가에도 갈 거예요. 우리는 통나무 다리 아래에 있는 샘을 드라이어드 샘이라고 부르기로 했어요. 정말 우아한 이름이죠? 언젠가 그런 이름을 가진 샘 이야기를 읽은 적이 있거든요. 드라이어드는 아마 숲의 요정이 아닐까 싶어요."

마릴라가 끼어들었다. "그래, 언제까지 그렇게 다이애나 얘기만 늘어놓을 셈이냐? 아무튼 무슨 계획을 세우든 이건 기억해라, 앤. 넌 그렇게 항상 놀 수만은 없단다. 먼저 네가 해야 할 일을 해놓고 다음에 놀아야 해."

그리고 이렇게 행복으로 가득 찬 앤의 마음은 매튜 덕분에 기쁨이 차고도 넘칠 정도가 되었다. 카모디에 있는 가게에 갔다 막 돌아온 매튜는 쑥스러운 듯 주머니에서 작은 꾸러미를 꺼내 마릴라의 눈치를 살피며 앤에게 건넸다.

"네가 초콜릿 과자를 좋아한다고 해서 좀 사왔단다." 매튜가 말했다.

마릴라가 코웃음을 쳤다. "나 참, 그런 건 이와 위장에 나빠. 이런, 이런, 그렇게 울상 짓지 마라, 얘야. 매튜 아저씨가 이왕 사오셨으니 몇 개는 먹어도 된다. 박하사탕이 몸에 더 좋긴 하다만 말이다. 한꺼번에 다 먹고 배탈이나 나지 않게 하렴."

앤이 신나서 말했다. "어머, 아뇨. 안 그래요. 오늘 밤엔 하나만 먹겠어요, 아주머니. 절반은 다이애나한테 주고 싶은데, 그래도 될까요? 다이애나에게 반을 준다면 나머지 절반은 두 배로 더 맛있을 거예요. 다이애나에게 줄 게 있다고 생각하니 정말 기뻐요."

앤이 다락방으로 올라가자 마릴라가 입을 열었다.

"저 아이에 대해서 이거 하나는 분명한 것 같구나. 인색한 아이는 아니야. 난 인색한 아이가 제일 싫거든. 이거야 원, 저 아이가 온 지 겨우 3 주밖에 안됐는데 마치 오래전부터 같이 살았다는 느낌이 드는구나. 저 애가 없는 집은 이젠 상상조차 할 수가 없단다. 그렇다고 '그러게, 내가 뭐랬어요.' 하는 표정은 짓지 마라. 그런 말을 하는 사람이 여자라도 기분 나쁜데, 남자가 그러면 더 못 참지. 어쨌든 솔직히 털어놓자면, 네 말대로 아이를 데리고 있길 잘했다 싶다. 저 아이가 점점 좋아지는구나. 하지만 이 일 가지고 계속 놀려댈 생각은 생각도 말아라, 매튜."

2 시

 Love is Not All (Sonnet XXX) by Edna St. Vincent Millay
(사랑이 전부가 아니에요)

사랑이 전부가 아니에요. 먹을 것도 마실 것도
잠도 아니고 비를 막아주는 지붕도 아니에요.
물에 뜬 통나무도 아니에요.
가라앉다 떠오르고 가라앉다 떠오르고 다시 가라앉는
사람을 구하는.
사랑은 굳어진 폐에 숨을 채워 넣지도 못하고,
피를 맑게도, 부러진 뼈를 맞추지도 못해요.
하지만 수많은 사람들이 죽음과 기꺼이 함께 하기도 하지요
사랑 하나 때문에. 내가 말하는 이 순간에도.
모를 일이죠. 내게 힘겨운 시간이 오면,
고통의 못 박혀 벗어나려 신음하거나
결심의 힘만으론 불가능한 궁핍함에 시달린다면,
그대의 사랑을 팔아 치워 평온을 구하거나
오늘밤의 추억을 먹을 것과 바꾸려 들지도.
그럴 수도 있겠죠. 그럴 거라고 생각하지는 않지만

To Science by Edgar Allan Poe (과학이여!)

과학이여! 그대는 진정 해묵은 시간의 딸이로다!
그대가 노려보는 눈으로 모든 것을 바꿔 버리는구나.
지루한 현실의 날개를 가진 독수리야,
그대는 왜 그리 시인의 심장을 파먹는 것이냐?
어떻게 그가 그대를 사랑하겠나? 혹은 어떻게 그대를 현명하다고 하겠나?
그대가 그를 방황하도록 내버려 두지 않는데.
보석 박힌 하늘에서 보물 찾을 수 있도록,
그가 담대한 날개로 높이 치솟았음에도 불구하고?
그대가 사냥의 여신 다이애나를 그녀의 수레에서 끌어내리지 않았던가?
그리고 나무의 요정 하마드리아드를 숲에서 몰아내어
어떤 더 행복한 별에서 은식처를 찾게 하지 않았나?
그대는 물의 요정 나이아드를 강으로부터 떼어내고
꼬마 요정 엘핀을 푸른 풀밭에서 떼어내고
내게서 타마린드 나무 밑의 여름 꿈을 빼앗아 가지 않았느냐?

Under the greenwood tree by William Shakespeare
(푸른숲 나무 그늘 아래)

푸른숲 나무 그늘 아래
나와 함께 누워
사랑스러운 새의 노래에 맞추어
즐거운 목소리로 노래하고 싶은 이여,
여기 오라, 여기 오라, 여기 오라.
     여기에는
        어떤 적도 찾아 볼 수 없으니
겨울과 폭풍을 제외하고는.

헛된 야심을 버리고
자연 속의 삶을 사랑하고,
들과 산에서 양식을 구하고
얻은 것에 기뻐하는 자여,
여기 오라, 여기 오라, 여기 오라.
     여기에는
        어떤 적도 찾아 볼 수 없으니
겨울과 폭풍을 제외하고는.

I Should Not Dare To Leave My Friend by Emily Dickinson
(내 친구를 두고 차마 떠날 수 없어요)

내 친구를 두고 차마 떠날 수 없어요.
만일 내가 떠난 사이에 그가 세상을 뜬다면
나를 원했던 그의 가슴에
나는 너무 늦게 도달하게 될테니까요.

내가 만일 그의 눈을 실망시킨다면
그렇게도 간절히 나를 찾던,
나를 보기 전엔– 나를 보기 전엔
차마 감지 못하던 그의 눈을 실망시켜야만 한다면.

내가 만일 그의 충실한 믿음을 배신한다면,
내가 올 것이라고 확신했던 그의 믿음을,
그 믿음은 듣고 또 들으며, 잠을 청하겠지요.
여전히 오지 않는 내 이름을 부르며.

내 심장은 차라리 그 전에 터져 버렸으면,
왜냐하면 그런 후에 터지는 심장은
간밤에 서리 내린 곳을 비추는
다음날 아침 햇살처럼 헛된 일이기 때문이지요.

3 희곡

희곡 01 The Crucible by Arthur Miller (시련의 도가니)

(프록터가 나간다. 헤일은 잠시 동안 난감해하며 서 있다.)
패리스: (재빨리) 제 딸 좀 봐 주시겠습니까? (헤일을 침대로 안내한다.) 우리 애가 창밖으로 뛰어내리려고 했습니다. 오늘 아침에는 큰길에서, 마치 날아가려고 하는 것처럼 두 팔을 퍼덕거리는 걸 발견했지요.
헤일: (눈을 가늘게 뜨며) 날아가려고 했다?
퍼트넘: 주님의 이름을 듣는 것조차 견디지 못합니다. 헤일 목사님. 마녀들의 마법이 온 사방에 있다는 분명한 증거입니다.
헤일: (두 손을 쳐들면서) 아니, 아닙니다. 제 말을 들어 보세요. 이 문제를 미신에 의지할 수는 없습니다. 악마는 치밀합니다. 악마가 존재한다는 증거는 너무나 명백합니다. 그리고 제가 여러분 모두에게 분명히 말해 둘 것이 있습니다. 제가 이 일을 진행하기는 하겠지만, 단 제가 이 처녀에게서 지옥의 흔적을 찾아내지 못한다 해도 제 말을 믿겠다는 마음의 준비는 되어 있어야 합니다.
패리스: 동의합니다. 목사님, 동의합니다, 우리는 목사님의 판단에 따르겠습니다.
헤일: 그렇다면 좋습니다. (침대로 가서 베티를 내려다보고는 패리스에게) 저, 이 이상한 일이 가장 먼저 나타난 조짐은 무엇이었습니까?
패리스: 음, 저, 저 아이를 보았지요. (애비게일을 가리키며) 그리고 제 조카와 십여 명의 처녀 애들이 간밤에 숲 속에서 춤추는 것을 목격했어요.
헤일: (놀라서) 평소에도 춤을 허락하십니까?
패리스: 아니, 아닙니다. 그건 비밀리에 ...
퍼트넘 부인: (기다리지 못하고) 패리스 목사님 댁 노예는 혼령을 불러 올 수 있는 능력이 있어요.
패리스: (퍼트넘 부인에게) 그렇다고 장담할 수는 없어요.
퍼트넘 부인: (겁에 질려서, 아주 낮은 목소리로) 난 알고 있어요. 목사님. 내 딸을 보냈거든요. 누가 우리 딸들의 생명을 빼앗아갔는지 티투바에게 알아 오라고요.
레베카: (깜짝 놀라며) 앤 부인! 죽은 혼령을 불러내겠다며 딸아이를 보냈단 말인가요?
퍼트넘 부인: 하나님한테야 면목이 없지만. 당신이 나설 일이 아니에요, 절대 아니죠, 레베카! 당신한테 더 이상 날 비난하는 소리 듣고 싶지 않아요! (헤일에게) 일곱 아이들이 단 하루도 살지 못하고 죽는 것이 자연스러운 일인가요?
패리스: 쉿!
(레베카, 크게 고통스러워하며 고개를 돌린다. 잠시 아무도 말이 없다.)
헤일: 일곱 명의 아기가 태어나자마자 죽다니.
퍼트넘 부인: (낮은 소리로) 그래요. (목소리가 갈라진다. 헤일을 쳐다본다. 정적이 흐르고, 헤일은 놀란 듯하다. 패리스가 헤일을 쳐다본다. 헤일은 책이 있는 곳으로 가서 한 권을 펼치고 책장을 넘긴 뒤 읽는다. 다들 숨죽이고 기다린다.)
패리스: (낮은 목소리로) 무슨 책인가요?
퍼트넘 부인: 거기 뭐라고 쓰였나요?
헤일: (지적 탐구에 대해 고상한 애정을 가지고 있다는 듯이) 이 책에는 보이지 않는 모든 세상이 포착되고, 정의되고, 계산되어 있답니다. 이 책에는 악마의 모든 악랄한 가면이 벗겨진 채 드러나 있습니다. 이 책에는 여러분이 익히 알고 있는 모든 악귀들의 이야기가 있습니다. 즉, 꿈 속에서 이성들을 유혹하는 모든

남자 마귀들과 마녀들, 땅이나 공중 아니면 바다로 돌아 다니는 마녀들, 낮과 밤의 남자 마법사들의 이야기가 다 들어 있습니다. 이제 두려워하지 마십시오. 악마가 우리들 사이에 나타난다면, 우린 그 놈을 찾아낼 겁니다. 악마가 얼굴을 보이기만 하면 완전히 박살을 낼 작정입니다! (침대로 걸어간다.)

레베카: 저 애가 다치지는 않을까요?

헤일: 그건 알 수 없습니다. 만약 정말로 저 애가 악마에 사로잡혀 있다면 우리는 그 놈을 찢어 내서라도 아이를 구해야 할지도 모릅니다.

레베카: 그렇다면, 난 가 봐야겠군요. 그런 짓을 하기엔 난 너무 늙었으니. (레베카가 자리에서 일어난다.)

패리스: (확신하고자 애쓰며) 레베카, 오늘 우리는 우리 모두에게 고통을 주고 있는 종기를 찢어 내야 할지도 모릅니다.

레베카: 다 같이 그렇게 되기를 바랍시다. 당신을 위해 하느님께 기도하겠어요.

Man and Superman by George Bernard Shaw (인간과 초인)

아나: 당신이 말하는 것은 부도덕한 충동이라는 거군요.

돈 후안: 부인, 소위 부도덕하다는 것이 자연의 본성입니다. 내가 그걸 부끄럽게 생각해도 어쩔 수는 없죠. 자연은 채홍사이고, 시간은 파괴자이며, 죽음은 살인자예요. 난 늘 이런 사실에 과감히 맞서고 그런 인식을 바탕으로 여러 제도를 세우고 싶었습니다. 반면에 당신은 이들 세 악마들을 정절, 검약, 애정 어린 친절이라고 선언하여, 그들의 비위를 맞추고 그런 아부에 바탕을 두고 당신의 세상을 만들어 가고 싶어 하죠. 그러니 잘 굴러가지 않는 것이 당연한 것 아닌가요?

석상: 부인들은 주로 뭐라고들 하던가요, 후안?

돈 후안: 자! 이제 서로 비밀을 털어놓기로 합시다. 우선 당신이 부인들에게 하곤 했던 얘기를 해주시지요.

석상: 나 말이요! 아, 난 맹세했지. 죽을 때까지 충실하겠다고, 날 거절하면 죽어 버리겠다고, 내게는 어떤 여자도 결코 그녀와 같지 않다고.

아나: 여자라니요! 누구요?

석상: 누구든 우연히 그 당시 내 옆에 있게 된 여자 말이다. 내가 늘 사용하는 말들이 있었단다. 그 중 하나는, 내가 여든이 되어도 내가 사랑하는 여자의 흰 머리카락 하나가 가장 아름답고 젊은 여자의 숱 많은 황금빛 머리결보다 더 가슴을 설레게 하다는 말이었지. 또 하나는 그녀 아닌 다른 어느 여자도 내 자식의 어머니가 된다는 생각을 하면 견딜 수 없다는 말이었고.

돈 후안: (반감을 드러내며) 이 늙은 바람둥이 같으니!

석상: (단호하게) 절대 그렇지 않소. 그 순간 난 영혼을 바쳐 정말로 그렇게 믿었고, 내게는 진심이 있었소. 당신과는 다르지. 그리고 내가 여자의 마음을 사로잡을 수 있었던 것도 이런 진심 때문이었소.

돈 후안: 진심이라니! 그렇게 터무니 없고 뻔뻔스럽고 밀도 안되는 거짓말을 믿을 정도로 어리석은 모습, 그게 소위 당신의 진심이라고요! 여자에 대한 탐욕이 너무 큰 나머지 그녀를 속이기 위한 갈망으로 스스로를 속이는 것, 그게 소위 당신의 진심이라고요!

석상: 아, 빌어먹을 궤변 같으니! 난 사랑에 빠진 한 사람의 인간에 불과하지, 변호사가 아니오. 그리고 그 때문에 여자들은 나를 사랑했지. 그들에게 축복이 있기를!

돈 후안: 당신이 그렇게 생각하도록 여자들이 유도한 겁니다. 내가 아주 냉담한 변호사 역할을 하고 있을 때에도, 그들은 역시 내가 그렇게 생각하도록 만들었다고 말씀드리면 뭐라고 하시겠습니까? 나 또한 무의미한 말을 내뱉고, 그걸 믿었던, 여자에게 심취했던 순간들이 있었어요. 때때로 아름다운 말을 해서 상대에게 기쁨을 주려는 욕구가 마음속에 홍수 같은 감정으로 일어나서 무모하게 말하곤 했죠. 또 어떤 때에는 내 속마음과는 달리 악마같이 냉정하게 설득해서 울게 만들었고요. 그렇지만 잔인해질 때 여자에게서 도망치는 것 역시 친절한 때만큼이나 어렵다는 걸 알게 되었지요. 여자의 본능이 내게 쏠리면 평생 노예 상태에 있거나 도망치는 수밖에 없었습니다.

희곡 03 A Streetcar Named Desire by Tennessee Williams
(욕망이라는 이름의 전차)

(스탠리는 전화를 끊고 식탁으로 돌아온다. 블랑시는 물 컵에 든 물을 재빨리 마시면서 자제하느라 안간힘을 쓴다. 스탠리는 블랑시를 보지도 않고 주머니만 뒤진다. 그러고는 천천히 다정한 척하며 천천히 말을 꺼낸다.)

스탠리: 처형, 내가 작은 생일 선물을 준비했어요.

블랑시: 어머나, 그랬어요, 스탠리? 나는 아무것도 기대하지 않았는데, 난, 난 스텔라가 왜 내 생일을 축하해 주려고 하는지 모르겠어요! 스물일곱이 된 다음부턴, 차라리 잊어버리고 싶던데! 글쎄, 나이란 차라리 잊고 살고 싶은 건데!

스탠리: 스물일곱 살이요?

블랑시: (재빨리) 뭐예요? 그게 내 건가요? (스탠리가 작은 봉투를 블랑시에게 내민다.)

스탠리: 그래요, 처형 마음에 들었으면 좋겠는데!

블랑시: 아니, 아니, 아니, 이건……

스탠리: 차표요! 로렐로 돌아가요! 그레이하운드 버스를 타고! 화요일에 떠나요! (바수비아나」음악이 조용하게 들리기 시작하다가, 계속된다. 스텔라가 갑자기 일어서더니 돌아선다. 블랑시는 미소를 지으려고 애쓴다. 그러고는 웃어 보려고 한다. 그러다 다 포기하고 식탁에서 벌떡 일어나, 옆 방으로 뛰어 들어간다. 블랑시는 목을 움켜쥔 채 욕실로 달려 들어간다. 기침과 구역질하는 소리가 들린다.) 저런!

스텔라: 그럴 필요까지는 없었잖아.

스탠리: 내가 당신 언니에게 어떤 취급을 받았는지 절대 잊지마.

스텔라: 언니처럼 외로운 사람한테 그렇게까지 잔인하게 굴 필요는 없잖아.

스탠리: 하기야 연약하기는 하겠지.

스텔라: 그래. 옛날에도 그랬고, 당신은 소녀 시절 블랑시 언니가 어땠는지 몰라. 언니처럼 부드럽고 남을 잘 믿는 사람은 아무도, 아무도 없었어. 하지만 당신 같은 사람들 때문에 언니가 고통받고 변하게 된 거야. (스탠리는 침실로 들어가 셔츠를 벗어 던지고 화려한 색깔의 볼링 셔츠로 갈아입는다. 스텔라가 스탠리의 뒤를 따라 간다.) 당신 지금 볼링치러 갈 셈이야?

스탠리: 물론이지.

스텔라: 당신, 볼링 치러는 못 가. (남편의 셔츠를 붙잡는다.) 언니한테 왜 그랬어?

스탠리: 내가 누구한테 뭘 어쨌는데? 내 셔츠 놔. 찢었잖아.

스텔라: 왜 그랬는지 알고 싶어. 왜인지 말해 봐.

스탠리: 우리가 처음 만났을 때. 당신과 나 말이야. 당신은 내가 상남자라고 생각했지. 그래 맞아, 여보, 나는 흙 구덩이에서 굴러먹던 상남자였어. 당신은 당신이 살았던 대저택의 사진을 보여줬지. 나는 당신이 그 저택에서 벗어날 수 있도록 해 주었고, 당신은 그래서 오히려 더 좋아했어. 오색찬란한 전등을 화려하게 켜 놓고 말이야! 그리고 우리 둘은 행복했잖아? 당신 언니가 나타나기 전까지 모든 게 좋지 않았어? (스텔라가 조금 움직인다. 그녀는 마치 내면의 소리가 자기 이름을 부른 듯 갑자기 생각에 잠긴 표정을 짓는다. 스텔라는 천천히 힘없이 다리를 끌며 침실에서 부엌으로 걸어간다. 멍한 얼굴과 무슨 소리를 듣는 듯한 표정으로 의자 등받이와 탁자의 가장자리에 기대고 의지하기도 하면서 움직인다. 스탠리는 셔츠를 갈아입느라 아내의 반응을 눈치 채지 못하고 있다.) 우리 둘이서 행복하지 않았어? 모든 게 다 좋지 않았어? 저 여자가 잘난 척하면서 나타나 나를 짐승 취급하기 전까지는 말이야. (스탠리는 스텔라의 표정이 갑자기 바뀐 것을 알아 차린다.) 이봐, 무슨 일이야, 스텔라? (스탠리가 스텔라에게 다가간다.)

스텔라 (조용하게) 병원에 데려다 줘. (스탠리는 스텔라에게 다가가, 그녀를 팔로 부축하며 바깥으로 나가는데, 알아들을 수 없는 말들을 중얼거린다.)

The Glass Menagerie by Tennessee Williams (유리 동물원)

짐: (갑작스럽게) 내가 볼 때 당신의 문제가 뭔지 알아요? 열등감이에요! 열등감이 뭔지 알아요? 열등감은 자기 자신을 비하하는 겁니다! 나도 열등감이 있었기 때문에 잘 알아요. 물론 내 경우는 로라처럼 그렇게 심하지는 않았지만 말이죠. 대중 연설 수업을 듣고, 발성 훈련도 하고, 과학에 소질이 있다는 걸 알게 되기 전까지는 나도 그랬어요. 그러기 전에는 결코 내가 어떤 면으로도 뛰어나다고 생각하지 못했거든요!

로라: 아, 그래요?

짐: 과학을 정식으로 공부한 적은 없었어요. (오른 쪽에 있는 안락 의자에 걸터 앉는다) 그런데 친구 녀석이 나보고 정신과 의사들보다도 더 사람들의 심리분석을 잘 한다고 그러더라고요. 그게 꼭 맞는 말이라고 주장하는 건 아니지만, 나는 사람의 심리를 잘 파악하는 편이에요. 로라! (씹던 껌을 꺼낸다.) 실례해요. 로라. 껌을 씹다가 항상 단물이 빠지면 뱉어 버리죠. 이 종이로 껌을 싸둘게요. 신발에 붙으면 안 되니까요. 그게 로라의 가장 큰 문제점이라고 생각해요. 자기 자신에 대한 자신감이 없다는 점 말이에요. 내 이야기는 그 동안 로라가 말한 몇 가지 사실과 내가 관찰한 바에 근거한 겁니다. 예를 들어 고등학교 때 그토록 끔찍했다고 말했던 쿵쿵 소리 말이죠. 교실 안으로 걸어 들어가는 게 두렵기까지 했다고 말했지요. 그 다음에 당신은 어떻게 대처했나요? 쿵쿵 소리 때문에 학교를 중퇴하고 교육을 포기했어요. 내가 아는 한 그런 소리는 실제로 있지도 않았다고요! 물론 약간의 신체적 결함이 있기는 하지요. 거의 눈에 띄지도 않아요! 그런데 당신은 상상을 통해서 수천 배나 확대해서 생각하는 겁니다! 내가 간곡히 충고 하나 하고 싶은데 뭔지 아세요? 자기 자신이 어떤 면에 있어서는 뛰어나다고 생각하라는 거예요.

로라: 어떤 면에서 그렇게 생각할 수 있을까요?

짐: 이런, 이것 봐요, 로라! 자기 주위를 조금만 살펴봐요. 뭐가 보이나요? 다들 별로 그렇게 특별한 사람들이 아니에요! 사람은 누구나 태어나면 죽게 마련이잖아요! 그 사람들 중에 로라가 가진 장점의 십 분의 일이라도 가지고 있는 사람이 얼마나 될까요? 혹은 내 상섬이나, 다른 어느 누구의 장점의 십 분의 일이라도 말이죠. 누구나 각자 남보다 잘하는 것이 하나는 있어요. 물론 여러 가지를 다 잘하는 사람도 있기는 하지요! 내 경우를 이야기해 볼게요. 나는 우연히 전기 역학에 관심을 갖게 되었어요. 야간학교에서 무선 공학 과정을 배우고 있어요. 로라. 물류창고에서도 꽤 중요한 일을 하고 있구요. 나는 무선 공학 강좌를 듣고 대중 연설을 공부하고 있어요.

로라: 그렇군요.

짐: 왜냐하면 텔레비전의 미래를 믿으니까요! 나는 텔레비전이 발전하면서 기회가 많아질테니 그 기회를 포착할 생각이에요. 그래서 초기 단계에서부터 적극적으로 참여할 계획이에요. 인맥들도 어느 정도 구축해 놓았고 이제 남은 것은 사업 자체가 본격적으로 진행되어 가도록 하는 거죠! 공부 많이 해서 지식을 쌓으면, 다음에는 돈, 또 그 다음에는 권력이 따라 오겠죠. 민주주의가 만들어진 과정이 바로 그런 과정이니까요! (짐의 태도는 빈말이 아니라고 생각할 정도로 자신만만하다. 로라는 그를 빤히 쳐다보는데, 그의 자신감에 감탄해서 수줍음까지도 잊고 쳐다본다. 짐이 갑자기 미소를 짓는다.) 내가 스스로를 과대평가한다고 생각하는 것 같네요!

로라: 아니. 절대 그렇지 않아요.

임용고사 합격에 반드시 필요한
일반영어 및 문학에서 만점을 추구한다.

Reading Writing & Booster

합격을 넘어
평생 가는 영어 실력!

초판 1쇄 발행 2025년 01월 10일

저자 김병두
발행인 공태현 **발행처** (주)법률저널
등록일자 2008년 9월 26일 **등록번호** 제15-605호
주소 151-862 서울 관악구 복은4길 50 (서림동 120-32)
대표전화 02)874-1144 **팩스** 02)876-4312
홈페이지 www.lec.co.kr
ISBN 978-89-6336-983-9 (13740)
정가 15,000원